MW01119892

THEATRE AND CITIZENSHIP

The History of a Practice

'Citizenship' is a contested term which today inspires both policy-makers and radical activists. David Wiles traces this ideal to its classical roots, examining both theatre and citizenship as performative practices. Wiles shows how people function collectively rather than as individuals, for example through choruses or crowd behaviour in the auditorium. He explores historic tensions between the passivity of the spectator and the active engagement of a citizen, paying special attention to dramatists like Aristophanes, Machiavelli and Rousseau who have translated political theory into a theatre of and for active citizens. The book is a fresh investigation of familiar and less familiar landmarks of theatre history, revealing how plays function as social and political events. In this original approach to theatre history, Wiles argues that theatre is a powerful medium for building community, and that attempts to use it as a vehicle for education are very often misplaced.

DAVID WILES is Professor of Theatre at Royal Holloway University of London. He has published extensively in the fields of classical and Elizabethan theatre, and his *Short History of Western Performance Space* was published by Cambridge University Press in 2003. This is his ninth book, and previous books have been shortlisted for the Criticos, Society for Theatre Research and Runciman prizes. He was a contributor to the *Oxford Illustrated History of Theatre* (1995) and is currently, with Christine Dymkowski, editing *The Cambridge Companion to Theatre History*. The focus of his teaching and research has always been the relation of theatre to society, particularly in respect of festival, and the present book builds on the breadth of his intellectual interests. Its genesis lies in a keynote lecture which he was invited to give to the International Federation for Theatre Research at the University of Maryland in 2005.

THEATRE AND CITIZENSHIP

The History of a Practice

DAVID WILES

Royal Holloway University of London

CAMBRIDGE
UNIVERSITY PRESS

CAMBRIDGE UNIVERSITY PRESS
Cambridge, New York, Melbourne, Madrid, Cape Town,
Singapore, São Paulo, Delhi, Tokyo, Mexico City

Cambridge University Press
The Edinburgh Building, Cambridge CB2 8RU, UK

Published in the United States of America by Cambridge University Press, New York

www.cambridge.org
Information on this title: www.cambridge.org/9780521193276

First published 2011

A catalogue record for this publication is available from the British Library

Library of Congress Cataloguing in Publication Data
Wiles, David.
Theatre and citizenship : the history of a practice / David Wiles.
p. cm.
Includes bibliographical references and index.
ISBN 978-0-521-19327-6 (hardback)
1. Theater and society. 2. Theater – Political aspects. I. Title.
PN1643.W45 2011
306.4′848 – dc22 2010041961

ISBN 978-0-521-19327-6 Hardback

Contents

Plates

Acknowledgements

Completion of this project was made possible by a grant under the AHRC Research Leave scheme. Tom Postlewait kindly refereed my application, and it is thanks to him that I first bent my thoughts to the citizen-artist. I am grateful to my colleagues in the Department of Drama and Theatre at RHUL for allowing me sabbatical leave, and for providing an intellectual environment that stimulates lateral thought. In particular, Helen Nicholson encouraged me to consider 'citizenship' a topic relevant to practitioners today. My research students have kept pointing me to new lines of enquiry, and proved a welcome diversion from labour over the word-processor. I have spoken on citizenship at seminars or working groups in Athens, Delphi, Leeds, Lisbon, Maryland, Oxford, Plymouth and at RHUL, and I am appreciative of helpful discussions that ensued. N. P. Ashley, Jacky Bratton, Margret Convery, Zachary Dunbar, Helen Nicholson and Ellen Wiles have spared the time to give me feedback on draft chapters or sections. Dick McCaw got me interested in Laban and found the photos. Vicki Cooper at Cambridge University Press supported this project from its inception. Thanks finally to Gayna, without whose support I could not have written this book about public life.

CHAPTER I

Introduction
Citizenship and theatre

Citizenship is the preoccupation of today. As I write these words in February 2010, the *Guardian* newspaper has just launched an online pamphlet on
Citizen Ethics, prompted by Michael Sandel's 2009 Reith Lectures, with
many figures from public life contributing their views.[1] The Marxist literary critic Frederic Jameson in 2002 lamented the re-emergence of political
philosophy 'trailing after it all those ancient issues of constitutions and
citizenship, of civil society and parliamentary representation, of responsibility and civic virtue, which were the hottest topics of the eighteenth
century just as surely as they are no longer our own. It is as though nothing
had been learned from the challenges of the revolutionary century just
concluded . . .'[2] Jürgen Habermas was, I believe, closer to the mark in dubbing modernity 'an unfinished project' rooted in the eighteenth-century
Enlightenment.[3] Citizenship is a contested term that has resonances for
people of many different persuasions, potentially a liberal rallying point,
potentially despite Jameson's protestations part of an agenda for radical
change. So why has this concept, rooted in antiquity and in the eighteenth
century, become again so necessary?

In the first instance, most readers of this book will inhabit a multicultural
society where ethnicity and cultural tradition do not marry up with any
homogenizing concept of nationhood. The idea of 'citizenship' unhooks
the state from ideas of nation, whilst affirming that ethics and feeling
cannot be separated from membership of a particular political community.
It offers a language through which to address fraught issues like the wearing
of Islamic headscarves in schools, or the placement of rehabilitation centres
within the 'community'. The term 'citizen' was not a watchword of the
American Revolution because citizens by definition have to be citizens
of somewhere particular, and unlike centralized France the USA was a

---

[1] www.guardian.co.uk/commentisfree/2010/feb/20/citizen-ethics-time-of-crisis
[2] Jameson (2002) 2.   [3] Habermas (1996).

I

federation of states; it was the Fourteenth Amendment of 1868 that gave the term resonance, asserting that black and white alike, if born in the USA, were automatically 'citizens of the United States'.[4]

Secondly, the collapse of the Marxist project, to which Jameson looks back, has left a certain vacuum. In my student years it was axiomatic that 'good theatre' and 'subversive theatre' were synonymous terms, and the promise of alternative ways of living was harnessed to the ideal of 'alternative' theatre performed in dark basements. Today the planet has shrunk and boltholes no longer exist. The problem of the future is how we can live together in a world of diminishing environmental resources, where communication technologies have made the boundaries of the nation-state increasingly porous. Citizenship addresses the fundamental problem of cohabitation.

Third is the issue highlighted by the *Guardian* pamphlet, the perceived lack of a shared ethical framework in societies stripped both of religious consensus and of the passions engendered by nationalism. In its printed text, the *Guardian* highlights Michael Sandel's phrase: 'The hollowing out of the public realm makes it difficult to cultivate solidarity.'[5] I shall return at the close of this book to the idea that in a world of media manipulation and personality politics there is no space for any serious public engagement with moral issues. The *Guardian* seeks to position its own forum within this public realm, a realm which includes theatre as we infer from the *Guardian*'s choice of contributors. Jude Kelly tells the reader that 'art is a fundamental right of every human being', while Kwame Kwei-Armah declares that when writing for the National Theatre his job is to 'hold a mirror up to nature'.[6] I shall not unpack at this point the assumptions that lie behind such statements, beyond asking the obvious questions: what is this thing 'art' that like food we have a right to consume? And is theatre primarily a mimetic representation, or is it a social event? The relationship between theatre and the public realm needs historical investigation if satisfactory answers are to be found for the contemporary problem of how theatre configures with citizenship.

Do we need citizenship? Do we need theatre? Let us return to first principles with the help of a nineteenth-century novelist. Leo Tolstoy places the seduction of Natasha Rostov at the centre of *War and Peace* as the pivot upon which the plot turns. Natasha enters the Moscow Opera House as an innocent, and at first all she can see on the stage is artifice: canvas

---

[4] See Heater (2004) 70.　　[5] *Guardian* 20 February 2010.
[6] Kelly's text in the newspaper version, Kwei-Armah in the online pamphlet.

backdrops, cardboard sets, an overweight prima donna. Her interest is in Moscow's social elite around her, and her own flesh exposed in an unfamiliar evening gown. The atmosphere progressively catches her up; she forgets her fiancé and surrenders without resistance to the seducer who invades her box. The action on stage mirrors her downfall: the woman carried off and lamenting, the male strutting his dance, a final vision of Hell. The theatre is a space of social performance, and a site of seduction where morality collapses. Natasha ends the novel learning from Rousseau about natural breast-feeding, and avoiding elegant French codes of female behaviour. The novel, not theatre, was the medium through which Tolstoy felt he could articulate truths both about unique individual Russians and about what Rousseau termed the 'general will', the transpersonal force which took Russians to victory against Napoleon. In Tolstoy's novel the aristocrats of St Petersburg are torn between their nationalism and their love for the French institution of theatre. In a Russia defined by its vast rural estates, Tolstoy celebrates the household and the relations of landlord and peasant as a form of society more natural than any aristocratic salon or confraternity of burghers. Although Moscow organically regenerates itself after its burning, we do not find in Tolstoy any notion akin to 'citizenship', for there was, and some would say there remains, no room for this republican and secular ideal in a society shaped by Czarist and Orthodox cultural traditions. Tolstoy's Russia defines its identity in opposition to France, and republicanism is a feature of the French other, an inadequate creed that collapses into Napoleonic imperialism.

Tolstoy's critique of theatre echoes Plato and Rousseau whose thinking I shall examine in the course of this book. His premise is that theatre is a social event which under the guise of cosmopolitanism binds together a certain social class, and its power lies not in any appeal to reason but in its seductive hold upon the emotions. Art for Tolstoy is at root 'a means of union among men, joining them together in the same feelings'.[7] Richard Rorty takes a similar view of the world when he contends that the principle of loyalty is always prior to the principle of reason, rationality being but a device to ensure the survival of large groups.[8] For Tolstoy, ethical values should be formed not in the public realm but in the intimate environment of the home, where novels like *War and Peace* will be read. It follows that it is an illusion for *Guardian*-reading theatre-goers to imagine their experiences will somehow generate a better world, for they attend the National Theatre

---

[7] *What is Art?* in Feagin and Maynard (1997) 171.   [8] Rorty (1998).

merely to be reassured in their pre-existent convictions, and in their social position. Such is the Tolstoyan challenge.

Let us consider in this light a recent National Theatre venture, Mark Ravenhill's play *Citizenship*. A typical review accessed via the National Theatre website records:

I Went To Watch Citizenship Last Night With My School @ The National Theatre. It Was Awesome. The Way Mark Ravenhill Managed To Use Comedy To Show An Actually Quite Meaningful Piece Of Drama Was Really Good. And His Characterisation Of All The Teens Were Pretty Much Spot On. Me And My Class Mates Were Left Comparing The Characters To Other School Mates. Definatley A Good Job Well Done.[9]

The spectator treats the play as a reflection of her social reality and transmits by the word 'meaningful' some recognition of thematic content. But it is clear that the spectator is echoing a certain academic discourse, and we have no means of knowing whether this mirroring of reality and sense of a lurking meaning will allow her 'to go out into the world and ask some new questions of it', as Ravenhill hopes.[10] The word 'awesome' catches an emotional reaction, hinting at an experience shared with classmates, perhaps affecting the dynamics of that group. I saw Ravenhill's play when it toured to the Oxford Playhouse, sitting near the front amid a small group of older spectators some of whom had obviously come by mistake. The auditorium behind was filled with teenage groups, mostly female, vociferous in their enthusiastic response and creating a sense of engaged participation and interchange with the stage more familiar to me as a theatre historian than as a patron of the Playhouse.

We can analyse Ravenhill's play on two levels. We can focus on the text, or dramatic content, and consider how the play *represents* teenage sexuality, portrays a world where young people are excluded from the public realm, and satirizes government attempts to teach citizenship via essays on multiculturalism and lifeskills training in motherhood. There is an available academic toolkit which makes this kind of analysis quite straightforward. Much harder to pin down is the performance as social event. What kind of bonding united the auditorium as a whole, or the teenage subgroups inclusive or exclusive of their teachers or youth leaders? Were the teenagers being educated in theatre-going so they will become regulars in later life? Were they all bound for university, aware that they do not themselves sit at the bottom of the social heap but finding cathartic liberation in seeing their sexual anxieties articulated on stage, and social liberation in the shared recognition of those anxieties? These questions confront us when we think of theatre as a social practice, and the answers are far from obvious.

In respect of modern citizenship, Ravenhill's *Citizenship* poses a further question. The play was commissioned as part of the National Theatre's 'Connections' programme, which included training sessions for teachers and directors of youth theatre groups, and it was written for amateur performance.[11] How do we compare participation in a community activity with the watching of a skilled professional production? We are thrown back on competing definitions of 'citizenship'. If we impose a local frame upon the term, we shall think of teenage actors exercising a kind of citizenship when they perform Ravenhill's text for their peers, functioning as active members of their community, not passive consumers of culture. On the other hand, if we give the term a national frame, we shall sense something rather valuable in the teenagers' participation in a wider cultural world. Though virtual encounters through blogs and iPhones complicate the old dichotomy of local and national,[12] such networking cannot in my view substitute for the complexity of human interaction generated by a shared physical presence in a public space.

Today this Arts Council policy statement of 1996 sounds quaintly archaic:

For five hundred years, drama has been at the heart of England's creative life... England is rightly regarded as a world centre for drama and its plays are exported throughout the world... In recognition of this the Arts Council of England spends a large proportion of its funds on drama... Just as German culture has found its highest expression in its musical tradition – or the Italian renaissance in its visual arts – so the English genius has been seen above all on stage.[13]

Though Ravenhill is certainly esteemed abroad, government funding of the arts in England can no longer be justified, at least publicly, on such aesthetic or nationalistic grounds, but a play that educates the young in citizenship is consistent with modern political values and is eminently fundable. Whatever Ravenhill may do to satirize the citizenship education provided by an uncaring state, he is trapped in a circle that positions him as part of that education, and the intensity of his writing no doubt reflects his awareness of being ensnared. The National Theatre has to reconcile the twin ideals of democratic diversity and national homogeneity which justify

---

[11] On the context and implications, see Deeney (2007).   [12] See for example Gray (2001).
[13] Arts Council (1996). On arts policy, cf. Everitt (2001).

its funding, and the director of that theatre, Nicholas Hytner, chooses his
words carefully. 'We want to tell the stories that chart the way the nation
is changing. We want to bring front-line reports from new communities
and generations, and we want to see the present redefined in the context
of the past.'[14] As a front-line report on the state of the nation, Ravenhill's
play happily fits this twenty-first-century agenda.

Although we may wince now at the rhetoric of 1996, unhooking citizenship from nationhood is not so easily accomplished. Advice to would-be
immigrants to the UK sets out the paradox. 'Britain is a country where people of many different cultures and faiths live. What brings British people
together is that they listen to different points of view, they have respect for
equal rights and they believe that community is important.'[15] A coherent
national identity is deemed at once to exist and to not exist. A 2008 government report by Lord Goldsmith recommended that school leavers in a rite
of passage should swear an oath of allegiance to Queen and Country, and
that a British national day should be established.[16] These proposals were
derided in the press for epitomizing the very antithesis of Britishness – the
sort of thing that Americans do and *we* don't. The national 'we' refuses to
be eradicated.

No study of citizenship can ignore the phenomenon of national difference. Since De Tocqueville, individualism has been recognized as a
distinctive feature of a USA that is at once a state and a union of states.[17]
The American rhetoric of citizenship emphasizes inclusiveness, asserting
that every minority has its place in a land that is understood to be diverse,
and attention to minorities helps to explain why the United States has never
generated a 'National Theatre' on the European model. The German *Bun-
desrepublik* is likewise formally a federation, and the term *Staatsbürgerschaft*,
the nearest approximation to 'citizenship', is federalist in the way it links
the state (*Staat*) to the burgher of an autonomous city. Ethnicity rather
than political membership has over a long period shaped the sense of
being German. Conversely, in France, with its history of centralization and
imperialism, Frenchness has long been regarded as a product of cultural
assimilation: to absorb French language and literature and relinquish other
cultural bonds is to become French.[18] England, with its mixed Anglo-Saxon
and Gallic background, and uneasy relationship to Anglophone Scotland,

[14] www.nationaltheatre.org.uk/?lid=7083
[15] www.lifeintheuktest.gov.uk/textsite/test_intro_20.html
[16] 'Citizenship: our common bond', published 11 March 2008: www.justice.gov.uk/docs/citizenship-
report-full.pdf
[17] Bellah *et al.* (1996) is a classic study.   [18] On France and Germany, see Brubaker (1992).

Wales and Ireland, is currently looking to the United States for a notion of citizenship that accommodates cultural and ethnic diversity, while at the same time it is unwilling to relinquish a more European idea of the 'nation' which implies an element of *natio*, common 'birth'. In an England that still proclaims itself not a republic but part of a United *Kingdom*, heaping moral value onto the term 'citizenship' is a novel project.[19]

It is never possible to shake off bonds created by history, even in a republic formed of immigrants like the USA, and the role of theatre in creating communal memories is often an important one.[20] I recently had the task of chairing a seminar that brought together an Austrian and a Polish theatre practitioner, and I found the mutual incomprehension revealing. For the Austrian, the Polish work made no sense and appeared regressive in its insistent rhythms and mythopoeic bricolage of classical material. From the Polish point of view, conversely, the idea that we can strip human beings down in Beckettian fashion to the minima of language and body seemed nihilistic. I could only reconcile this clash of principles by looking at national traditions. In a Germanic context, anything that smacks of the *Volk* is suspect because of the way national myths were manipulated by Fascism, and any valid aesthetic must now be founded on minimalism and first principles. In Poland, on the other hand, where the cultural trauma of Stalinism followed two centuries of state dismemberment, religion and folk tradition seemed to rescue Poles from a sense of dehumanization or non-being. An aesthetic based on residues of cultural memory appeared therefore to be a natural form of creative expression. There is manifestly less attachment to nation in long-established nation-states like Britain than in newly autonomous nations, and any account of citizenship needs to take note of this difference. Poland, with its history of incursions from Prussia, Russia and Austro-Hungary, finds sources of solidarity in its language, literature and religious practices that may appear incomprehensible to native speakers of a globalized English language.

Such diversity makes the work of the historian all the more important.[21] Citizenship is a function of the spatial unit to which the citizen belongs, and that unit can take different forms, including the local community, the city, the city-state, the nation, the republic, and arguably the 'world'. Of all these, it is the 'republic' that has been tied most strongly to the moral ideal of the 'citizen'. While 'democracy', rule by the collective *demos* or public,

---

[19] For the English political context, see the introduction to Brannan, John and Stoker (2007).
[20] On nation and memory, see Smith (1999).
[21] Useful historical surveys of citizenship include Riesenberg (1992), Heater (1999), Faulks (2000), Heater (2004) and Magnette (2005).

was an invention of Athens, the ideal of the 'republic', which implies
ownership of the *res publica* or 'public thing', was a creation of Rome.
Rome was too big for democracy, and the senatorial class was entrenched
in its power, but within the Roman Republic an element of face-to-face
encounter and democratic voting was powerful in symbolic terms, offering
a moral right to riot when senators forgot that the state ultimately belonged
to the people. Emotions attached to a *republic* are not the same as emotions
attached to a *nation*, since the one term traditionally implies ownership,
the other nativity.[22] 'Civic republicanism' is today the standard label given
to the school of political thought that opposes individualistic liberalism,
and includes figures like Michael Sandel.[23]

Republics are self-evidently human constructs, unlike 'nations' and
'communities'. Benedict Anderson in *Imagined Communities* developed
an influential critique of nationalism, from a republican perspective. His
argument is that 'all communities larger than primordial villages of face-
to-face contact (and perhaps even these) are imagined. Communities are to
be distinguished, not by their falsity/genuineness, but by the style in which
they are imagined.'[24] In Anderson's historical model, 'imagined' religious
and dynastic communities were replaced in the Age of Enlightenment by
'imagined' national communities, powerfully influenced by the medium of
print. My own point of departure is different, for I believe we should not
undervalue the phenomenological experience of false and genuine communities. Thus, for example, the proposal that all British school leavers should
swear allegiance to Queen and Country was widely perceived as a ceremony
that would create false community. Anderson's parenthesis '(and perhaps
even these)' points to a philosophical hole at the core of his method: what
relationships, then, are not 'imagined'? By inference we are pointed back to
the unique authenticity of familial and neighbourly relationships. Anderson's historiography focuses upon discourse and textuality at the expense of
performance, and he has many perceptive things to say about the impact
of print-capitalism, but he is not interested for example in how the reading
of a newspaper in an eighteenth-century coffee-house might constitute a
performance, creating a small community of minds and bodies within the
public sphere. It is, I shall argue, the very nature and purpose of theatre
to create communities, and most forms of pre-modern theatre maximized
the audience's awareness that it embodied a community that transcended
familial and neighbourly relations.

---

[22] In defence of nation as an ideal, see e.g. Miller (2000), Kymlicka (2001) 203–64. On the tension
between republic and nation, see Taylor (2004).
[23] Kymlicka (2002) 294–9, Finlayson (2005) 108–13.   [24] Anderson (1991) 6 – first published in 1983.

British sensibilities have long responded to the dream of connection to a community rooted in time immemorial. Seventeenth-century English radicals, for example, claimed that the people were still subject to a 'Norman yoke' in the belief that somewhere in an earlier and uncontaminated Anglo-Saxon past lay a world akin to Eden.[25] Raymond Williams, in *The Country and the City*, showed how British writers repeatedly manufactured fakes of country life, but paradoxically he laid bare at the same time continuities in the desire of writers to fight the logic of profit with an ideal of rural community. Material traces of the past visible through his Welsh study window reminded him of an enduring 'structure of feeling' which pitted a communal country life against urban alienation.[26] Jean-Luc Nancy from a French perspective argues that historians too easily postulate lost communities, whereas it is actually the experience of loss that constitutes communities. Rousseau is a paradigmatic figure here, inventing the citizen of a free, sovereign community in response to the harsh and godless reality of modern 'society'.[27]

In 1960 John Arden and Margaretta D'Arcy wrote a 'community' play for a Somerset village in which they were living.[28] Neither so English as to trouble the Irish D'Arcy, nor so spiritual as to trouble the secular Arden, the story of Christ's nativity seemed to be the perfect vehicle for community theatre. However, the centuries-old nativity play is now in crisis. Defending himself in the right-wing press in December 2007 against charges of repressive political correctness, Trevor Phillips, Chair of the Equality and Human Rights Commission, roundly supported the school nativity play: 'In spite of its growing consumerist tinge, Christmas is a moment when our whole nation can celebrate the story of hope, togetherness and compassion symbolized by the Christian tale; you don't have to be a Christian to share the values of community and family. There is room for everybody at this inn.'[29] The rhetoric of 'nation' fuses with the rhetoric of 'community' in this secularizing, assimilationist rhetoric, but however attractive Phillips' metaphor of an inn with many guests may be, British policies of multiculturalism are increasingly hard to reconcile with the idea of 'one nation', as we are reminded when Phillips notes that 'Mohammed' is 'the second-most-common name for new babies in England'.[30] It was once assumed that modernity entailed the decline of religious belief, but in most parts of

---

[25] Hill (1964). [26] Williams (1975). [27] Nancy (1991) 9–10.
[28] *The Business of Good Government*.
[29] 'Why be ashamed to celebrate Christmas?' *Evening Standard* 10 December 2007.
[30] The statistic incorporates multiple spellings.

the world the case has proved otherwise, with religion very often a foundation for the feeling that one belongs to this and not that community. The secular notion of 'citizenship' has, and has long had, a role to play in providing an ethical counterweight to the metaphysical claims of religion and of nation.

Citizenship was for many centuries not only a secular but also a masculine ideal. Attesting to the value of public life, it implicitly downgraded domestic life, which along with forms of ritual activity comprised the traditional sphere of women. Until the twentieth century, republicans commonly identified the citizen as a man who takes his place in the ranks to fight for his city, while nationalists, because of their emphasis on birth, were more inclined to develop female hagiographies, around figures like Joan of Arc or Good Queen Bess. Though public life continues to be dominated by men, the ideal of citizenship evolved in the twentieth century to underpin the moral case for equality. It was logical enough that advocates of citizenship who had long resisted essentialist arguments about nation and religion should also learn to resist essentialist arguments about gender. Aimee Beringer in 1900 looked back nostalgically to the eighteenth century when women were able to flourish in the 'public' profession of dramatist. In the Victorian period, she lamented, women succeeded as novelists, but had no access to the life experience needed for the stage, so as to 'listen to the heart of the world, and get the echo of its throbs over the footlights'. Today, Beringer concluded, the aspiring female dramatist 'must first become a citizen of the great world, and then serve her apprenticeship to the lesser, that of the theatre'.[31] Her speech reveals how the eighteenth-century ideal of citizenship was already being used at the start of the twentieth century to demand a place for women in public life, a public life that included the public realm of the theatre. The gap which Beringer takes for granted between the private world of the novelist and the public transactional world of the theatre has shrunk since 1900. More women now write more plays, but theatre is less connected to the public sphere of the citizen.

The republican arguments of the German-Jewish political theorist Hannah Arendt (1906–75) have proved something of a challenge to feminism, since Arendt's resolute attachment to the public realm with scarcely any mention of gender can be seen either as masculinist or as liberating.[32]

---

[31] Beringer (1900) 368 – a paper read to the Society of Women Journalists. My thanks to Anna Fokas for this reference.
[32] Cf. Warner (2002) 58. See Arendt (1958) 8 for her most striking discussion of gender, related to the parallel creation stories in Genesis.

The difficulties raised by her position relate to the problem of identity, for Arendt appears to downgrade both the inner world and the biological world. Any serious engagement with the figure of the 'citizen' needs to begin with the nature of the person. Michael Sandel as a civic republican challenges the liberalism of John Rawls who built his theory of justice upon a conception of the human subject as bounded and unified. When Rawls perceives society as the convergence of already individuated persons, then according to Sandel he separates our identity as citizens from our identity as persons, for he is more interested in right, and by extension individual human rights, than in wider conceptions of the good life which provided the foundation for classical theories of justice.[33] Rawls' position is characterized as the theory of 'atomism' by Charles Taylor, who insists that 'the identity of the autonomous, self-determining individual requires a social matrix'.[34]

Those like Taylor and Sandel who see self in collectivist or communitarian terms trace their thinking back to Aristotle's famous statement that the human being is a *zōon politikon*, a political animal. Aristotle postulates an evolutionary process whereby humans moved from households into villages and thence into the polis or 'city-state', arguing that humans have an innate impulse towards partnership, and that humans in isolation are incomplete. Aristotle's conception of pre-history differs sharply from Rousseau's romantic picture of the natural savage who went fishing in the woods in splendid isolation, prior to his corruption by society.[35] The polis, Aristotle maintains, 'is both natural and prior to the individual', and his definition of justice is founded not on individual rights but on the basis of what makes a right society.[36] He argues in his *Ethics* that 'the good of the individual is to be cherished, but finer and more sacred is the good of the tribe or polis'.[37] The theatrical correlative to Aristotle's theory lies in the idea that the chorus is historically prior to the individual actor,[38] since it is a deeper human instinct to replicate the movements of others in dance than to step out from the collective and like Oedipus ask who one truly is. A theatrical counterpart to modern atomism can be found in Erving Goffman's *The Presentation of Self in Everyday Life*, where Goffman uses

---

[33] Sandel (1998).
[34] Taylor (1985) 209. On the tension between communitarianism and liberalism, see Kymlicka (2002) 208ff.
[35] See especially Rousseau's treatise on the origins of inequality: Rousseau (1992) 230.
[36] Aristotle *Politics* I.ii (1252b). Here and elsewhere in this book, translations are my own unless referenced to a translated source.
[37] Aristotle *Nicomachaean Ethics* I.ii.8 (1094b).
[38] On Aristotle and the origins of drama, see Depew (2007).

the metaphor of a theatre to distinguish a frontal area of social performance from a secret back-stage area where one can be one's authentic self.[39] This metaphor made sense in relation to theatres that might be found on a 1950s American campus, but in the choral mode of Greek theatre the important action takes place in the visible public domain, the sphere of the *zōon politikon*.

Hannah Arendt attributes to Christianity the idea that the essential human freedom is freedom of the individual will, citing Augustine's account of conflicts which took place in the dark chamber of his heart.[40] In the earlier Graeco-Roman world, Arendt argues, freedom could be exercised only within the political community, and she insists we should not translate Aristotle's *zōon politikon* in the Roman fashion simply as *animal socialis*, a social animal.[41] Aristotle, she maintains, was arguing not that selfhood is a function of social bonds but that self-realization is only possible within the public realm of the polis. Driven by horror of Fascist and Stalinist totalitarianism on the one hand and American corporate capitalism on the other, and against her own background as a stateless Jew, Arendt argues that inner freedom is a function of public freedom. Freedom should be understood by analogy with the performing arts as a performance which requires a certain 'virtuosity', and it must constantly be acted out if it is to be preserved.[42] Citizenship, for Arendt, is not an abstract moral ideal sustained by an atomized individual, but is a performance practice.

Arendt draws a rather clear line between the performance of the politician in the assembly and the performance of the actor in the theatre, approving Cicero's philosophical ideal of spectatorship which involves no desire to win or make money.[43] However, in Cicero's accounts of attending the theatre, we learn how the words of actors were transformed into political statements by the response of the spectators, and sitting in a prominent seat Cicero was never the disinterested spectator he hoped to be.[44] An active and expressive engagement with theatre was part of public life for a citizen of the Roman Republic. Arendt's distinction between the political animal and the social animal turns out upon inspection to be too clean. Theatre is a messy activity which cannot be reduced to any single category of the aesthetic, the political or the social, but involves the interpenetration of all three.

[39] Goffman (1959).   [40] Arendt (1961) 158.   [41] Arendt (1958) 23.   [42] Arendt (1961) 154.
[43] Arendt (1961) 219, citing *Tusculanian Disputations* v.iii.9 (where the ideal is traced to Pythagoras).
[44] Wiles (2003) 174.

Arendt argues that where freedom exists, it 'has always been spatially bounded', the product of specific human groups,[45] and she has no truck with the idea that human rights are natural or god-given and that true 'citizenship' is therefore citizenship of the world. The counter-argument on behalf of cosmopolitanism is well set out by the philosopher Kwame Anthony Appiah, born to an English mother and to a father who was African, or rather Ghanaian, or rather Ashanti. Appiah maintains that he has no difficulty in acknowledging emotional loyalties to different forms of nation, like the Ashanti, and at the same time participating in the democratic political culture of the USA. He welcomes the fact that the USA is not centred on a common national culture, because this allows him to choose his own identity. He accuses theorists like Arendt of being 'overly influenced by the view of politics taken by some in the small self-governing town of Athens in the fifth century B.C.E.',[46] and welcomes the fact that the USA is a 'state' but not a 'nation' since this allows him freedom to choose who he will be. The corollary of this classically American liberal position is that Arendt's ideal of a public realm shared by all can never be realized. It was Arendt's encounter with the modern USA that made her feel she could not realize herself as a human being without active membership of a more circumscribed political entity. Jefferson, she argues, recognized that 'the Constitution had given all power to the citizens, without giving them the opportunity of *being* republicans and of *acting* as citizens', and regrets that he never fulfilled his plan to embed a system of miniature republics in the form of wards to create a more participatory democracy.[47] Appiah and Arendt help us focus upon competing liberal and communitarian ideals for makers of theatre: on the one hand, the propagation of universal moral values linked to an assumption that people choose their identities; on the other, the formation of communities bonded by an obligation to participate. Theatre can be played *to* an audience, or it can be played *with* an audience.

The autonomous and bounded individual self flies in the face of all that we learn from modern neurology. The brain has been widely understood as a multiplicity of parallel activities, following Daniel Dennett's demolition of the homunculus, the lonely inner spectator of a 'Cartesian theatre' who views images supposedly thrown up in the mind by the senses.[48] The discovery of 'mirror neurons' in macaque monkeys in the early 1990s then

---

[45] Arendt (1963) 279; cf. Arendt (1967) 290–302 on the limitations of 'human rights'.
[46] Appiah (1998) 101, 107. Arendt is not mentioned by name.
[47] Arendt (1963) 256.　　[48] Dennett (1992) esp. 107–8.

revealed, to the excitement of many in the world of theatre, that the human brain is wired to imitate, so that when we sit watching actions in the theatre our bodies experience physical impulses which mirror those of the agent on stage. The tears and laughter of an audience are spread contagiously because that is how the social human brain functions. We cannot help ourselves functioning as part of a collective because that is the nature of the human species.[49] If we relinquish the idea of the atomized self in favour of a collectivist self, a self that derives from the social brain, then we have to rethink in a rather fundamental way how to describe theatre spectatorship, and we must try to understand audience response in terms of group processes rather than multiply upwards the cognitive processes of individual spectators.

Scholarship in Theatre Studies has made little attempt to theorize the phenomenon of collective audience behaviour. The best book in English on theatre audiences remains Susan Bennett's study of 1990, inspired by the proposition of reader response theory that an 'interpretive community' pre-exists the solitary act of reading. Bennett cites the claim of semioticians that individual spectators check their own decoding against the decodings of others in a theatre audience and adjust accordingly to create a collective response, but is wary of endorsing this account and concludes in rather vague terms: 'It is surely the case that while the theatre audience is a collective consciousness composed of the small groups in which spectators attend theatrical events, it is also a specific number of individuals.' Though the collective response may be homogeneous, she maintains that 'the individual's response to performance undoubtedly constitutes the core of the spectator's pleasure'.[50] Bennett intuits but is unwilling to conceptualize a transpersonal level of response. It is effectively a modern article of faith that the individual pre-exists the citizen.

To challenge this article of faith we must return to Aristotle, who links the *zōon politikon* to a theory of friendship whereby the friend is a *heteros autos*, which is to say an 'other self' or 'alter ego'.[51] The concept of being self-sufficient or under your own control 'relates not just to your living a solitary life but to your parents and children and wife, and broadly to friends and citizens, since mankind is by nature a political thing'.[52] There is a rather small quantitative limit to real friends, a larger limit in the bond of citizenship, though the polis itself must be of limited size, with 10 plainly

[49] See Emery, Clayton and Frith (2008), especially the essays by Gallese and Frith.
[50] Bennett (1997) 154–5; text unchanged from the first edition: Bennett (1990) 164–5.
[51] Aristotle *Nicomachean Ethics* IX.ix.10 (1170b).   [52] Aristotle *Nicomachean Ethics* I.vii.6 (1097b).

too small a number and 100,000 too vast.[53] Part of what defines friendship with one's *heteros autos* is the condition that Aristotle terms *synaisthēsis*, co-perception. 'Given that one lives with many, one would choose co-perception with the maximum number; but since this is very hard, it is a necessity that the activity of co-perception should be with fewer.' We notice that co-perception is active not passive, and the term *energeia* which I have translated as 'activity' evokes the energy of an audience. Aristotle sees living together as essential to the good life and thus a moral duty, and he contends that the goal of *koinōnia* or 'community' involves not only working together but also *syntheōrein*, 'co-spectatorship' as in a festival.[54] Aristotle's active concept of co-perception, which stems from his sense that selfhood is not bounded by the individual, offers a useful foundation for a more communitarian account of theatre spectatorship.

The idea of communal spectatorship emerged again with romanticism. When Goethe visited the Roman amphitheatre of Verona in September 1786, he imagined how the Roman crowd once formed the only backdrop in a space 'perfectly suited for impressing the populace with itself'. Instead of functioning, according to the old metaphor of the hydra, as the 'many-headed multitude', Goethe believed that the Roman crowd was 'united into a noble body, induced into oneness, bound and consolidated into a mass, as if it were one form, enlivened by one spirit'.[55] This experience helped him adjust to the communal spirit of theatre-going in Italy, so different from Weimar. Just outside the walls of the Roman amphitheatre he found an improvised sporting arena created by benches, carts, barrels and knolls, where a crowd of several thousand responded noisily to every stroke of the ball, and the postures of the players suggested to him the classical aesthetic that once shaped performances inside the amphitheatre. At the Opera he could not enter into the mood of the Italian audience, and was reminded of the role he once played as Aristophanes' human hero amid a chorus of birds, concluding 'I feel I shall never make a good bird.' He was happy, however, with his lonely bird's eye perspective from the rim of the amphitheatre at sunset, looking down at tiny figures beneath.[56] Goethe, like Rousseau, yearned for an experience of organic collectivity while being fearful of losing his selfhood in the crowd, and feeling condemned to personal isolation.

---

[53] Aristotle *Nicomachean Ethics* IX.x.6 (1171a), IX.x.3 (1170b).
[54] Aristotle *Eudemian Ethics* VII.xii (1245b). On *synaisthēsis*, see Sorabji (2006) 236. On *theōria*, see Wiles (2007) 237–9.
[55] Goethe (1994) 37. [56] Goethe (1994) 40–3.

Goethe's ambivalence points us towards two conflicting ideals of the citizen spectator. On the one hand there is the philosopher who stands above the performance space and outside the choral dance, determining his or her autonomous moral actions; and on the other there is the participant who surrenders individual self-interest to the larger organism. It is one of the paradoxes faced by the theatre historian that unselfconscious collective behaviour can only be analysed by the philosophical outsider, by the likes of Goethe standing alone on the crest of his amphitheatre. In Aristophanes' comedy, the chorus of innocent birds has the moral edge over the rationalistic and scheming individual, but the post-classical world has long preferred the perspective of the individual.

Crowd theory was popularized by Gustave le Bon in *La psychologie des foules*, published in 1895 and inspired by memories of rampant crowds in the Paris Commune. Le Bon's thesis is that: 'Whoever be the individuals that compose it, however like or unlike be their mode of life, their occupations, their character, or their intelligence, the fact that they have been transformed into a crowd puts them in possession of a sort of collective mind which makes them feel, think, and act in a manner quite different from that in which each individual of them would feel, think, and act were he in a state of isolation.'[57] For Le Bon, the theatre audience constituted an exemplary crowd, experiencing the same emotions at the same moment, only inhibited from action by the fleeting awareness of illusion. Crowd theory explains for Le Bon why readers so often find it impossible to anticipate which texts will work in the theatre, or why a given play succeeds in one country and fails in another.[58] While Le Bon points to the dangers of the crowd which responds to feelings rather than ideas, he also claims that a crowd may be led to a higher level of feeling than its aggregated individual members could ever attain. The fine moral sentiments of melodrama were no doubt in his mind.

It is hard for us in the twenty-first century to think of audiences as 'crowds' because we tend to forget how different the nineteenth-century auditorium was from its disciplined modern successor. In another classic study of the crowd, Elias Canetti distinguishes a 'rhythmic' crowd, such as he finds in a Maori choral dance or a Shi'ite Mystery play, from a 'stagnating' crowd which simply takes pleasure in its own density. Spectators in the modern European theatre feel only a mild form of crowd pressure which 'scarcely ever gives them a feeling of inner unity and togetherness'. Like

---

[57] Le Bon (1960) 27. On crowd theory, see McPhail (1991).
[58] Le Bon (1960) 68, 52. *Charley's Aunt* is cited as an example of unanticipated success.

classical concert-goers they are the product of 'a long and artificial training in stagnation'. Canetti remarks that 'there are few phenomena of our cultural life as astonishing as a concert audience. People who allow music to affect them in a natural way behave quite differently; and those who hear it for the first time, never having heard any before, show unbridled excitement.'[59] This observation applies equally to the theatre, and historians need to keep reminding themselves what a strange creature the modern bourgeois theatre audience has become.

Le Bon's argument was taken up by Freud in his 1921 study of *Massenpsychologie*. Purging Le Bon of his latent racism, Freud fought a rearguard action on behalf of the ego, arguing that the crucial factor in crowd behaviour was identification with a common object.[60] Freud was fighting collectivist tendencies in Germany that I shall examine in my final chapter. Richard Wagner was one such collectivist who held that it was impossible to be 'free in loneliness' and subscribed to Nietzsche's belief that modern egotism marks a loss of ancient wholeness.[61] He disliked the tiered nineteenth-century auditorium, which forced theatre managers to find a lowest common denominator satisfactory to all social classes, and sought a spontaneous theatre of the German *Volk* where social divisions would be erased.[62] Le Bon, Nietzsche and Wagner (but not of course Freud the Jew) were read with enthusiasm by Hitler, and Le Bon's ideas about theatre also impressed Mussolini.[63] Hitler understood how individuals became suggestible under the influence of mass meetings, where a man entered in doubt and left as 'a member of a community'.[64] The success of Fascism in inducing the surrender of ego brought crowd theory into disrepute, and Brecht's warning that we surrender cognitive responses at our peril shaped European thinking about theatre for a generation. The swing of the pendulum towards individualism has brought its own dangers, and the idea of citizenship allows us to admit the virtues and indeed the necessity of the collective impulse, as we try to strike the right balance between personal moral responsibility and the surrender of personal egotism.

To recapitulate, I have in this discussion identified citizenship as the nexus in respect of two major oppositions. Firstly, I have distinguished the idea of nation from the idea of a republic, both partially subsumed since Machiavelli by the idea of the 'state'. While national 'citizenship' has only a thin technical meaning, relating to the holding of a passport, republican

---

[59] Canetti (1962) 36–7.
[60] Translated as 'Group psychology and the analysis of the ego' in Freud (1985) 91–178.
[61] Wagner (1892) 98.   [62] Wagner (1977) 40–3, Wagner (1892) 207.
[63] Moscovici (1985) 63–4, 89.   [64] *Mein Kampf* cited in Berghaus (1996) 60.

'citizenship' carries a thicker moral meaning, invoking obligations towards fellow owners of the public thing, the *res publica*.[65] Secondly, I have distinguished a bounded individual self from a permeable social self. We can start from the premise that we are essentially individuals who acquire our cultural identity through selection and accretion, and are capable of making autonomous rational choices that determine our actions; or we can start from the premise that we as human beings are components of a cultural matrix, so the language we speak, the religion we practised as a child and the music that stirs us become essential parts of who we are, from which it follows that our moral choices are rooted in cultural norms, and theatre must engage us not as individuals but as members of a community.

Étienne Balibar writes of the 'indetermination' of the citizen: 'The citizen is unthinkable as an "isolated" individual, for it is his active participation in politics that makes him exist, but he cannot on that account be merged into a "total" collectivity.' The citizen for Balibar is a utopian figure who 'can only be thought if there exists, at least tendentially, a distinction between public and private'. The citizen is at once the constitutive element of an abstract State, and the actor of a permanent revolution, endlessly calling for equality.[66] It is the indeterminate and contested nature of the citizen which makes it important that she or he be subjected to historical examination.

My enquiry necessarily begins in Athens where theatre and the democratic citizen emerged at the same historical moment, apparently as part of a single process. I shall focus on Aristophanes' *Frogs*, where Dionysus seeks a playwright to save the city in its moment of crisis, and political discourses merge with aesthetic discourses in a manner that is likely to bewilder the modern reader. I shall juxtapose Aristophanes' portrayal of tragedy as a means of saving the city with Plato's claim that tragedy disrupts the harmony of the perfect city. While the cacophonous frogs of Aristophanes' chorus symbolize a dysfunctional body politic, Plato seeks a choral performance that will not be interrupted by the pain and dissidence of heroic individuals. Choral dancing tied the practice of theatre to the democratic polis through collective and embodied participation, but Aristotle provided a rationale for spectatorship of a more passive kind, writing as a cosmopolitan intellectual for whom Athens was but a temporary home.

The Roman Republic had a much greater impact than democratic Athens on subsequent conceptions of citizenship, until the twentieth century. I shall view Rome through the lens of the Florentine republic, where Livy's idealization of republican Rome shaped Machiavelli's vision of a free

---

[65] For the metaphor, see Faulks (2000) 10–11.   [66] Balibar (1991) 51–4.

Florence, released from the tyranny of the Medici. When forced to become a man of letters rather than an active servant of the state, Machiavelli sought to rebuild the dramatic structures of republican Rome, just as he had sought to reconstitute Roman political structures. He rejected not only the tyranny of the Medici but also the Christian republicanism of Savonarola, and this secularism cut him off as an intellectual from the common population. He refused to allow that traditional Christian morality in the private sphere had any bearing upon the competitive and manly virtue characteristic of the true citizen, while also rejecting Cicero's principle that the good man and the good citizen are one and the same. Inheriting from Rome the idea that comedy is an imitation of domestic life, he worked through the idea that drama has an educative function, before deploying it finally as a source of collective amoral laughter. His pursuit of good citizenship led him to an uncompromising rejection of the idea that theatre should teach morality.

My geographical focus in the next chapter switches to England, and my theme is the shift from citizen to subject once the nation-state ruled by an absolute monarch replaced the autonomous walled city as the frame for political identity. I begin with the Coventry Corpus Christi play, where theatre was intertwined with both urban citizenship and Catholic Christianity. Reformed Christians charged with city government in the Elizabethan age found theatre incompatible with a protestant faith that focused on personal responsibility rather than collective action, and Elizabethan theatre flourished in London because despite the opposition of those who governed the city it enjoyed the support of those who governed the nation. In this context I shall examine how two of the great myths of republican Rome played out on the London stage, amid competing claims on the loyalty of the citizen. The assassination of Julius Caesar was enacted at the Globe by a company that leaned towards court, while the rape of Lucrece, which resulted in the ousting of a despotic Roman monarchy, was played at the Red Bull, a theatre characterized by civic pride. I shall end by turning to John Milton's dream of writing *Paradise Lost* in the form of a tragedy, when religion was again as in medieval Coventry deemed the proper foundation for citizenship, and harnessed to a republican future a different theatrical future seemed possible.

It was in the French Enlightenment that the ideal of citizenship crystallized, as men looked back to the lessons of classical antiquity, and forward to a better and more rational future. The dilemmas of Rousseau lie at the core of this book. Torn between two competing identities, as cosmopolitan Parisian and citizen of the small Genevan republic, Rousseau attempted to resolve the tension between truth to self and surrender of self to the community. In his *Letter to M. d'Alembert on his article 'Geneva' in the VIIth volume of the Encyclopaedia, and specifically on the project of establishing a playhouse in that city*, Rousseau argued, against Voltaire, that the establishment of a public theatre in Geneva would only serve to entrench the power of a patrician class which, like the Senate in republican Rome, was locked in a long power struggle with the people. Inspired by Plato's *Republic*, Rousseau claimed that a system of participatory festivals would engender solidarity, while theatre would be socially divisive. Settled in Genevan territory, Voltaire fought for the theatre as a space of free expression, and hoped his plays would implant the radical ideas of the Enlightenment. While Voltaire was interested in dramatic content, Rousseau attended to the social institution of theatre. Festivals, he believed, could be quintessentially Genevan, but theatre would never be anything other than a French institution, generating a cosmopolitan rather than a localized world. Arendt's argument that freedom is spatially limited relates to Rousseau's argument on behalf of localism. In his *Social Contract* Rousseau struggled to reconcile the romantic ideal of personal freedom with the republican ideal of political freedom. He placed proudly beneath his name on the title page the words 'Citizen of Geneva', but soon found himself forced by the censorship of his book to renounce that citizenship. Religion was the crucial faultline that brought about the collapse of his utopian dream.

Voltaire and Rousseau became the twin heroes of the French Revolution, their bodies carried in state to the Pantheon. Rousseau's ideal of the civic festival inspired the projects of Jacques-Louis David, while in the theatre the Roman tragedies of Voltaire celebrated republican notions of 'liberty'. The tension between passive spectatorship and active participation was never reconciled, and in practice the theatre may have provided a more participatory environment than the festival. I shall track the career of Marie-Joseph Chénier, who found himself at the epicentre of the revolution as tragic dramatist, festive lyricist and politician devoted to the cause of public education. In the longer term it was neither Rousseau nor Voltaire but Diderot, the third great philosopher-dramatist of the Enlightenment, whose principles triumphed. Diderot's voyeuristic naturalism was secular, democratic and scientific in spirit, but left scant space for the classical ideal of citizenship.

Participatory happenings, the drama of ideas, the representation of real life ... Our choices in the twenty-first century have not in essence moved on from those available in the Enlightenment. Our social order continues to be constrained by religions that refuse to be rationalized out of existence, by the dominance of large nation-states and by the gap between dreams of democratic participation and a political system that is felt to be disempowering. We have not reached any more settled consensus about human nature: whether we are essentially atomized individuals, or whether it is legitimate to postulate some equivalence to Rousseau's transpersonal 'general will'. In the final chapter I shall examine the collectivist impulse in Germany prior to the Second World War, and the communist-inspired work of the Indian People's Theatre Association in the era of Indian independence, addressing the difficulties that arise when an idea of the 'people' or *Volk* is not attached to an idea of citizenship, but also the power, pleasure and potential of collective action. The post-war swing of the pendulum towards individualism has entailed the erosion of what is variously referred to as the public sphere, the public realm or the public square. I shall argue in a theoretical conclusion that only in this domain can the practice of theatre coalesce with the practice of citizenship.

CHAPTER 2

Athens

The performing arts... have indeed a certain affinity with politics.
Performing artists... need an audience to show their virtuosity, just
as acting men need the presence of others before whom they can
appear... The Greek polis once was precisely that 'form of government' which provided men with a space of appearances where they
could act, with a kind of theatre where freedom could appear.[1]

For Hannah Arendt, as for most other modern theorists of citizenship,
classical Athens is a necessary reference point when she tries to imagine
what citizenship might mean today in a regenerated public sphere. The
phrase 'form of government' is qualified by quotation marks because the
polis was nothing but the sum of its self-governing citizens, and there was
no abstract conception of the 'state'. The citizen's life finds its justification
through a public demonstration of virtuosity – a word better rendered by
the Italian *virtù* or the Greek *aretē*. The polis exists, as Aristotle puts it,
not merely to allow the cohabitation of families and villages but for the
sake of fine actions. It is not the rich or well-born who have most share in
the polis, but those who are superior in political virtue because they put
most into the *koinōnia*, the 'community'.[2] We should not underestimate
the difference between the participatory democracy of Athens, organized
on the basis of lottery and rotation to maximize participation, and our own
representational system which separates the active few who govern from
the passive majority who consent to being governed. Rousseau was one
of the last major political theorists to challenge the electoral principle. He
has a French dance instructor comment on the submissive body-language
of an Englishman who thinks he is a citizen: 'No, sir: this lowered face,
this timid look, this hesitant stance announce a mere slave with the title of
Elector.'[3]

[1] Arendt (1961) 154. Cf. above p. 12.   [2] Aristotle *Politics* III.ix.14–15 (1290b–1281a).
[3] Rousseau (1969) 667. On types of democracy, see Manin (1997). Cf. also Rousseau's *Social Contract*
IV.3.

DEMOCRACY AND CHORALITY

It has often been remarked that theatre and democracy emerged simultaneously in fifth-century Athens. Recent classical scholarship has offered some cautions, however. Tragedy seems to have emerged as a genre in the pre-democratic period known as the age of the tyrants.[4] Aeschylus died in Sicily, and it is likely that his play *The Aetneans* was written to support the foundation of a Greek colony under Mount Aetna, non-democratic and ruled by a 'tyrant'.[5] Euripides provided a mythic ancestry for the Hellenizing king of Macedonia in his *Archelaus*, and it is widely assumed that he wrote *The Bacchae* while in exile at Archelaus' court.[6] Once we imagine *The Bacchae* performed in Macedonia, we shall find it hard to see what is inherently democratic about this story of failed kingship. If we think of tragedies as textual containers, then we rapidly become caught in a hermeneutic circle: we pride ourselves on looking at the past through democratic eyes, and thus readily interpret the text as a vehicle for the democratic ideology we approve. If we look at tragedy and comedy not as abstract containers of meaning but as material and embodied practices, we may find ourselves on less slippery ground.

For Aristotle, the polis comprises those capable of collective self-rule, and the citizen (*politēs*) is one who shares in the processes of decision-making within the law-court and the assembly, and who 'exists especially in a democracy; elsewhere his existence is feasible but not inevitable'.[7] Democracy is always a relative term, dependent on how widely membership in the body politic extends, and we should not be supercilious about Athens' exclusion of slaves and women, given most 'democracies' in Europe and North America only abandoned property qualifications in the nineteenth century, and extended the vote to women in the twentieth. The remarkable features of Athenian democracy were its systematic participatory structure, and the unprecedented rights it gave to manual workers. Though there were many other democracies in the Greek world, Athens is the best documented. While our historical sources are writers and theoreticians, speaking out and doing were the basis of democracy, so it is not surprising that we have no extant treatise which proselytizes democracy or defines its ideology. Like theatre, democracy was both an embodied practice and a process, constantly engaged in renewal.

Athens was the product of 'synoikism', the coming together of towns and villages in the region of Attica to form a single political conglomerate.

---

[4] Wilson (2000) 18, Rhodes (2003).   [5] Documentation in Poli-Palladini (2001).
[6] See Revermann (2001).   [7] Aristotle *Politics* III.i.6–12 (1275a–b).

A mass evacuation at the time of Xerxes' invasion did much to support the feeling that Athens comprised its people more than its land, and to make possible a decision in the Peloponnesian war to concentrate resources on command of the sea rather than defence of borders. Athens was much the largest city in the classical Greek world, with some 30,000 adult male citizens when the democratic structure was set up at the end of the sixth century BC, a number that had grown substantially, perhaps doubled, by the time of Pericles in the mid fifth century. In the later years of the century the Peloponnesian war took a terrible toll on numbers, and we return to a figure of around 30,000 in the fourth. To these numbers we must add women, children and youth, a population of free immigrants amounting to perhaps half the number of citizens, and a large but unquantifiable number of slaves, with some 10,000 working in the silver mines alone.[8] For Mogens Hansen, on the basis of such figures, Athens cannot be described as a 'face-to-face' society, yet Paul Cartledge has insisted that face-to-faceness is one of the key principles of Greek democracy.[9] For Aristotle, scale was critical, and a polis had an optimum size, like a ship, an animal or indeed a tragedy. The minimum size is determined by self-sufficiency, the maximum by the need of citizens to know each other, since they would otherwise deliver bad judgements, appoint the wrong people and lack control over civic membership. Likewise a general cannot command too large an army, for his herald would need the voice of a Stentor.[10] 'Voice-to-voice' might be a better description of Athenian society than 'face-to-face'.

The emergence of tragedy relates to demography, and to the challenge that faced Athenians wanting to capitalize on the cohesive benefits of a face-to-face society, when numbers meant that you could no longer recognize all the faces of fellow citizens. In the Greek world at large, choral dancing was the fundamental device for social bonding. Different social groups, defined by age, gender and sometimes birth, would dance in honour of relevant gods or goddesses, and these dances would narrate myths touching the particular deity. Plato in his *Republic* and more conspicuously in his *Laws* attempts to reinstate a traditionalist order of choral dancing that embodies the order of society. Aristotle gives less attention to the cultural and religious domain within the polis, but nevertheless uses the chorus as a metaphor for social order. He ponders what defines the polis, given the amount of immigration and constitutional change, and proffers the

---

[8] See Davies (1992) 296–300, Hansen (1991) 55.
[9] Hansen (1991) 60; Cartledge in Raaflaub, Ober and Wallace (2007) 156–61.
[10] Aristotle *Politics* VII.iv (1326b); cf. *Poetics* II.vii (1250b–1251a).

analogy of a constant group of dancers who present a tragedy and a comedy, thereby picturing the polity as a genre of collective dance.[11] With regard to leadership, Aristotle argues that, just as the body needs to be governed by the soul, the woman by the man, and the slave by the master, so some individuals are capable of a different sort of civic virtue, by analogy with the chorus, where the chorus leader has superior skills to the dancer in the ranks.[12] These analogues raise interesting questions about chorality in democratic Athens a century earlier: who exactly were the dancers? And how distinctive was the leader expected to be?

Barbara Kowalzig has thrown valuable light on Athenian chorality, demonstrating not only the centrality of choral dancing in the Greek polis, but also its creativity and fluidity. The polis was constantly responding to change, manufacturing new rituals that created the illusion of longevity and employing poets at great expense.[13] When we look at Greek tragedy through this lens, the old dichotomy between ritual and art becomes unsustainable. Tragedy and comedy were in common parlance simply another form of *choros* or 'choral dance'. Kowalzig calls our attention to the distinctive nature of chorality in democratic Athens, where public choral dancing was concentrated around the cult of a single god. Since Dionysus was male, there was no place for public dancing by women of the kind that one saw in Sparta and most other Greek cities, while the payment of dancers meant that it was no longer just an elite who could commit the time to training.[14] With regard to the narrative content of tragedy, Kowalzig describes an assimilative process, consistent with Athenian imperialism, which used the medium of tragedy to incorporate non-Athenian myths in an Athenian ritual.[15] The strength of Kowalzig's analysis lies in its demolition of the conceptual divide between play and ritual frame, allowing us to see how and why participation in the worship of Dionysus was an act of Athenian citizenship. Dionysus the wine-god was well suited to a democratic role since his alcoholic pleasures are available to all alike and break down social constraints.[16]

The major city festival of Dionysus took place in the spring. In addition to five comedies and three tetralogies the festival incorporated twenty dithyrambs, musically elaborate circular choral dances.[17] We have two examples by Bacchylides from the Aeschylean period, one culminating in the birth of Dionysus, the other a dialogue concerned with Theseus and

[11] Aristotle *Politics* III.iii.7 (1276b).   [12] *Politics* III.iv.6 (1277a).
[13] See the introductory chapter to Kowalzig (2007a).   [14] Kowalzig (2004).
[15] Kowalzig (2007b).   [16] See e.g. Seaford (1994) 245–7.
[17] A tetralogy = three tragedies + a satyr play. Pickard-Cambridge (1988) is the standard sourcebook.

Athens.[18] While tragedy and comedy have enjoyed a high profile in the later history of western culture, classical dithyrambs left little mark, perhaps because their meanings seemed too local, and music was too central in their performance. Nevertheless the dithyramb was far more significant than tragedy in fifth-century Athens in terms of mass participation, financial outlay and victory monuments. Renowned Greek poets were commissioned to write them, and each tribe competed with a chorus of fifty boys with unbroken voices and fifty men.[19] The ten 'tribes' were the basic building blocks of fifth-century democracy, each one an arbitrary mix of three 'demes' or pre-existent local communities, one from the urban centre, one from the coast and one from the hinterland, in a system designed to create common identity in a diverse population of traders, fishermen and peasant farmers. The willingness of Athenians in the Peloponnesian war to sacrifice their farmland for the sake of naval supremacy demonstrates the success of the tribal system in building a shared sense of the collective good. The dithyrambic competition was one of the key institutions in building civic solidarity, giving religious sanction to a tribal structure that shaped both warfare and the executive.[20] At the start of the Dionysia, the spectacular masked procession which culminated in sacrifice and feasting was organized on a tribal basis,[21] and seating was later organized by tribes, though we have no evidence for the fifth century.[22]

Comedy may well have been organized on the same basis, given that the quota of five comedies incorporated ten hemi-choruses, but tragedy sat outside that structure, for unlike comedy its subject matter was not overtly Athenian. While the dithyramb was a vast logistical enterprise, tragedy was economical, requiring only three choruses of twelve, or later fifteen, and we should think of it as a solution to the problem of scale, for its emotional power ran a vast assembly of people through the same gamut of shared emotion so they could experience collectivity, shedding tears in a vicarious form of participation. The surrender of individuality to group emotion was a demonstration of Dionysus' power, and thus a tribute to the god. Kowalzig examines a number of passages in tragedy which seem to reflect back on the theatrical event and so 'project the audience back into the orchestra and make it part of the "ritual" occurring on stage'.[23]

[18] Bacchylides *Dithyrambs* 19 and 18. On the dithyramb, see Wilson (2000) 66–7, Csapo (2004) 214–16. Wilson (n. 202) surmises that the 'Theseus' dithyramb was intended for performance on Delos.
[19] Standard information in Pickard-Cambridge (1988) 66, 74–9.
[20] On the tribal system, see Hansen (1991) 46–9.   [21] Wilson (2000) 24.
[22] Wiles (1997) 37.   [23] Kowalzig (2007b) 236.

Until recently it was possible to state categorically that Greek tragedies were vast one-off events. Simon Goldhill, for example, in *The Cambridge Companion to Greek Tragedy* of 1997 offered an account of the Athenian audience where he argued that 'to be in an audience is above all *to play the role of democratic citizen*'.[24] He does not dismiss Plato's figure of 30,000 spectators out of hand but offers 14,000–17,000 as a plausible estimate, and describes this as the largest annual gathering of citizens, more than twice the size of the Assembly. He points to seats of honour (*prohedriai*) at the front and the presence of 500 members of the Council en bloc as evidence for construing the auditorium as a map of the body politic, arranged in a semi-circle to maximize public self-awareness, and he favours the hypothesis of tribal seating. The audience for him constitutes 'the civic gaze'.[25] Current fashion in archaeology will have none of this. The fifth-century theatre is held to be rectilinear, and the audience limited to 7,000 at most.[26] I do not find these arguments persuasive. The circularity of dithyrambic dancing makes rectilinear reconstructions hard to credit.[27]

Nonetheless, some rethinking of Goldhill's account is required. Spectators had to pay for seats on wooden stands erected by contractors, so maybe some of the poor would have watched from higher up the slope, and late sources mention a famous tree under which men stood,[28] so the performance may not have gathered the whole community within an architectural emblem of civic harmony. Foreign residents comprised about a third of the free population and, as tradesmen concentrated in the urban centre, would have provided a substantial presence, reminding us that being Athenian and being a citizen were not identical. If we accept an audience figure of around 17,000, and then allow for the presence of foreign visitors, non-citizen residents, males under the age of twenty-one and possibly a few women and slaves, it is hard to imagine that more than a quarter of the citizen body was present. Archaeological finds have also prompted scholars to give more attention to performance in local communities. In the larger

[24] Goldhill (1997) 54 – Goldhill's italics.
[25] Goldhill (1997); cf. Plato *Symposium* 175e. Wiles (1997) offers a similar perspective.
[26] Moretti (2000) is the most influential statement of the new orthodoxy. Hans Goette gains authority from providing an appendix to Csapo (2007). The evidence is not adequately published. Two domestic wells found half-way up the slope of the stone auditorium provide the main argument for reducing the scale of the classical auditorium, but given chronic overcrowding within the city walls during the Peloponnesian war, it is likely that empty slopes would have been requisitioned for domestic use outside the festive season. On rectilinearity, see Wiles (2010).
[27] For example, the models in Munich Theatre Museum extensively reproduced in Moraw and Nölle (2002). The 'rectilinear' argument rests mainly on a few fifth-century stone seating blocks built into the later structure. See also Wiles (2010).
[28] See Csapo (2007).

demes, each of which functioned as a polis in miniature, there was a flourishing circuit of theatre festivals in honour of Dionysus taking place in the
months leading up to the City Dionysia. We know now of some nineteen
festivals across Attica, and must take seriously Plato's sarcastic reference
to enthusiasts who 'as it were rent out their ears and run to hear all the
choruses at the Dionysia, omitting neither towns nor villages'.[29] It is clear
that plays could be tested or reproduced in deme performances. Many who
could not see tragedies in Athens could see them locally, and it is likely that
many danced in tragic choruses when their deme could afford to buy in
the actors. The theatre extended like modern mass media beyond the range
of a single Stentorian voice, and transferability was one of its democratic
advantages. The Dionysia was not a gathering of the entire community,
but it was the centre from which ripples spread.

Rousseau was far more sympathetic to Athenian actors than he was
to their later French counterparts, and he lists six reasons why Athens
honoured actors:
(1) Theatre was new so there was no prejudice.
(2) Actors were regarded as priests.
(3) Actors were 'educated citizens who before the eyes of their compatriots
    performed the history of their country'.
(4) The Athenians were passionate about liberty, so respected the organs
    of instruction.
(5) There were no female performers.
(6) Theatre was neither commercial nor 'enclosed in dark prisons'.
Greek plays, he concludes, being 'large, proud spectacles performed in the
open air before a whole nation, provided nothing else but contests, victories,
prizes, goals that would inspire the Greeks to ardent emulation, warming
their hearts with sentiments of honour and glory'.[30] Rousseau recognizes
here that the competitive framework of theatre festivals was linked to
the dramatic content of tragedy, and his understanding of Greek theatre
as a medium of historical and political education would have a modern
ring but for his antifeminism, and a language of 'nation' which elides
Athenian patriotism with panhellenism. Rousseau's ultimate preference is
for Spartan chorality over an Athenian theatre centred on the actor, for
it is choral dance that will provide the foundation for a renewed sense of
citizenship in Geneva. Though Athens was passionate about liberty, and

---

[29] Jones (2004) 124–58; *Republic* 5.475d. Wiles (1997) 23–34 examines some of the settings. The deme
   theatre at Acharnai is currently being excavated.
[30] *Letter to d'Alembert*: Rousseau (2003) 130–1.

he cites Iphigeneia's famous speech in Euripides to reinforce the point,[31] Rousseau did not in the last analysis consider Athens to be a true democracy, for the demagoguery of Pericles did not generate an authentic expression of the General Will.[32] Rousseau could not accept, either in politics or in theatre, that listening to rhetoric should be an important component of citizenship. He was more pragmatic, however, when he pondered how to create citizenship in a land as vast as Poland, and here conceded a place to spectatorship. Having praised the tragedies of Aeschylus, Sophocles and Euripides because they helped bring the courage and virtues of the Greeks to a pitch no longer imaginable, he concluded that the building of Polish patriotism would require such spectacles, with the Spanish bullring providing a better model than eighteenth-century court theatres.[33]

The interpretation of Greek tragedy has undergone many vicissitudes. While figures like Nietzsche and Frazer steered readers and producers in the first half of the twentieth century to see Greek tragedy as a religious ritual, the ongoing work of philologists editing Greek texts has invited readers to view the text as a self-contained entity with its own internal coherence. The trend in the last thirty years, a period influenced by figures like Brecht and Arthur Miller, has been to read Greek plays as political engagements,[34] and two essays have had a seminal influence. Jean-Pierre Vernant in 1972, explaining why tragedy and democracy emerged at the same moment, argued that an old heroic and mythic world collided with a new legal and political environment that stressed individual responsibility, leaving a gap in social experience, a gash in human consciousness to which tragedy responded. For Vernant, the formal divide between actor and chorus correlated with a tension between aristocratic heroism and the civic community.[35] While French scholarship took an anthropological and psychoanalytic turn, Anglophone scholarship showed more interest in political institutions, and Simon Goldhill's essay of 1987 'The Great Dionysia and civic ideology' has been much cited. Goldhill called attention to formal civic aspects of the festival which included the display of revenues, the appearance of the ten elected generals, the proclamation of public honours and a parade by orphans adopted by the state after their fathers had died fighting for the city. Interpreting these pre-play rituals as an ideological expression of the normative relationship between an

---

[31] *Iphigeneia in Aulis* 1375ff. – noted in the posthumous edition of the *Letter* – Rousseau (2003) 130.
[32] Rousseau (1964): article on political economy.   [33] Rousseau (1964) 958, 963.
[34] Saïd (1998) helpfully sub-divides the political currents, but cannot herself escape a text-based reading.
[35] 'The historical moment of tragedy in Greece: some of the social and psychological conditions' in Vernant and Vidal-Naquet (1988) 23–8; first published in English in 1981.

individual citizen and the democratic polis, he reads the plays as transgressive, arguing that 'the tragic texts seem designed to leave an audience
with a question... It is here in the potential *undermining of a secure and
stable sense of norm*... that the most unsettling thrust of tragedy may be
located.'[36] Goldhill's citizen-spectator is a man who asks himself awkward
questions, and Vernant similarly explains how 'the hero has ceased to be a
model. He has become, both for himself and for others, a problem.'

It is salutary to move from Goldhill back to the eighteenth century
and to see how Greek tragedy looked from a perspective other than our
own. Voltaire believed no less fervently than Rousseau and Goldhill in the
educational benefits of Greek tragedy. Citing some of his own triumphs,
he argued: 'These subjects move the coarsest as the most delicate of souls;
and there would be fewer coarse, hard souls if the people attended decent
performances. This is what made the Athenians a superior nation. Artisans
did not waste on lewd farces the money that should have fed their families. At glorious festivals, the magistrates summoned the entire nation to
performances which taught virtue and love of country.'[37] While Voltaire,
on the basis of his own experience, conceives of a feeling spectator, Goldhill prefers a thinking spectator who corresponds with modern ideals of
'deliberative democracy' which emphasize public debate and the benefits
of an informed, thinking electorate.[38] The flaw in Goldhill's model of the
atomized thinking spectator who picks apart ambiguities in civic discourse
is that rationalistic spectators do not function collectively and cohesively.
The Athenians were devotees of debate in the law-court and the assembly,
not to mention philosophical schools, but they were no less remarkable for
their ability to act en masse and follow through collective decisions. Viewing Greek tragedy through the lens of the eighteenth century, Rousseau
and Voltaire were more attuned than we are to the emotional power of
Greek tragedy.

When Vernant and Goldhill encourage us to read tragic texts in the
historical and political context of performance, they leave in place the
conceptual split between text and context. Vernant's essay distinguished
'ritual' from the new 'aesthetic' role of the theatrical mask, and saw choral
lyric in tragedy as qualitatively different from work by Simonides and
Pindar, noted authors of dithyrambs. In a companion essay, Vernant tells
us that although 'each play constitutes a message, enclosed within a text',
only a mental context made it possible for the playwright to communicate

[36] Revised text in Winkler and Zeitlin (1990) 97–129, p. 128 (Goldhill's italics).
[37] Letter to Capacelli, 23 November 1760: Voltaire (1963–93) no. 6393.
[38] See Dryzek (2002). Barker (2009) develops a similar line, linking tragedy to the impossibility of any
   final moral reconciliation.

with his public.[39] Goldhill provides a more clear-cut distinction between the norm established by the ritual frame and the transgressive intrusion of tragedy. Rousseau broke down this text/context binary through his insistence that Greek tragedy was essentially a competition, and that the spirit of emulation imparted by the festival was inseparable from enactment of a heroic story. The assumptions of Vernant and Goldhill rest upon democratic liberalism, postulating a morally autonomous spectator who engages more or less successfully with a problem play. The assumptions of Rousseau rest upon civic republicanism, and a conviction that the dance of the citizen out there in the public sphere is of far greater human value than the individual's private reflection upon an art-object.

Diagram 1

SOKRATES DEDICATED	
EURIPIDES TAUGHT	
TRAGEDIANS	AMPHIDEMOS
PYTHON	EUTHYDIKOS
EKHEKLES	LYSIAS
MENALKES	SŌN
PHILOKRATES	KRITODEMOS
EKHYLLOS	KHARIAS
MELETOS	PHAIDON
EMPORION	

We learn much about the competitive structure of festival from an inscription carved on the base of a statue, probably a statue of Victory, found in the coastal deme of Anagyrous.[40] The grandeur of the monument implies that it commemorates a victory won in Athens, not locally (see Diagram 1). The statue was set up by Sokrates as *chorēgos* ('leader of the chorus') to celebrate his successful 'liturgy'. Liturgies were allocated each year to rich Athenian individuals, who had no choice but to part with some wealth unless they could point to someone indisputably richer who had been overlooked. The performance of liturgies offered them a road to public honour, which in an aristocratic environment they would have secured through other forms of conspicuous consumption. Peter Wilson constructs a plausible scenario for Sokrates' liturgy around the hypothesis that this was the first victory of Euripides, which took place in the spring of 441 BC. Two years earlier this same Sokrates had been threatened with 'ostracism', a democratic device that sent into exile individuals thought to

---

[39] 'Tensions and ambiguities in Greek tragedy': Vernant and Vidal-Naquet (1988) 29–31.
[40] Wilson (2000) 131–6.

have overreached themselves, and a month or so after the 441 Dionysia he was elected to the post of general. His production of Euripides' tragedy was a critical event in his public career.

The inscription names fourteen 'tragedians' – in Greek *tragōidoi*, 'singers [for the prize of a] goat'. These are the chorus, who normally had to be citizens. We know that in the dithyramb a rival *chorēgos* could wreak havoc by identifying a dancer who was not a registered citizen.[41] The tragic com-petition was formally a contest of choruses, and the three speaking actors attached to each chorus were technically ancillaries, their citizenship of no relevance, and there is no mention of them on this monument because they were paid by the state, not by the *chorēgos*. Since there were normally fifteen in a tragic chorus, it is hard to resist the inference that Sokrates was 'chorus leader' in a double sense: not just the sponsor leading his chorus to the theatre in the grand procession but also the actual leader of the dance, positioned at the centre of the front file and demonstrating to the Athenian public not only his munificence but also his voice and athleticism.[42] The evidence of vases suggests that the dancers of tragedy were young men, replicas of the beautiful beardless Dionysus, and the bare names on this monument suggest that these were local men who needed no further identification. Sokrates would have recruited young men from his own community so he could train them in his home over a period of many months. Since he paid and fed them, they could be chosen more for their skills than their wealth, though we cannot be sure how far these skills extended to poor fishermen. The erection of the monument locally rather than centrally testifies to the strength of the deme, reminding us that citizenship is always layered. While dithyrambic victories in Athens were commemorated by grand monuments on the road to the theatre, tragic victories were commemorated in the city by a simple plaque, for the competitors in dithyrambs were civic units and the monuments fos-tered collective zeal, whereas tragic victories reflected more directly on the individual *chorēgos*, whom it behoved to display public modesty.

Euripides was the *didaskalos* or 'teacher'. Plutarch has an anecdote about a chorus man giggling when Euripides taught him to sing in the elaborate, emotional and orientalizing 'half Lydian' mode, reminding us that cho-reography and music sat alongside words as the elements which the poet created or 'taught'.[43] We should not rule out the possibility that at this

---

[41] Wilson (2000) 77, 148.
[42] Wilson (2000) 97–8, Wiles (1997) 95. The term *coryphaeus* is normally used to distinguish the chorus leader in performance.
[43] 'On listening' in Plutarch *Moralia* 46b.

early stage of his career Euripides interacted with the chorus as *hypokritēs* –
the leading actor, literally 'answerer'. His function as teacher of dancers
slid imperceptibly into teaching the Athenian public, offering the public
knowledge parallel to the cultural expertise gained by a dancer. The idea
that the poet is a *didaskalos* is central to Aristophanes' conception in
The Frogs. In this comedy Dionysus develops a yearning for Euripides,
who had died in the previous year, and pursues him to the underworld,
where he becomes judge in a competition, obliged to choose whether
Euripides or Aeschylus is the poet to save the city in its moment of crisis.
Artist and citizen coalesce in this debate. Before we examine *The Frogs*,
however, we need to understand the historical circumstances, at the start of
405 BC.

THE FROGS

Athens overreached itself in the Peloponnesian war with a bold but rash
assault on Syracuse in 413 BC, undertaken with the aim of controlling Sicily.
Nicias was one of Athens' most renowned *chorēgoi*, his victory monuments
a conspicuous feature in the sanctuary of Dionysus, but his generalship
was not of the same quality.[44] In the backlash to defeat, democracy was
overthrown and a regime of 400 men took control in a coup in 411,
presenting itself nominally as rule by the 5,000 hoplites, i.e. those citizens
rich enough to arm for warfare on land. Thanks to the democratic passion
of the navy, dominated by oarsmen of lower social status, the oligarchy
was ousted and its perpetrators stripped of their citizen rights. The site
chosen for a ceremony of reconciliation – Thucydides' term is *homonoia*,
'being of the same mind' – was the Theatre of Dionysus.[45] This detail
reveals something important about theatre in democratic life: a sacred place
that engendered same-mindedness rather than divisive argument. Soon
afterwards Alcibiades returned from exile. Alcibiades had used flamboyant
displays as *chorēgos* to win mass popular support, and one account of
his return tells how he rowed into Athens with a famous actor in full
tragic costume setting the rhythm of the oars, accompanied by an *aulos*-
player who had made his fame at Delphi.[46] The anecdote, true or not,
reminds us of the strict parallelism in democratic life between the naval

[44] On Nicias, see Wilson (2000) 137–8, 228–9.
[45] Thucydides viii.93. The oligarchic regime was instituted at Colonus, a shrine sacred to upper-class 'knights' and lent further significance by Sophocles: see Wiles (1997) 150.
[46] Duris of Samos, cited in Plutarch *Alcibiades* 32. On Alcibiades, see Wilson (2000) 148–55. The *aulos* was a reed instrument with double pipes.

trierarch, who recruited, paid and trained members of his tribe to row as an ensemble to the controlling and energizing music of the *aulos*, and the task of the *chorēgos* responsible for competitive displays of physical synergy in the theatre. Alcibiades found Athens an unsafe place to be because the dominance of one charismatic individual led inevitably to accusations of 'tyranny'.

The war was going badly, the empire was crumbling and control of the sea was critical for the supply of corn to an urban population. The main residual fleet was trapped in Mytilene and needed rescue. All resources were concentrated on the construction of a new fleet, but there was a shortage of able-bodied citizens. Rowing in the fleet carried a small stipend, and some citizens had always brought slaves to row beside them, and some non-citizens had always made up numbers. With the enemy occupying Attica, many slaves had deserted the city and their loyalty was at risk. Morale was of the essence at this moment of emergency, and citizen numbers needed to be enhanced, so slaves were apparently promised citizenship before they enlisted to row. Citizenship had been a closed category since Pericles in 451 restricted membership to the children of two citizen parents, and this rule was now loosened, making bastards legitimate.[47] Another unprecedented feature of the fleet was that some of the knights swallowed their aristocratic pride and abandoned their horses to join ship in a display of solidarity. The marshalling of the emergency fleet involved a significant reconceptualization of citizenship.

In the ensuing battle of Arginusae, the Athenians outrowed and out-rammed the opposing crews, who were well paid with Persian money but were not citizens or future citizens with their city at stake. Twenty-five Athenian ships were lost, and in the storm that followed the battle the Athenians were unable either to attend to sinking ships or to administer a coup de grace to the enemy. Some 1,500 Athenians must have died, and the victory was an occasion for relief rather than celebration. Diodorus records that on the eve of the battle the Athenian commander-in-chief dreamed that he and six of his fellow generals were performing *The Phoenician Women*, competing against the Spartans who were performing *The Suppliant Women*. These two Euripidean tragedies feature the seven Argive commanders who died in their assault on Thebes, and the prophet interpreted the dream to mean that seven generals would die, even though victory would be won.[48] True or not, the anecdote reveals again the convergence of competition in the theatre and in warfare. It was not intellectual debate but images of

---

[47] On the slave presence see Hunt (1998) 87–95.   [48] Diodorus xiii.97.6.

war and death that are supposed to have haunted the imagination of this Athenian spectator.

Diodorus recorded the dream because of the ironic manner in which it came true. In October 406, an unconstitutional meeting of the assembly condemned the generals to death, and the six who had returned to Athens were at once executed. According to the ever-practical Xenophon, the crime of the generals was their failure to rescue the living, but for Diodorus their principal crime was failure to bring back the corpses of the dead for burial in Athens. Euripides' *Suppliant Women* is one amongst many tragedies that reminded the Athenians how important burial was, both for individuals concerned with the afterlife and for a community's sense of renewal. The Athenians rapidly repented their hasty action, and turned on those who had whipped up their emotions,[49] though they did not accept Spartan overtures for peace. It was in this atmosphere of hysteria and in-fighting, panic and defiance that Aristophanes wrote his *Frogs*, performed some three months after the unconstitutional assembly.

The play was performed not at the Dionysia but at the winter Lenaian festival, when it was permissible for the *chorēgoi* and their dancers to be resident foreigners.[50] 'Athenian' was never a straightforward category. The presence of two choruses suggests that, as in the Dionysia two months later, the *chorēgia* was divided because no single individual was rich enough to sustain the liturgy alone.[51] The chorus of frogs is more spectacular, while the chorus of pilgrims, who make a jest of their ragged costumes, has a longer role. While one of the rival comedies performed at the festival was called 'The Muses' and dealt with the arts, and the other focused on the politician Cleophon,[52] Aristophanes yoked these themes together, and as part of a collective endeavour to create theatre when food was scarce and energy sapped, he explored why theatre was necessary to a community's survival.

There are two reading strategies we must beware of when examining *The Frogs*. The first splits the play into two: a picaresque journey to the underworld followed by a contest of literary giants. The 1975 Sondheim version, which makes Shakespeare triumph over a modernizing George Bernard Shaw, struggles to reach beyond the aesthetic domain.[53] We need different conceptual frameworks to make sense of Aristophanes' world,

---

[49] Kagan (2003) offers the fullest modern narrative account.   [50] Pickard-Cambridge (1988) 41.
[51] Sommerstein (1996) 192.   [52] Sommerstein (1996) 1.
[53] In a reworking of this version in New York in the wake of 9/11, the audience gathered that 'the creative artist should be admired for the gently plangent comfort of nostalgia and the affirmation of collective memory': English (2005) 133.

where artist and citizen were one and the same. Second is the quest for Aristophanes' political message.[54] The privileged status of the authorial text as the element transmitted to posterity encourages critics to search for the intent behind the words, or an ideology enshrined in discourse, but the 'message' always proves elusive. The historian struggles to explain the vagaries of an Athenian public which awarded Aristophanes first prize for his caricature of Cleon, predecessor of the populist Cleophon, yet promptly elected Cleon general.[55] Perhaps theatre attracted a social elite unrepresentative of the masses, perhaps the political message as so often in theatre proved counterproductive, or perhaps influencing votes was incidental to the main purpose of the performance event. It is my broad argument in this book that we should avoid interpreting theatre as a channel whereby a playwright conveys a predetermined message to a receiver, but should try to see a play as a shared experience made by all its participants.

The Frogs is articulated around a series of theatrical metaphors, and my analysis will focus on four of them. In the first, the title scene of the play, Dionysus is ferried to the underworld, but Charon the boatman inverts hierarchy by insisting that not he but Dionysus should take the oar. While he rows across the orchestra, Dionysus engages in a musical contest with a chorus of marsh frogs, and succeeds in outcroaking his opponents. On a ritual level the scene alludes to the worship of Dionysus at his shrine 'in the marshes', which may have become an unsafe area in 405.[56] On a political level it relates to Athens' famous warships. The slave Xanthias is not allowed on board because he did not fight at Arginusae (191). Dionysus was a soldier at Arginusae (48), in other words a member of the hoplite class affluent enough to serve on deck in armour without the need to row, and so through rowing himself to the underworld this hoplite engages in manual labour he would normally spurn. Rowing in the manner of a commoner, Dionysus sings the harsh music of the mob more effectively than the mob themselves. Music, religion and questions of citizenship merge in an image that evokes the city's recent trauma.

During his brief spell back in Athens, one of Alcibiades' achievements was to lead the annual procession of initiates to Eleusis across lands that a foreign army of occupation had made unsafe, and this procession is commemorated by the arrival of the second chorus.[57] Aristophanes' audience

---

[54] McGlew (2002) 12–16 and Van Steen (2007) offer sensible overviews of the problem.
[55] Aristophanes won the prize for his *Knights*: see Sommerstein and Barrett (1978) 33–4.
[56] Parker (2005) 56 infers that the shrine lay outside the city walls.   [57] Kagan (1987) 291–2.

needed no reminding of how many Athenians had now been consigned the underworld, and his chorus of pilgrims now enjoy a utopian afterlife. They enter in a procession which we might compare to the grand procession of the Dionysia, where tribal groupings, foreign residents identified by red robes and at least a token woman created an image of the civic community.[58] Aristophanes' chorus of pilgrims offers a slightly different image of the inclusive community, because women feature on more equal terms, and because the Mysteries were open to the disenfranchised;[59] it is also overtly exclusive, the chorus banning, for example, those who have failed to dance with the Muses and those who have created faction among the citizens, and many individuals are singled out for their different forms of sexual, political or artistic deviance. The major force of the Aristophanic image lies in its reminder that what makes a person Athenian is participation in the religious cults of the city, not the niceties of voting rights.

In the third metaphor, Dionysus and his slave Xanthias exchange costumes as each in turn pretends to be the master. Since the evidence of slaves was admitted in court when given under torture, both are tortured in a vain attempt to establish which is master. The scene alludes to Arginusae where slaves merged with citizens, but also more broadly to a democracy where aristocracy and *dēmos* have become indistinguishable. What the scene does not define is an authorial verdict. We can take the metaphor to imply that the distinction between master and slave is a product of convention, opposing the view later held by Aristotle that slavery is enshrined in nature; or we can take it as an expression of outrage against the erosion of natural distinctions. Spectators of all persuasions could unite in laughter, on the basis of varied interpretations, and experience themselves as a homogeneous crowd.

In the ensuing *parabasis*, the demarcated direct address to the audience, the chorus voice political opinions in unusually direct terms.[60] They begin by setting out the privileged status of their utterance, making it clear that the advice they give is both collective and sacred, not simply the view of one individual: 'It is right for the holy chorus to join-in-advising and to teach good to the city' (686–7), and continuing: 'So first it seems good to us to equalize the citizens and take away their fears' (687–8). The chorus recall the disenfranchising of citizens after the collapse of the oligarchy, and the

---

[58] On the procession, see Wilson (2000) 97–8.
[59] On women in this scene, see Dover (1993) 67–8; on the Mysteries, see Parker (2005) 342–3.
[60] Good analyses in Goldhill (1991) 201–22 and McGlew (2002) 163–70.

enfranchising of slaves after Arginusae, affirming: 'we should willingly take all men as our kin, with rights and as citizens, who fought with us at sea' (701–2). The image of Dionysus pulling on his oars while Xanthias remains ashore resonates here as much as the image of master/slave symmetry under torture. In the second half of the *parabasis*, the chorus develop a new metaphor. The city has abandoned its traditional gold and silver for coinage of silver-plated bronze (718ff.), and alas Athens has behaved as it did in debasing its coins: 'Those who are true-born and moderate men, just, fine and virtuous, brought up in gymnasia and choruses and music, we reject, but the bronze and foreign and redheads and the base and base-born we use for everything, and the newest arrivals' (727–32). The 'message' here, the advice sanctified by ritual, is less a product of the individual poet's voice than of comedy as an institution. The term *kaloi kagathoi* which I have translated with the moral terms 'fine and virtuous' has an elitist political ring, and is used to evoke the class of those who practise athletics and dance in choruses. Athens could not have *The Frogs* without the expert athletic dances furnished at great expense by the city's *kaloi kagathoi*. The impoverished attire worn by the chorus as they delivered the *parabasis* was a reminder of what it meant to exclude the rich from the polis.[61]

The conventions of comedy gave all males the same grotesque body incorporating a hanging phallus, pot belly, breasts, prominent buttocks and a large mouth, so the genre was premised on biological human equality.[62] At the same time, the name 'Xanthias' alludes to blond, Slavic hair colouring, identifying him as the human equivalent of bronze coinage, and a reddish wig probably distinguished the slave and non-oarsman from the god. The performance could be taken as a proclamation of human equality or of ethnic difference, according to taste. The play's overt message about inclusiveness affirms what is already implicit in the structure of the festival, that theatre is a space designed to create *homonoia* and to equalize the citizens. Sharing in collective laughter and fantasizing a shared utopia were instrumental in bonding the citizen body, as was the provision of choruses by the elite. We can no more say whether *The Frogs* had an elitist or a populist message than pronounce whether the *chorēgia* was a democratic or a residually aristocratic institution. The play was not about democracy, it *was* democracy in action.

The final image is the contest of the two poets, the old-fashioned Aeschylus versus the modernizing Euripides. Dionysus started off in quest of Euripides, whose *bons mots* he delights in, but returns with Aeschylus. As

---

[61] On costume, see Dover (1993) 62–3.   [62] See Foley (2000).

he explains to the god of the underworld: 'I came for a poet. To what end? That the city, being saved, may produce choruses.' Theatre was not just a means of representing the city, it was the life of the city. To understand the terms of the contest, we should recall the influential figure of Damon, who was both a political consultant to Pericles, advising him that paying jury-men for their services was the best way to create a participatory democracy, and a theorist of music, working out how different rhythms and harmonies shaped character.[63] We know of his views mainly through Plato: 'Beware of endangering everything through changes to a new *form* of music; nowhere do types of music alter in isolation from major political *nomoi* – so Damon says, and I am convinced by him.'[64] The Greek word *nomos* was used both for laws that governed the city and for forms of music, while the word *mousikē* ('music') relates to the whole spectrum of activities dedicated to the Muses, including tragic and comic performance. The contest in *The Frogs* is ultimately about two kinds of music, based on the premise that the harmonies of 'music' were inseparable from the harmonies of citizenship.[65]

Euripides defines his writing as 'democratic' (952) because he makes everyone speak, and he invites the Athenian audience to support his case:

I introduced these people [*the audience*] to such considerations, adding logic to my craft, and speculation, so now they think of everything, and have a real grasp of domesticity, so they investigate how's this? wherever's that? who took this? (971–9)

Democratic theatre, in other words, has become a *drame bourgeois*, a play about private rather than public life. Later in the contest Aeschylus sings a parodic Euripidean aria about a stolen cock (1329ff.), a demotic song since the voice belongs to a woman who goes to market, but a sign of individualism since it is sung by one virtuoso performer rather than a chorus. Challenged to say why a poet (*poiētēs*, literally 'maker') deserves admiration, Euripides responds that a poet must display 'cleverness and put things in mind, so we may *make* better men in cities' (1009–10). Making citizens is the ultimate goal of the poet, and Aeschylus counters Euripidean intelligence and verbal fluency with his own claim to have *made* fighters, to have created heroes like Patroclus and Teucer 'so I could rouse the citizen himself to kill like them, whenever he hears the sound of the trumpet' (1041–2). Few would endorse today this militaristic ideal of citizenship, though the equation of citizen with warrior made perfect sense to Machiavelli and Rousseau. It is a democratic assumption entirely alien

[63] See Wallace (2004). [64] Plato *Republic* 4.424c.
[65] On the 'new music' see Zimmermann (1993), Csapo (2004).

to post-war modern concerns for individual freedom of thought and the right to dissent.

The debate of the playwrights exposes the absurdity of any simple theory of mimesis, whereby people learn through identification with what they see. Aeschylus' *Seven against Thebes* is alleged to have made Thebans brave, not Athenian spectators, and a claim that *The Persians* made Athenians zealous to conquer is undermined by Dionysus' pleasure in lament (1021–9). In broad terms, the contest pits larger-than-life Aeschylean heroism against a Euripidean taste for debate and argument. Evoking the ragged costumes of an under-funded chorus, Aeschylus maintains that potential trierarchs now dress in rags to avoid funding warships – a failure of civic heroism. The oarsmen of Athens' vessel-of-state, the *Paralus*, on the other hand, played a critical role in undermining the oligarchy in 411, and are said to have learned their insubordination from Euripides[66] (1065–73). The democratic city requires its elite but also its argumentative oarsmen. Aeschylus wins as the voice of tradition, and Cleophon the leading spokesman of the *dēmos* is castigated as no true-born Athenian (680–2).[67] Yet this same Cleophon wanted to retain the policy of reliance on naval strength that Aeschylus espouses in his final statement (1463–5),[68] and while Cleophon the man is vilified in the last two lines of the play (1533–4), his militaristic policy is endorsed by the choice of Aeschylus.

The Athenians decided to revive the play a year later, and the extant text incorporates passages of rewriting. The starving city was now on the brink of surrender, Cleophon had been or would soon be executed and Aristophanes was publicly crowned with olive. We are told that the revival was because of the *parabasis*, but this detail sounds like a scholarly surmise.[69] It is clear that the Athenians liked the play because it united and fortified them, but can we really accept that it gave them *advice*? The fact that all Athenians with their bitter divisions and differing levels of despair could laugh at this play together is surely the key factor behind the revival and crowning. David Konstan identifies Aristophanic comedy as a site where social contradictions are enacted, and as a postmodern critic is happy to see the double function of 'Aeschylus', as exemplar of aristocratic style and emblem of democracy, in terms of 'seams and sutures' in democratic

---

[66] Thucydides viii.73.

[67] This charge was also levelled in the play *Cleophon* performed at the same festival: Sommerstein (1996) 1.

[68] Aristotle *Constitution of Athens* 34.1.

[69] Dover (1993) 73–6; Sommerstein (1993). The information is attributed to Dikaiarchos who chronicled the festivals.

ideology.[70] Whilst *The Frogs* can certainly be read for its seams and sutures, the point of the live performances in 405 and 404 was surely not to enact contradictions but to overcome them. James McGlew is closer to the mark when he comments that 'Old Comedy played to individual self-reflection about as well as Socrates played to crowds'.[71] The goal of the performance was to engender an interactive experience, built upon the rhythms of the gags and the dances. The chorus accuse fashionable tragedians of prattling at the feet of Socrates (1491–5), because tragedy and comedy were not about the contemplative world of ideas. They belonged to the world of the active citizen.

The satire of individual politicians was a feature of democracy and was intended to cause offence,[72] but there was no question of Aristophanes attacking the democratic system itself. While Chris Carey sees Aristophanes as a man who responded to public opinion and voiced communal anxieties, Jeffrey Henderson sees him as an assertive political figure who used his democratic freedom of speech to voice minority opinion.[73] These critics reflect contemporary views of citizenship, with English and American emphases respectively. The historian should not, in my view, see Citizen Aristophanes either in terms of a mass medium, or as a brave individual expressing unpopular opinions. Comedy created group solidarity by excluding deviant individuals, and Citizen Aristophanes was an active builder of that solidarity. In *The Frogs*, audience members were reminded that tragedy had provoked not only their collective tears, but also their shared intellectual ferment. The contest between Aeschylus and Euripides mirrors the contest between Aristophanes and two fellow comedians, part of a competitive structure that united through dividing.

PLATO AND ARISTOTLE

When the Spartans occupied Athens in 404, democracy vanished only temporarily, and it survived in a stable form for another eighty years, along with the choregic system. No longer, however, could democracy equate with utopia. Plato and Aristotle reflected on theatre and citizenship in an effort to imagine a more perfect social system. In *The Laws* Plato pictures Athenian tragedy as an act of 'blasphemy', for social order and musical order are of a piece.

---

[70] Konstan (1995) 5, 73.   [71] McGlew (2002) 19.
[72] See 'The Old Oligarch' *Constitution of Athens* 18; also Euripides *Suppliants* 435.
[73] Carey (1994), Henderson (1998).

Whenever some authority makes sacrifice before the people, a chorus thereupon arrives, not one but a bevy of choruses, and standing near the altars, often right beside them, they pour sheer blasphemy over the ceremony, with speeches and rhythms and mournful harmonies tugging at the souls of the listeners; whichever is best at drawing instant tears from the city at sacrifice carries off the prize. Should we not vote out a system (*nomos*) of this kind? If the citizens must become listeners of such laments, when the days are not pure but malign, then choruses paid for their singing should come from abroad just as at funeral processions people are hired to send off the deceased with something like Carian music. Such music would I'm sure be appropriate to these songs. Moreover the attire suited to funeral song would not be garlands and gilded outfits but, in a word, quite the reverse.[74]

The existing Athenian theatre festival, in Plato's conception, was an addendum to the people's sacrifice to Dionysus. Since lament was a recurrent feature of hero cults in the Greek world, Plato could not rule out collective expressions of grief in a ritual context, but what galls him in Athens is the competition to make an audience weep, the participation of citizen dancers and the splendid costumes which signify that this weeping is false and pleasurable. He wants the citizens of his republic imbued with music that will shape their identities, and so he distinguishes the exotic music of tragedy from the indigenous music that will be absorbed by the bodies of his citizens. Each social category in *The Laws* – boys, girls, young men, women, mature men, old men – has its own music and dance, harnessed to traditional narratives, and the music of slaves should be different again.[75] This is to be a stable society where everyone knows their place, not a melting-pot like democracy where the world is in constant flux. Plato defines tragedy as essentially the representation of a fine and virtuous life, and pictures himself as a dramaturg who will realize in the political constitution which he has devised a more authentic mimesis of the good life than any itinerant poet could provide.[76]

In his earlier *Republic*, Plato was even more austere. He abolished the *aulos*, the instrument of ecstasy, and confines his citizens to two modes of song and dance, one militaristic, the other pacific and restrained.[77] Whereas in *The Laws* he focuses on participatory chorality, in *The Republic* his interest lies rather in the stories told by tragedians which slander the gods. In his utopia, poets will be allowed to represent only virtuous human beings so citizens can learn by imitation.[78] Perhaps Plato recalled *The Frogs* when he developed his myth of the metals. Among the earth-born mortals of his republic, the ruling class of Guardians will have traces of gold,

---

[74] Plato *Laws* 7.800.   [75] *Laws* especially 2.664–5, 669; cf. Kowalzig (2007a) 1ff.
[76] *Laws* 7.817b.   [77] Plato *Republic* 3.399.   [78] *Republic* 3.401b.

the Auxiliaries who maintain their power have silver, while peasants and labourers have iron and bronze in their make-up.[79] Democracy is shunned by Plato as a world where all natural relations of authority are erased, including those between master and slave, male and female, father and son.

Observation taught Plato that democracy regularly degenerates into dictatorship, and Alcibiades was a well-known instance of this phenomenon. At the end of *The Frogs* Euripides inclines towards rejection of this charismatic leader who held the mob in sway,[80] but Plato associates Euripides above all his peers with admiration of the god-like 'tyrant' or dictator. The tragic poets are ordered to leave the utopian republic, whereupon: 'Touring to other cities, I suspect, gathering crowds, and hiring fine, loud, persuasive voices [i.e. actors], they will draw constitutions towards tyranny and democracy ... They will receive their fees and prizes mainly, of course, from tyrants, and to a lesser extent from democracies.'[81] Given the volume of modern scholarship on tragedy as democratic ideology, it is on the face of it surprising to see tragedy presented by Plato as a vehicle for 'tyranny'. The logic lies in the cash nexus and the seductive voices of actors which correlate with dramatic texts that, according to Plato, eulogize dictatorship. The most famous 'tyrant' in Greek theatre is doubtless 'Oedipus tyrannus', chosen as ruler of Thebes by popular acclaim because he saved the people from the Sphinx; and we must recall that when Sophocles portrayed this exceptional politician, he also created an exceptional role for a star actor. Plato recoiled from the whole culture of stardom, seeking to rewrite the civic script in order to emphasize choral participation and banish charismatic individuals.

When Aristotle in his turn tried to define the ideal polis, he began by defining the *politēs* or 'citizen' and, as an itinerant philosopher with no ancestral roots in Athens, he took a comparative approach. He starts from the assumption that the true citizen cannot be a *banausos*, an artisan, since citizenship requires leisure in order to take up political office, and the *banausos* is perforce a kind of slave whose master is the community.[82] He much regrets that in democratic cities like Athens the *banausoi* do in fact exert varying degrees of power and are considered citizens.[83] Aristotle then opens up a gap inconceivable to Plato between the good citizen and the good man, since moral virtues belong to all social classes. Aristotle's division

---

[79] *Republic* 3.415. On autochthony, see e.g. Loraux (1986).   [80] Aristophanes *Frogs* 1422–32.
[81] Plato *Republic* 8.568.   [82] Aristotle *Politics* iii.1278a.13.   [83] *Politics* iii.1278a.9.

between true citizens and a quasi-citizen working class has implications for the theatre.

Since the spectator is of two kinds, the one free and educated, the other vulgar and composed of *banausoi*, thetes and so forth, the latter too should be allowed contests and spectacles for their relaxation. These people are perverted, as are their souls, from nature's disposition, and likewise harmonies and melodies are deviant when sharp or coloured. Pleasure depends on your particular nature, and therefore licence must be granted to performers before this sort of spectator to use this category of music.[84]

The split between high and low culture, between an elite audience capable of appreciating art and a popular audience, has been a recurrent feature of political thinking about the arts ever since.

Given his binary divide in the body politic, one of Aristotle's resulting preoccupations is participation. Performance smacks of getting one's hands dirty in a way that does not befit a ruling class.

The Spartans do not learn to play but are by repute capable of judging correctly between good and not good performances. The same argument [as was applied to education] applies when music is used for a free man's enjoyment or pastime. Why should they play themselves rather than enjoy when others play? We might consider what image we have of the gods. Zeus is not one to sing and play the lyre on behalf of poets: '*banausos*' is the name we give to such musicians, for this is not the practice of a 'man', unless he be drunk or disporting himself.[85]

Aristotle concedes that some form of engagement in practice is necessary for children, if the adult citizen is to be equipped to judge the music of others, but he warns against the competitive structure of public festivals that is central to the Athenian educational system. Here the only criterion of merit is the pleasure of the public, and the vulgar spectator corrupts the performer, determining what sort of person he becomes, and encouraging certain forms of movement.[86] Aristotle's scorn for the *banausos* rests on the assumption that mechanical movements of the body degrade character.

While Plato was influenced by memories of the traumatic Peloponnesian war, Aristotle was a Macedonian with no emotional investment in the idea that a citizen body is in the first instance a fighting force bent on ensuring collective survival. The old symmetry between choral dance and warfare was no longer of interest to him, and the theatre he knew was dominated by itinerant star actors rather than citizen choruses. When Demetrius of Phaleron took power in 317 BC and abolished the *chorēgia*, his rule

---

[84] *Politics* viii.1342a.19–30.   [85] *Politics* viii.1339b.1–10.   [86] *Politics* viii.1341a–b.

was imposed by a Macedonian garrison and his principles of government derived from the Aristotelian school.[87] Aristotle's neglect of chorality in the *Politics* and *Poetics* is not an oversight, but a stance born of opposition to fourth-century democracy.

Aristotle's location of the arts in the sphere of leisure leaves open the question of what 'music' is for, and whether it has any direct bearing on the practice of citizenship. Arguing that its function must exceed such simple pleasures as sleep and inebriation, Aristotle offers a provisional triad: education (i.e. the building of a virtuous character), diversion and contemplative thought, though he gives little explanation of the last beyond remarking that it exceeds the capacity of children.[88] A few pages later, catharsis replaces contemplative thought as the third element, reason abruptly substituted by emotion. The *aulos* was the instrument that governed all choral performances, and Aristotle explains that it is an 'un-ethical' instrument suitable for catharsis rather than moral learning.[89] He justifies passive spectatorship on the grounds that if an emotion is powerful enough in one person it can be shared by others, examples being pity, fear and 'enthusiasm', i.e. religious possession. Just as the possessed find a curative catharsis through music, so catharsis may likewise benefit those subject to pity, fear and other emotions.[90] Aristotle here prepares the ground for his argument in the *Poetics*, where text rather than performance is his object of enquiry, the political and ritual context of performance is effaced, and the chorus is likened to a regular character.

In the *Poetics* Aristotle moves away from Plato by distinguishing a human instinct for mimesis from a human instinct for rhythm. This allows him to separate the content of a play from its poetic form, paving the way for the study of the 'dramatic literature' in today's world. In response to Plato, Aristotle offers three grounds in the *Poetics* for admitting tragedy to an ideal republic. Firstly, mimesis is a natural human pleasure, so is inherently worthwhile – an argument which relates to his concept of diversion in the *Politics*. Secondly, mimesis is educational, so we learn what things are like, or what people are like. And thirdly, tragedy is cathartic.[91] Critics from Rousseau to Boal have attacked the catharsis theory because it does nothing to promote active citizenship, and Rousseau put his finger on the central contradiction in his *Letter to d'Alembert*. The theory claims that you purge passions by arousing them, so in order to become temperate and wise,

---

[87] Wilson (2000) 270–2.
[88] Aristotle *Politics* viii.1339a. I have translated *phronēsis* as 'contemplative thought'.
[89] *Politics* viii.1341a.   [90] *Politics* viii.1342a.   [91] Aristotle *Poetics* iv.1–7, vi.2.

Rousseau supposes, you must first be made wrathful and mad. Not at all, reply others, we cannot share the emotions of every character in the play; it is an accurate painting of the passions that deters us from wrong. Thus Rousseau demonstrates an incompatibility between the emotional theory of catharsis and the educational theory of mimesis. Consulting his own heart at the end of a performance, Rousseau finds that his own passions are aroused but not conquered. Emotion can only be purged by reason, yet reason has no effect in the theatre, so theatre in the end 'purges passions you do not have, and foments those you do'.[92] The tension between moral judgement and emotional absorption is one that modern political theatre has never overcome, despite Brecht's best efforts.

The most important insight we derive from Greek philosophy is the principle that theatre educates through forming habits of mind and body. Aristotle toyed with the idea that the arts could generate thought in suitably educated adults, but found no way of proving his point. In his essay 'The distribution of the sensible', Jacques Rancière adapts this Greek premise. Plato, according to Rancière, distinguished three aesthetic practices: (1) the manufacture of surface signs, both in painting and the written word; (2) theatre, tied to the institution of democracy but unable to find a place for actors within the civic order; and (3) the chorus, which allows the community to sing and dance its own unity. Plato's interest lay not in the category of 'art' but in images which shaped the *ethos* or moral habits of individuals and communities. Aristotle belongs to a new regime of representation, where 'mimesis' carves out an autonomous space for art, an art that *contains* phenomena like perspectival depth and plot.

Let us take the example of the tragic stage. It simultaneously carries with it, according to Plato, the syndrome of democracy and the power of illusion. By isolating *mimēsis* in its own proper space and by enclosing tragedy within a logic of genres, Aristotle – even if this was not his intention – redefined its politicity. Furthermore, in the classical system of representation, the tragic stage would become the stage of visibility for an orderly world governed by a hierarchy of subject matter and the adaptation of situations and manners of speaking to this hierarchy. The democratic paradigm would become a monarchical paradigm.[93]

Rancière here moves from Aristotle to French neoclassicism, and in Chapters 5 and 6 I shall examine how Voltaire and Chénier lay at the far end of this tradition, voicing republican ideas in respect of dramatic content, but tied to an Aristotelian regime of representation that revered

---

[92] Rousseau (2003) 68–70. Cf. Boal (2000).   [93] Rancière (2004) 17–18.

higher forms of art, heroic subject matter, heightened language and, by extension, higher classes in society.

The *Poetics* was a political project, and its influence did not end with the French Revolution and the birth of what Rancière calls the 'aesthetic' regime of modernity. If we want to understand the relationship between Athenian tragedy and democratic citizenship, we have to think away from the *Poetics*, not through it. We think through it when we conceive of tragedy as a written genre, and seek out the political ideology embedded in its discourse. We think away from Aristotle when we conceive of tragedy as a mode of chorality, a dance form supplemented by the work of actors. A recent book entitled *Tragedy and Citizenship* argues that tragedy contributed to active citizenship through the way it 'offered fertile material for discussion'.[94] I have argued for a major shift of emphasis, seeing fifth-century tragedy as a performance practice that built community, with shared pleasure in discussion comprising but one aspect of communal polis life. Athens was of course a deliberative democracy, but more importantly it was a participatory democracy.

[94] Barker (2009) 15.

CHAPTER 3

Florence, Rome and Machiavelli

Rome's greatest dramatic legacy was comedy, and I shall examine that genre through its transmutation at the hands of Machiavelli. Machiavelli is one of the foundational theorists for modern civic republicanism, and he is at the same time author of *Mandragola*, long acknowledged as a masterpiece of renaissance comedy, yet these two aspects of his achievement are rarely linked. A common theme is of course the citizen, for comedy in the classical tradition represents the everyday world of the citizen, but it is not evident how Machiavelli's championship of the active republican citizen correlates with the apparently passive activity of theatre-going. Machiavelli's political and dramaturgical ideals rested alike on his passion for republican Rome, and his belief that Florence was heir to that city, so it is in Rome that we must seek the convergence that Machiavelli both intended and realized in his life as a citizen. I shall argue that both Machiavelli's dramatic activities and his republicanism can be understood as a rebellion against three competing ideals offered by popular Christianity, by Ciceronian humanism and by absolute princely rule.

MACHIAVELLI'S POLITICAL WORKS

Florence was formally a republic until the Medici established a Duchy in 1537, and, as in Venice, an economy based on commerce underpinned republican values. Italian republicanism was not only a political system but also a lifestyle, defining itself by codes of dress, of social interaction and of personal morality. The fourteenth-century constitution involved a rapid rotation by lot of senior offices amongst an inner group of some 2,000 men, and at the other end of the spectrum those who did not belong to a recognized guild formed an outer plebeian underclass, with no serious claim to the title of *cittadino*, 'citizen'. The republic was no democracy, but nevertheless a substantial group of men shared control of their city-state, an experience impossible in a pyramidal society with a monarch at the apex, and every man subject to another above him.[1] In the later fifteenth century the Medici family, enriched by international banking, became first among equals, and it was easy to draw parallels with republican Rome where Pompey, Caesar and others used their wealth to buy support among the poor, so Republic inexorably slid into Principate, the principal citizen becoming monarch by popular acclaim. In 1494, two years after the death of Lorenzo the Magnificent, the Medici were driven out of Florence and the republican constitution was reshaped with a strong but closed Grand Council of 3,000 men. The preaching of Savonarola gave a spiritual drive to this anti-aristocratic revolution, but the pendulum swung towards secularism in 1497/8, and it was now that the young Machiavelli gained an important public office as secretary to the Chancery. His family was an old one, though not affluent enough for him to number among the 3,000. Not a citizen in the fullest sense, he was nevertheless deeply engaged in the political world, until his role as a public servant ended with the return of the Medici in 1512. After a spell in prison, he retreated to his small farm and devoted himself to writing by default, unable to regain his place in the public sphere.[2]

Machiavelli wrote four major political works, but only *The Art of War* was published in his lifetime. Like Rousseau, the famous 'Citizen of Geneva', Machiavelli proudly published his book as 'Florentine secretary and citizen' despite having been ousted from office.[3] It is couched as a dialogue set in the Orti Oricellari, gardens planted with species of flowers and trees that grew in antiquity, and a meeting place for humanist intellectuals hosted by the young and syphilitic Cosimo Rucellai, where Machiavelli became a provocative Socrates for the young.[4] Machiavelli's soldier spokesman sets out his political aspiration:

> To honour and reward virtue, not to disparage poverty, to esteem the rules and methods of military discipline, to constrain the citizens to love one another, to live without factions, to esteem private less than public good ... He who ordains such a thing plants trees beneath the shade of which one lives more fortunate and happy than beneath these trees [i.e. those of the Orti in Florence].[5]

Machiavelli saw factionalism as the curse of Florence, and his lifelong preoccupation was the creation of a civic spirit such that individuals would

---

[1] Rubinstein (1990) provides a clear summary of a complex system. Trexler (1980) traces the results of exclusion.

[2] The standard biography is still Ridolfi (1963); on Machiavelli's public service see also Black (1990).

[3] Godman (1998) 235.

[4] On the gardens, see Gilbert (1949), Dionisotti (1993) and Cummings (2004) 15–78.

[5] Machiavelli (1997–2005) 1.536; translation adapted from Machiavelli (1989) II.572.

no longer fight each other in jostling for power. During his years of service to the republic, his greatest energies were devoted to the creation of a citizen militia that would secure the safety and autonomy of the city more effectively than mercenaries. The idea of arming the young men of the city was far too dangerous in the unstable republic that Machiavelli served, so he was only permitted to enrol peasants, whose loyalties were often to their village and crops rather than the Florentine republic. Machiavelli's militia had a moment of glory with the capture of Pisa in 1509, but ignominy in 1512 when its collapse at Prato led directly to the fall of the republic. His book was no pipe-dream, however. The potential of an urban militia became apparent three years after Machiavelli's death, when young armed Florentines fought tenaciously for their republican liberty after another brief ousting of the Medici.[6]

In *The Art of War* Machiavelli created a utopian equivalent to Plato's Republic, a perfectly ordered and disciplined community complete with a mobile city built around its central piazza. The rotation of authority is worked out to prevent relations of patronage, and the absence of women does much to make a perfect society possible: these soldiers will have no time 'for thinking of either Venus or games or any of the other things that make soldiers rebellious and useless'.[7] Machiavelli recognizes that wars provide only a temporary world of order, but regimental training on days of holiday will mop up surplus civic energies and make a fine public spectacle.[8] He risks offence to the Medici as patrons of art when his spokesman says how much better the Florentines 'would have done (be it said with due respect to all) to seek to be like the ancients in things strong and rough, not in those delicate and soft, and in those that are done in the sun, not in the shade'.[9] At the end of the book Machiavelli reviews recent military failings of the Italian city-states, following catastrophic invasions of Italy by the French, the Spaniards and the Habsburgs. The amateurism and phoney wars of the past will no longer suffice if the freedom of the city-state is to survive in this new context, and what Italy has achieved in the arts, it should also achieve in war, 'because this land seems born to raise up dead things, as she has in poetry, in painting and in sculpture'. In an ironic reference to his own dramatic activities in the Orti Oricellari, he compares Macedon with Athens: 'While the rest of Greece was at leisure and attended to the performance of comedies, Philip by means of this order and these exercises became so powerful that in a few years he was

---

[6] On Machiavelli and the militia, see Bayley (1961).   [7] Machiavelli (1989) II.691.
[8] Machiavelli (1989) II.591.   [9] Machiavelli (1989) II.570.

able to conquer her completely.'[10] Comedy is a soft Grecian indulgence, and any citizen concerned with liberty should have rougher, more important concerns.

Machiavelli's *Discourses* were published posthumously, attributed again to the author as 'citizen and Florentine secretary'. Livy's history of the foundation of the Roman Republic provides the basis for reflections on the strengths and weaknesses of Florentine republicanism. The work grew out of pro-republican discussions in the Orti, and there was nothing abstract about these debates for the Orti was shut down as an organization after some participants (including a dedicatee of the *Discourses*) plotted an anti-Medicean coup. In this classical environment, an assassination plot against the Medici seemed like a re-enactment of Brutus' heroic killing of Caesar.[11] The overarching theme of the *Discourses* is the superiority of collective rule over individual rule. The first normally yields decisions which serve the interests of the city, while the second tends towards a tyranny that infects the body politic with its own corruption. Machiavelli builds on the newly discovered work of Polybius to argue that political conflict is a necessary condition of republican liberty, and he interprets the power struggle between plebs and Senate in Rome, like that between the populace and the wealthy of Florence, as a sign of vigour, and a source of dynamism if faction can be avoided. Where Plato dreamed of harmony and stability in the perfect society, Machiavelli saw a need for constant renovation through conflict. Sparta failed for lack of citizen numbers, but Rome was able to renew itself through expansion, not tyrannizing conquered peoples but assimilating them as new citizens. He understood that the days of the small Italian city-state were numbered.

Dedicated to Giuliano de' Medici, *The Prince* had a very different context. Having been arrested and tortured in 1513 for his supposed role in a plot against Giuliano, Machiavelli needed Medicean patronage if he was again to serve his city, and it is unclear how much irony lies beneath his notorious argument that ends justify means in the acquisition of princely power. The themes of the citizen army and the possibility of a well-ruled Florence dominating a united Italy relate more clearly to the agenda of the *Discourses*. The Medici rejected Machiavelli's vision of princely rule, but took him into their fold when they commissioned him to write a history of Florence. Machiavelli couched this *History* as an analysis of factionalism and the evils it had wrought, pushing his critique of the Medicean rise to

---

[10] Machiavelli (1997–2005) I.689; translation adapted from Machiavelli (1989) II.725.
[11] Skinner (2000) 56, Cummings (2004) 23, 36.

power as far as he dared, and the book can be read as a plea for enlightened leadership in a republican context. The overt aim of his narrative is to show how 'citizens having grown wise through the sufferings of others, can keep themselves united'.[12]

Machiavelli's *History* tells the story of armed conflict and resolution, and we only glimpse the cultural processes that bond citizens into a unity. A group of Florentine Signiori, opposing the incipient tyranny of a fourteenth-century French Duke, explain that their love of liberty cannot be destroyed because it is embedded in tradition; even if liberty is removed for a generation, symbols remain such as public buildings, banners and titles that renew the desire for it. They urge the Duke not to put his trust in the common people, who of course do not partake of the citizen's liberty, but the Duke responds by fostering maygames, providing the common populace with banners and money so their plebeian processions and feasting can fill the city. A generation later these same commoners rise up in the 'revolt of the *ciompi*' and briefly take control of Florence, their egalitarian code holding that men are all alike when naked, and nobility is just a matter of external clothing.[13] Republican citizenship for Machiavelli relied on some measure of social equality, but never equated with social levelling or championship of the poor. Public ceremonies are portrayed as a means of control rather than an expression of solidary citizenship. In the vacuum left by the death of Cosimo de' Medici in 1464, his successors set up an enactment of the Epiphany that took over the whole city, with each sector of the city equated to a part of the Middle East, and the Medici inserted as latterday Magi, aiming 'to give men something to think about that would remove their thoughts from government'.[14] Lorenzo consolidated his power by treating Florence to jousts, triumphs and other festivities in order 'to keep the city abundant, the people united, and the nobility honoured',[15] wooing the common people away from republicanism towards the values of aristocracy.

Machiavelli's Lorenzo is a schizophrenic individual comprising 'two different persons joined', wise and virtuous in public life but witty, frivolous and sexually adventurous in private.[16] Latin plays performed at Lorenzo's

---

[12] *History of Florence*, Preface – Machiavelli (1989) iii.1031.
[13] *History of Florence*, II.34, 36, III.13 – Machiavelli (1989) ii.1124, 1127, 1160.
[14] *History of Florence*, VII.12 – Machiavelli (1989) iii.1052; Trexler (1980) 401–3. Cf. another subversion of religious tradition when the Duke of Milan was entertained by a Pentecost play performed unseasonally in Lent: *History of Florence*, VII.28 – Machiavelli (1989) iii.1372.
[15] *History of Florence*, VIII.36 – Machiavelli (1989) iii.1433. Translation adapted.
[16] *History of Florence*, VIII.36 – Machiavelli (1989) iii.1434.

wedding in 1469 anticipate his patronage of humanist intellectuals,[17] and inhabit an unresolved middle ground between civic and private courtly worlds. Machiavelli applied to his own life the moral that if a man is thought wise by day, he will not be dismissed as mad for any doings at night,[18] and this ethical divide between public and private living informed his understanding of comedy and its place in society.

CICERO

The renaissance found in Cicero the best exponent and finest embodiment of Roman republican morality, and examination of Cicero's influential treatise *On Duties* will reveal how far Machiavelli opened up a new concept of citizenship.[19] Like Machiavelli, Cicero wrote in political exile, forced out of public office by the collapse of the Republic, and turning by default from engaged citizenship to the act of writing. The treatise is formally addressed to Cicero's son studying in Athens, offering him a slice of Roman wisdom, and it was written in the aftermath of Caesar's assassination when there were still hopes of resurrecting republicanism.

Cicero writes from the premise that humans are social animals before they are individuals, expressed in a complex sentence that deserves quoting in full. The Latin word *patria* captures far better than the English 'country' the idea of place as parent.

> But since, as Plato famously wrote, we are not born for ourselves alone, and the *patria* claims part of our begetting, our dear ones a part, and, since as the Stoics hold, all that grows on earth is created for human use, so humans are born for the sake of humans, that amongst themselves all may help others, in which we must follow the lead of nature, pooling our shared gains from the exchange of duties, through reciprocity, by our skills or our labour or our talents, to bind the society of humans with humans.[20]

On this collectivist foundation Cicero constructs a nest of identities. First, necessarily, is our common humanity, and like the Greek Stoics Cicero has no truck with Aristotle's notion that some are born to be slaves, supporting this humanist creed with a famous line in Terence which states that nothing

---

[17] *History of Florence*, VII.21, VIII.36 – Machiavelli (1989) III.1364, 1433. These are otherwise undocumented, so Machiavelli may be trying to claim primacy for Florence over Ferrara in reviving ancient theatre.

[18] Letter to Vettori of 5 January 1514 – cited in Hulliung (1983) 115.

[19] On Cicero's influence, see MacKendrick (1989) esp. 262–3.

[20] Cicero *On Duties* [*De Officiis*] i.22. My translation of the Latin is informed by Plato *Epistle* ix.358a. On the background see Mitchell (1991).

human can be alien to man.[21] The next layer is provided by race, nation and language, and after that and prior to kinship comes *civitas*, 'citizenship'. Places like the forum and the temple combine with institutions and social relationships to create the emotional bonds of citizenship. Family is the *seminarium* or seed-bed of the republic, and domestic relationships exist for the sake of the city, not vice versa, allowing the city to reproduce itself. Our relationship to our *patria* or *res publica* subsumes friendship and other relations, and patriotic duty equates with duty to parents, greater than our duty to wives and children.[22] There is a slippage between the notions of city, *patria* and republic, and in his treatise *On Laws*, Cicero reflects upon his own circumstances. Born in Arpinium many miles from the city of Rome, he has two *patriae*, one by birth and one through citizenship. Just as Ithaca was dear to Odysseus, so Cicero's germinal *patria* is very dear to him, with its rituals and the graves of his ancestors, yet the republic (which by his day included over 900,000 voting citizens[23]) subsumes his birthplace and is even dearer.[24]

It is hard for liberal westerners today to find more than empty or dangerous rhetoric in Cicero's declaration that he would not hesitate to give his life to serve his country, yet Cicero's public service did indeed cost him his life when Antony's assassins caught up with him, and countless common Roman men died during their mandatory sixteen years in the legions. The sense that in your deepest being you are part of a *res publica*, and that activity in this public sphere gives life its value, has become foreign to us, and requires a certain leap of the historical imagination. There is no reason to doubt Machiavelli when he declared near the end of his life that 'I love my native city more than my soul', and it was easier for him than for Cicero to conflate city, birthplace and republic.[25] While Cicero wrote as an optimist, believing that cooperation is part of human nature, Machiavelli was reared in a religion that taught of original sin. He set out his own version of the Fall in a poem 'On Ambition', and in one of his carnival scripts fallen angels descend and demonstrate to Pluto and his beautiful bride that sexuality is inseparable from sin. In a poem inspired by Lucian's *Golden Ass*, but lacking Lucian's redemptive Platonist finale, the protagonist finds the life of a hog less blighted than the life of a human.[26] Machiavelli had no sympathy for the messianic republicanism of Savonarola, but his

[21] Cicero *On Duties* i.30, citing *Heautontimoroumenos* 77, a text cited also in Cicero *On Laws* i.33.
[22] *On Duties* i.53–8.   [23] Millar (2002) 160, 193.   [24] Cicero *On Laws* [*De Legibus*] ii.3–5.
[25] Letter to Vettori of 16 April 1527: Atkinson and Sices (1996) 416.
[26] Machiavelli 'On Ambition', 'By the Devils Driven from Heaven' and 'The Ass': Machiavelli (1989) II.735–6, 878, 772.

theory that conflict must be part of a free society relates to Christian rather than pagan assumptions about human nature. Cicero followed Plato in assuming that the ideal statesman cultivates a perfect soul that will last to eternity,[27] and he ignored Aristotle's conceptual divide between the good citizen and the good human being. Machiavelli turned Aristotle's divide into a chasm, defining good citizenship by its results not by its means, with cruelty and kindness simply alternative strategies for creating civic order amongst self-interested human beings.

Cicero follows Aristotle as much as Plato in his concept of the 'liberal' man, the man who is free because he is liberated from labour to pursue a political life. This class-based perspective, harnessed to a Stoic belief in the control of emotion, yields the ethical and aesthetic principle of 'decorum'. Cicero wants art to be urbane rather than obscene, and *honestum* ('decent') like the games of children, but as a traditionalist he allows Aristophanes and Plautus to be acceptable, and concedes that jesting and *ludus* ('play'), like sleep and rest, have their place when the serious things of life are done.[28] His taste for Terence points, however, to another view of comedy based not on the ludic principle of play but on the educative principle of *mimesis*. Donatus gave currency in the renaissance to the Ciceronian adage that comedy is an 'imitation of life, a mirror of custom, an image of truth'.[29] There is a tension in Cicero between a Roman view that comedy is playful relaxation from the important things of life, and a Greek view that comedy is a mode of public education, and we shall see later how Machiavelli responded to this dilemma. Nostalgic though he was for the 'severe' music of early Roman drama,[30] Cicero rejected Plato's proposition that musical change yields political change. If drama was to shape the citizen, then it would have to be on the cognitive level. Cicero argues in *On Duties* that pupils learn when their teachers imitate vices for the sake of correcting them.[31]

Cicero repeatedly turns to the theatre to find analogues for citizen behaviour, since citizens are performers in the public sphere of the forum. Decorum in the theatre means that the actor will fit his performance to whatever character he is given, good or bad, while in public life the citizen must conform to the *persona* or 'mask' that nature has given him, with temperance and restraint moderated by more individual traits. As stage convention demands an acting style that is neither effeminate nor rustic,

---

[27] See 'Scipio's dream', the finale to Cicero's *Republic*.   [28] Cicero *On Duties* i.93–6, 103–4.
[29] Donatus *On Comedy* 5.1. Cf. Cicero *For Sextus Roscius* 47.
[30] Cicero *On Laws* ii.39.   [31] Cicero *On Duties* i.146–50.

so the social actor must find a decorous middle course. Greek men in public life wore only a cloak to cover their nakedness, but Cicero notes that in comedy (played in Greek costume) actors sport underwear to avoid any risk of exposure, and the Roman citizen should be equally modest.[32] The metaphor of the theatre came easily to Cicero because as a political figure he was himself regularly on public display in the theatre.

For all his championship of *humanitas* and the equality of political rights, Cicero held private property to be sacred, and never seriously questioned the principle that wealth should be a means of buying power, for example through securing networks of clients. This left him in a dilemma when it came to the funding of theatre and other public spectacles. On his way up the political ladder, Cicero performed the office of aedile which involved organizing and subsidizing public spectacles, and in *On Duties* he takes pride in the modesty of his expenditure. He explains how Alexander the Great was warned by his father not to shower money on his subjects to buy popularity, and quotes a text by Alexander's tutor Aristotle which states that the delectation of the multitude lasts but a moment and is quickly forgotten, theatre being merely the pleasure of boys and girls, slaves and the slave-like, and not of serious men. Cicero takes issue with Aristotle's successor, Theophrastus, who praised the opulence of Athenian public performances, with sponsorship the best way of using private wealth,[33] and his aedileship was a case where the end justifies the means. If the 'people' demand entertainment, then 'good men' must concede.[34]

Cicero tolerated Pompey's theatre-building to pre-empt the greater evil of Caesar's dictatorship, but Machiavelli could not approve Lorenzo's sponsorship of popular festivals, distinguishing public means that bring a citizen renown, such as warfare or diplomacy, from private means that include artistic patronage and laying on games for the masses, which ultimately breed social division.[35] He saw the cultural policy of the Medici, on both a populist and elite level, as part of their assault on traditional republican values, arguing that war generates *virtù* while leisure generates corruption, for 'the strength of armed souls cannot be corrupted by a more honest leisure than that of letters, nor could this leisure penetrate well-ordered cities with a greater and more dangerous duplicity'.[36]

[32] *On Duties* i.97–8, 129.
[33] *On Duties* ii.55–7. The work by Aristotle is lost, but cf. Aristotle *Politics* v.1309a.
[34] *On Duties* ii.57.   [35] Machiavelli *History of Florence* VII.1 – Machiavelli (1989) III.1337.
[36] *History of Florence* V.1: Machiavelli (1997–2005) II.519; cf. Machiavelli (1989) III.1232. The word for leisure is *ozio*, from Latin *otium*.

If Machiavelli took a different view of the theatre from Cicero, the main reason may lie in the form which the theatre event took in Rome, where the citizen-statesman was obliged to display himself beneath the eyes of an assembled people. Cicero remarks in one of his speeches that the theatre is a place where the populace makes its views known, exactly like political meetings and elections in the forum.[37] Cicero was obligated to repay the masses because they had voted for him to be aedile, while Lorenzo enjoyed no such democratic legitimacy. Plutarch has a revealing anecdote to illustrate Cicero's political skill:

Formerly the knights were mixed up with the masses in the theatre, sitting randomly amid the people. Marcus Otho, when praetor, was first to privilege them over other citizens, and assigned them the special seating which is still kept for them today. The people found this demeaning, and when Otho appeared in the theatre, they assailed him with hissing, while the knights cheered him with loud clapping, and so the people hissed all the more, and the knights went on cheering, whereupon they turned towards each other, insults were hurled, and the theatre descended into chaos. When Cicero heard of this, he came and called the people to the sanctuary of Bellona, where he admonished and exhorted them. When they returned to the theatre, the people clapped Otho loudly, and competed with the knights to show most honour and respect to his person.[38]

Theatre functioned as a site of political display, where politicians could bask in acclaim or endure humiliation. Public opinion could be expressed better in the theatre auditorium than in assemblies where the people stood on flat ground in tribal groupings with little opportunity to experience themselves as a singular organism. Plutarch describes a change in the configuration of the auditorium as the theatre ceased to be a place where social distinctions were dissolved, to become a map of the social hierarchy in a process that would be completed by the Emperor Augustus. The auditorium which once symbolized and embodied the equality of all citizens of the republic would soon embody the hierarchical order of Imperial society.[39] We notice that the Roman theatre was not a place for moral instruction, and unlike Greeks the Romans never doubled up theatres as places for political assembly. Cicero leads the turbulent audience from their temporary festive space into an adjacent sanctuary that commemorated civil war, in order to stand on the temple steps and educate citizens in civic virtue.

[37] Cicero *For Sestius* 106. Cf. Nicolet (1976) 479–94, Vanderbroeck (1987) 77–81.
[38] Plutarch *Life of Cicero* 13. The *lex roscia theatralis* was actually introduced by Lucius Otho, not Marcus.
[39] See Wiles (2003) 178–9.

TERENCE'S *ANDRIA*

Machiavelli's first dramatic text is not an original play but a translation, from Terence's *Andria*.[40] On the face of it, this is an archetypical humanist text and the least 'Machiavellian' of all Roman comedies. The characters are all good people, acting from commendable motives: the young man is faithful to the girl he loves, the father wants only what is best for his son, slaves choose whether to help the old master or the young master and the courtesan has been devoted to her protégée; when it turns out that the eponymous Andrian heroine is actually Athenian, and the hero can marry her, all the games of bluff come to an end. The heroine never actually appears onstage, which eases the problem of cross-dressing. In 1476 a pioneering performance of the *Andria* was given by schoolboys before the Signoria, and it was repeated in the Medici palace with a young member of the Medici clan probably amongst the actors.[41] Terence was 'rescued from Hades' by this production, and performances of his plays now had a respectable place within an elite education. Angelo Poliziano, principal humanist scholar in Lorenzo's entourage, edited and translated the play, and lectured on it in the university.[42]

Machiavelli's choice of text was a conservative one, and he may have been bidding for patronage, since several of his contemporaries at the Orti Oricellari were playwrights, and their moralistic classicizing plays were put on in the Medici palace.[43] The radicalism of Machiavelli's project lay in its language, and the only precedent was Bibbiena's *Calandria* written in colloquial Tuscan in 1513. Poliziano was a pedant, while Ariosto found himself more comfortable with classically inspired verse. Machiavelli's scrupulous yet performable translation was arguably a more important project than the writing of a new play. His text made the figures of Roman comedy talk not like coached schoolboys but like living people on the streets of Florence, demonstrating as in *The Art of War* that Florence could indeed be a latterday Rome.

The patriotic agenda behind the *Andria* translation is set out in Machiavelli's *Dialogue on Language*, where, relegated to his farm, the writer

---

[40] Machiavelli's plays are translated in Sices and Atkinson (1985).
[41] See Gareffi (1991) 24, Ventrone (1992) 221, Ventrone (1996); on Poliziano, see also Dionisotti (1993).
[42] Poliziano (1973).
[43] See Gareffi (1991) on Nardi and Strozzi. It has been suggested on inadequate evidence that *Mandragola* was performed at the Medici wedding of 1518, but *Andria* is a more plausible candidate. Stoppelli (2005) 75–9 reviews the scholarship.

engages in cultural combat on behalf of his country.[44] The playwright
Trissino on a visit to Florence had introduced the habitués of the Orti
to Dante's essay 'On the vulgar tongue', where Dante maintained that
he wrote his poetry in an Italian that was not Florentine but generically
courtly.[45] Machiavelli accuses Dante of parricide against the *patria*, and
challenges him to a debate, for he cannot agree that Brutus was sent to
the pit of Hell for his assassination of Caesar, and he cannot accept this
courtly description of Dantean language. Languages like states, Machiavelli
argues, are in perpetual flux, and Florentine has not been contaminated
by new words, but has enriched itself through assimilating new elements
on its path to linguistic dominance within Italy. The Roman army by
the same token always managed to be Roman, despite assimilating a huge
majority of foreign legionaries. He contrasts Florence with a corrupt and
heterogeneous Papal court, claiming that 'Where customs are perverted
language too must be perverted, and take on the effeminate lasciviousness
of those who speak it.' As home of the three literary giants Dante, Petrarch
and Boccaccio, Machiavelli's Florence has a moral claim to superiority over
other Italian states.

The climax of Machiavelli's dialogue is a discussion of comedy. Poliziano
had set out the traditional rationale for comedy as a 'mirror' of domestic
life, and thus a tool for instruction.[46] Machiavelli accepts this rationale,
but adds the qualification that men enjoy themselves during the comedy
and only afterwards savour the underlying lesson. To achieve its effect,
he argues, the language of comedy must be local, popular and easy to
understand. Ariosto, the pioneer of neoclassical comedy, failed because he
was not comfortable with the dialect of his native Ferrara and opted for a
language that was graceful but 'without any of the salt that such a comedy
demands'. The Florentine dialect has resources, evidenced no doubt by
Boccaccio, which allow it to be colloquial without offending decorum, but
in order to use it properly one has to be a native speaker. The dialogue
is a manifesto for Machiavelli's own dramatic style, and in the *Andria* he
adds not a few pinches of salt to Terence's neutral and purist Latin.[47] We
could argue with hindsight that the music of popular speech supplied by

---

[44] Translation in Machiavelli (1961) 175–90. On the language debate, see Martinez (2000) and Shell
(2000).
[45] Piccioli (1968) 63–6.
[46] Poliziano (1973) 8, with citations via Donatus from Cicero and Livius Andronicus. Poliziano's major
manifesto for theatre as education was a preface to Plautus *Menaechmi* (1488): Gareffi (1991) 19–20.
[47] Terence's own term is '*ingenius*' – natural or innate: *Heautontimoroumenos* 47.

Machiavelli compensates for the music of the *aulos* in Terence's play. The classic theory of comedy set out by Machiavelli, namely that it holds up a useful mirror to the cheating of servants, the unrestrained libido of youth and so forth, proves but a façade for the real function of his *Andria*, which is through language to celebrate and define a collective identity. Machiavelli's translation is not a humanist text but a patriotic text.

If we track back from Machiavelli to the original performance of *Andria* in Rome in 166 BC, a similar paradox confronts us. While Machiavelli made Romans talk like Florentines, Terence made Athenians talk (or sing) like Romans. The *Andria* was performed at the festival of the 'Great Mother' instituted in Rome in 204 BC on the authority of the Delphic Oracle, and should be seen as a Grecian ceremony performed in the context of a Grecian religious practice. The plays for the festival had to be new and the stock of Greek material was finite, so drawing on more than one original was profligate, and Terence was accused of 'contaminating' one text with another.[48] While Plautus assimilated and Romanized Greek material, Terence preferred to maintain the play's cultural otherness, offering *Andria* as a work by Menander that he has brought to a Roman audience. We can see this as a sign of cultural respect, but we can also see the play as a piece of cultural booty won by the conquering nation.

A year before *Andria* was performed, Aemilius Paulus returned to Rome in triumph from his conquest of Macedon, which formerly controlled the Greek mainland,[49] and brought back not only the captured monarch but also many works of Greek art, or 'religious objects' as we might better term them. Lorenzo a year before his death replaced the biblical pageant wagons that rolled through Florence on midsummer's day with a re-enactment of Paulus' pagan triumph, celebrating the way he had himself brought ancient cultural artefacts along with power and renown to the new Rome.[50] Machiavelli did not accept the Medicean parallel, but praised Aemilius Paulus as an exemplary republican hero who chose to enrich the republic rather than himself.[51] Paulus enslaved 150,000 Greeks, but showed respect for Greek cultural practices, and at his funeral six years later two plays by Terence would be performed. Paulus' son Scipio helped organize the funeral, but his expensive outlay on gladiators had disastrous consequences for Terence, whose scenic games lacked the same popular appeal.[52] Scipio had a Greek education, accompanied his father on the cultural tour of

[48] On *contaminatio*, see Goldberg (1986) 95.
[49] For Paulus' career and an evaluation of sources, see Reiter (1988).
[50] Trexler and Lewis (1981) 129–31.   [51] Machiavelli *Discourses* iii.25.
[52] Polybius 31.28; Terence *Hecyra* prologue.

Greece designed to win hearts and minds, and along with his brother took his pick from the royal Macedonian library, so here was an obvious source for new texts that could be passed to a writer for reworking. Terence's humanist text was perhaps quite literally a piece of colonial plunder.[53] Terence conspicuously failed to deny that Scipio was the real author of his plays.[54]

While Paulus was demonstrating his Greek-loving credentials in Macedonia in 167 BC, another conqueror of Greek cities presented in Rome a travesty of Greek theatre, importing Greek tragic choruses and forcing them to fight each other like gladiators, to the shock and humiliation of Polybius, a Greek in the entourage of Scipio. Polybius records the impact of all the wealth brought to Rome by Paulus, fostering decadence in the young, with the exception of course of Scipio.[55] To traditionalists, Greek wealth and Greek money were suspect. Cato, himself the product of a Greek education, took an anti-Greek stance which culminated in the expulsion of Greek intellectuals from Rome in 161 BC, and aristocratic banquets at the festival of the Great Mother were curtailed.[56] Terence's plays were caught up in a battle for the soul of Rome, fought around definitions of the Roman citizen, for the Romans had a clear choice: to maintain the disciplined, militarized lifestyle that had made them powerful, or to live the good life of Greeks now they had the means. The *Andria* purports to mirror an Athenian world characterized by warm affective relations both between father and son and between youths and sexual partners, quite alien to the authoritarian behaviour patterns of Rome. To applaud Terence was to applaud a new set of political values.

As we have seen in Cicero, there were two competing models of what comedy should be: *ludus* and jesting as respite after labour, or educational *mimesis*. Plautus emphasized the ludic dimension, Terence the mimetic, and Terence's prologues suggest that many in the audience did not share this taste. The Roman audience was not a passive recipient of messages, but a highly expressive body, and when Paulus was sick and unable to attend the theatre it made its feelings clear.[57] Cutting down the level of direct audience address that he found in his Greek originals, Terence shunned the interactivity that Plautus delighted in. The Greek-Roman cultural

---

[53] Plutarch *Aemilius Paulus* 28.
[54] Cicero thought the secret author was Laelius, a close friend of Scipio, while Quintilian and Suetonius were familiar with the story that the youthful Scipio was the true author. The sources are evaluated in Goldberg (1986) 9. I follow Leigh (2004) 158–91 in identifying a Scipionic link, against Gruen (1992) who pictures Terence as a mere freelance.
[55] Polybius 31.25.   [56] Polybius 31.24; Aulus Gellius 2.24.   [57] Plutarch *Aemilius Paulus* 39.

battle came to a head in the Senate when a move to Hellenize Rome by
building a stone theatre was defeated, and a counter-motion was passed
requiring the audience to stand in the theatre as men stood in Roman
political assemblies.[58] The Greeks sat in assemblies because they enjoyed
the art of oratory, and liked to debate ethical issues, but the Romans stood
because, as Cicero emphasized in *On Duties*, their cultural tradition was
one of action not contemplation. The experience of standing in the pit in
the reconstructed Shakespeare's Globe has been experienced as a revelation
by many, for it makes theatre-goers more expressive and aware of their
neighbours, with mental passivity impossible. Terence wrote at a moment
when Romans had a stark choice: passivity in accepting luxurious fruits of
conquest that included imported comedies, or remaining men of action.

The post-Aristophanic form known as 'New Comedy' represents scenes
of private life, and the genre implies, on the face of it, that citizenship
is only an incidental factor in the construction of personal identity and
ethical values. If we dig one layer deeper into the *Andria*, we return to
the lost original play by Menander, the most celebrated author of New
Comedy. Menander wrote to a formula evolved at a time when Athenian
citizenship was in crisis. Back at the beginning of the fifth century, citizenship roughly corresponded with the population of free adult males,
but membership was thereafter restricted to the descent group. This group
enjoyed the privileges of citizenship, such as financial subsidy, the right
to self-representation in court, the right to own land and the right to
dance in the Dionysia, but migration meant that many citizens no longer
lived in Attica, while many economically productive non-citizens now did.
Increasingly it seemed an accident of inheritance that some were citizens
and others not, which undermined the idea that the essence of citizenship
was a collectivist moral obligation.[59] After a long period of democratic stability in the fourth century, following the end of the Spartan occupation,
the franchise was again restricted at the end of the fourth century when
Athens was overwhelmed by the armies of Macedon. Many who had been
citizens but owned no property suddenly found that they were citizens no
longer, and abolition of the *chorēgia* coincided with a reduction in the pool
of those who would have been available to dance. It was in this political
environment that Menander's plays emerged.

Menander and his contemporaries established at the end of the fourth
century the convention that a comedy is a boy-meets-girl love story. In

---

[58] Rawson (1989) 470, Dillon and Garland (2005) 283–4.
[59] On Menander in the context of citizenship law, see Davies (1977–8), and more broadly Lape (2004)
    21–39.

Menander the young man is always a citizen while the *innamorata* is not, so long-term cohabitation may be possible, but there can be no production of legitimate citizen children. By some miraculous discovery the *innamorata* is always found to be of citizen birth so love can proceed to marriage. In *Andria*, typically, it is revealed that the heroine is the long-lost sister of the bride previously designated for the hero, and we never see her because the interpersonal love story was incidental to Menander's main purpose. The play allowed its audience the fantasy that status boundaries, which formed the basis of the democratic system, could somehow be reconciled with the order of nature.

Menander transferred the formal setting of comedy from the public sphere to the private sphere, and the audience were invited to gaze at a flattened mirror of bourgeois life, played out on a shallow stage.[60] Yet this same audience was also gathered in horseshoe formation so it could contemplate itself as a collective entity, and we could interpret Menander's comedies as public celebrations of the way the closed political community has managed to reproduce itself, the family being, as Cicero put it, the *seminarium* of the republic. The shift of focus from public life to private life undoubtedly implies a public recognition that the assembled Athenian polis can no longer determine its own destiny in a world shaped by larger political forces. The formulaic story-line which dissolves an Andrian into an Athenian also helped to idealize Greekness, and foreign slaves in the world of Menander's comedy remain emphatically other, capable of fine human feelings but fixed by their masks as different by nature.[61] When Terence sought to transpose Menander's plays for a Roman audience, part of the difficulty he experienced lay in the different nature of Roman citizenship. Rome steadily extended the geographical boundaries of citizenship, and freed slaves could aspire to citizen membership in numbers quite inconceivable in Greece.[62] The Romans had plenty of cultural anxieties, such as poverty, land reform, class and Greek decadence, but they did not have the same obsession with policing the boundary between citizen and non-citizen.

THE MANDRAKE AND THE SOCIETY OF THE TROWEL

Mandragola (*The Mandrake*) is generally considered to be Machiavelli's dramatic masterpiece. The hero Callimaco falls in love with Lucrezia,

---

[60] Wiles (1991) 36ff.   [61] See Wiles (1988).
[62] See e.g. Gardner (1993) 7, Dillon and Garland (2005) 329.

young pious wife of the elderly Nicia. Disguised as a doctor he prescribes the mandrake root as a fertility drug, the side effect of which will be the death of the first man with whom Lucrezia sleeps. Cajoled by her mother and her confessor, Lucrezia consents, and discovers the joys of adulterous sex when Callimaco disguises himself as a vagrant, swept off the streets and supposedly consigned to his death. The play illustrates the philosophy behind *The Prince*, that ends justify means. The characters without exception subvert every Ciceronian and Christian moral principle, and the consequence is that all parties are happy, no-one is hurt, and the Florentine republic is enabled to reproduce itself. The humanism of *Andria* is turned on its head. In the prologue Machiavelli tells his audience that he is contenting himself with these vanities because he has nowhere to show his face, no other tasks whereby to demonstrate his *virtù*, in other words writing as a refugee from public life. The question of intent cannot easily be sidestepped: did Machiavelli think of the play as an idle night-time diversion, a respite from the important matters of public life? Or did he intend that the audience should savour some useful lesson once their laughter had subsided?

The amoralism of Machiavelli's text remains troubling for anyone seeking to defend its place within a canon of great works, prompting critical searches for allegory or satire, and efforts to place the heroine as victim of a rape.[63] My concern here is not with textual meaning but with performance events, and different performances in Machiavelli's lifetime meant different things according to context. It now generally assumed that, after readings in the Orti, an amateur performance must have been given in the carnival season of 1520, or perhaps a couple of years earlier.[64] Performed in the context of republican discussions, the name Lucrezia evokes the famous heroine whose rape triggered the birth of the Roman Republic,[65] but it was also the name of Machiavelli's mistress, and an audience of intimates from the Orti might have associated old Niccolò Machiavelli with Lucrezia's husband Nicia. The audience are told that the Friar can be identified by his habit, and it is usually assumed that he is one of the Servites who controlled Florence's most celebrated cult, that of the Virgin Annunciate.[66] Molested

[63] Haywood (2002) 44–50 provides a convenient survey.
[64] Piccioli (1968) 85 and Ridolfi (1963) 173 envisage at least a reading. Rucellai's tragedy *Rosamunda* may have been performed in the Orti in 1515 – the evidence is reviewed in Cummings (2004). The recent dating of 1520 by Inglese is viewed sympathetically by Stäuble (2004) 37–8 and Stoppelli (2005) 76, though Stoppelli believes Machiavelli had been working on the play since 1513.
[65] Stoppelli (2005) 115 finds the allusion so obvious it no longer needs argument, while the allusion to Machiavelli's mistress at most adds another layer.
[66] Haywood (2002) 24.

by a friar as she pursues this cult, Madonna Lucrezia may be an analogue of the Virgin Mary, married to an old man and magically impregnated as at the Annunciation. Richard Trexler in his *Public Life in Renaissance Florence* examines the complex system of Christian ritual practices which once bonded the city, showing how the Medici undermined this structure by substituting themselves as the 'charismatic centre', until Savonarola created a fresh set of ritual forms around the innocence of boys in order to reconnect spirituality to public ethics.[67] The framework of Christian belief and practice that once cemented the bonds of citizenship was now vulnerable, and derived from a pagan culture Machiavelli's comedy was an assault on popular piety.

The success of the play in Florence yielded an invitation to Rome for a performance with the same cast and scenery before the Medicean Pope Leo.[68] The survival of a manuscript from 1519/20 bound up with poems by Lorenzo the Magnificent confirms that the play was not perceived as anti-Medicean. We may surmise that the Pope relished Nicia's command of Florentine argot, and was unmoved by the play's anticlericalism, an aspect emphasized by the placing of a church at the centre of the perspectival set.[69] Another courtly performance was planned in the carnival season of 1526, when Machiavelli's friend Guicciardini, governor of Romagna on behalf of Clement, the second Medici Pope, invited him to his provincial court at Faenza. Also invited was Machiavelli's current mistress, the singer known as Barbera, whose presence was necessary because she and her company were to sing songs between the acts. It is easy today to forget how crucial such *intermezzi* were in framing a comedy and completing the performance event. The songs were to be sung by nymphs and shepherds, and this mythological pastoral world created a context within which necessary compliments could be paid to the god-like virtues of the governor, and to Pope Clement who had imposed Florentine rule.[70] The neoplatonist framing device made it possible for the audience to see the urban world of the play as the antithesis of an ideal and natural world ruled by men of virtue and wisdom. Guicciardini told Machiavelli that he regarded the performance as necessary recreation amid the tumult of current events,

[67] Trexler (1980). Newbigin (1996) develops Trexler's perspective, with a detailed study of Medicean appropriation of the Annunciata cult, and broader transformations of lay piety.
[68] Sources in Stoppelli (2005) 78.
[69] Hayward (2002) 34 emphasizes the point. Cf. Serlio's placing of the church – Wiles (2003) 216–17; antecedents for this use of stage space include Plautus' *Aulularia*, adapted by Machiavelli: see Ridolfi (1963) 315–16.
[70] First Canzone. The lyrics survive because Machiavelli included them in a letter.

and wanted a new prologue that would pitch the play correctly for a non-Florentine audience.[71] In the event he was called away on a mission, the performance was cancelled and a year later Rome was sacked by an invading army. Guicciardini's Ciceronian view of comedy as a diversion from the grave affairs of public life denied *Mandragola* any function as a meditation upon morality, but the importing of a play from Florence was not without political significance.

The Rome performance was arranged through Leo's principal fixer, the Florentine Cardinal Bibbiena, whose *Calandria* may have inspired Machiavelli to turn playwright, being a successful Florentine play in the classical style with a flavouring of Boccaccio. It was produced in the Ducal court of Urbino in 1513 by Baldassare Castigliano, who would become famous as author of *The Courtier*, which promulgated across Europe a refined aristocratic lifestyle. Since 'courtier' and 'republican citizen' are antithetical terms, it seems worth pausing on this production. As a performance event, it framed or was framed by spectacular mythological *intermezzi* which provided an allegory for the state of Italy, and the shameless behaviour enacted in the comedy functioned as an anti-masque, indirectly glorifying the antithetical world of public affairs shaped by dukes not citizens.[72] Bibbiena's text differs in two obvious ways from *Mandragola*. Firstly, the stooge Calandro allows the spectator to empathize with the young well-bred hero, whereas Nicia's command of popular speech makes him not only a fall-guy but also a figure of strength and celebration. Secondly, it includes empowered women, and celebrates androgyny since male and female identical twins prove interchangeable. As in *Twelfth Night*, likewise written in the orbit of a feminized court, laughter invites recognition that there is nothing natural about male superiority, for court is by definition a place where men lay their weapons of war aside in favour of female arts like conversation. *Mandragola*, by contrast, is resolutely masculine in its plot and metaphorical language, and the hero's name means 'fine in battle'. Machiavelli throughout his life idealized a republic of virile men.

We hear of another performance of *Mandragola* in Venice in 1522. Available in a cheap printed edition without Machiavelli's name on the title page, the play was now a commodity, for the Venetian government had

---

[71] Letter by Guicciardini in Atkinson and Sices (1996) 372.

[72] Bentley (1964) 511–15 prints Castiglione's account of the event; the same volume includes a translation of *Calandria*. For the context, see Fontes-Baratto (1974).

given up attempts to ban commercial theatre by 1517, and it was performed on monastic premises to a paying audience as part of a carnival
season which also included *Calandria*. The actor-manager of the company
was from Lucca, and had discovered how to make money touring Latin
comedies in translation. He was known by the stage name of Cherea, after
the young hero in Terence who disguises himself as a eunuch in order to
rape the heroine,[73] and this 'Cherea' was probably now mature enough to
play the star role of Nicia. The packed audience crowded onto the stage,
making it impossible to play the final act, and the performance had to be
done again three nights later. The chaos is testament to the excitement
which the play generated, though we should not underestimate the interludes which framed or were framed by the play, not costly aristocratic
spectacle this time but vocal impressions by the popular comedian Zuan
Polo.[74] When a Venetian diarist identifies Machiavelli's comedy as the story
of a Florentine, we are reminded how important voices were in an Italy
united by its common language but segmented by dialects that echoed
political boundaries. Four years later Cherea came across an amateur production of *Mandragola* mounted by the local Florentine community in
Venice, and gave it a public showing. *Mandragola* in Venice was not a
play about citizenship in any ethical sense, but could be used to celebrate
Florentine identity, or perhaps to mock it when a Luccan spoke in Florentine to Venetians. The durability of comedy as a cultural form relates to
its versatility, requiring only a few actors and a canvas backdrop, pleasing
audiences of any social class in any city where its language can be compre-
hended. *Mandragola* was at once a local play and a play that transcended
locality. As Machiavelli wrote in his prologue when envisaging the afterlife
of his jaw-breaking play: 'This is your Florence, tomorrow it will be Rome
or Pisa.'

   The Venetian republic was never ashamed of its mercantile foundations, for out on the lagoon its nobility could never aspire to becoming
landed gentry, and the city was a natural seed-bed for commercial theatre.
Florentine republicans were more ambivalent about their relationship to
trade, and in his political writings Machiavelli studiously ignores the economic basis of his city's prosperity. The first documented performance of
Mandragola in Florence was mounted by the Compagnia della Cazzuola,
the 'Society of the Trowel' (or 'Tadpole', with a pun on *cazzo* = penis).

[73] On the Venetian performances, see Padoan (1978) 34–67; contextual material is in Muraro (1964).
Machiavelli once transcribed *The Eunuch*, an obvious analogue for *Mandragola*.
[74] On this comedian, see Petrini (1996) 107–9; Henke (2007) 71–3.

The Society was set up in 1512, shortly after the return of the Medici, who lifted the ban on such organizations which had been seen as a threat to republican openness. The name stems from a homoerotic foundation myth, and relates to a change of moral climate, for republicanism was not sympathetic to homosexuality.[75] The Society began as a gathering of creative artists, musicians, painters and performers of the spoken word, far removed from the intellectual habitués of the Orti, but accrued a number of wealthy afficionados, not only Giuliano de' Medici, but also a mercer, a cloth-shearer and a physician. It was bound by its original constitution to balance membership of minor and major guilds, and hierarchy was subverted at the first dinner when members took precedence on the basis of their carnival costumes. The purposes of the Society were convivial. In performative banquets, dining in Hades on toads and snakes, for example, would be accompanied by the howls of the damned. Evenings would be rounded off by a more formal neoclassical play mounted by the members. Machiavelli's contemporary, pagan and celebratory play was a natural choice for the Society, and a celebrated wit known as Barlacchia brought a distinctive Florentine voice to Nicia. The guild system placed him as a herald or town crier, but effectively he was a professional actor.[76]

The structure of the Society echoed that of religious confraternities which in earlier generations had put on sacred plays as an act of piety, part of the texture of republican life and characterized by mixing across social and local boundaries.[77] Machiavelli's levelling of all human beings to a single moral baseline was consistent with the confraternal and carnivalesque principles of the Cazzuola. The Society of the Trowel belonged neither to the corporate medieval city nor to the individualizing capitalist city, but sat on the faultline between them. Its members functioned neither as citizens of Florence nor as private individuals, but as refugees from the public world inventing a new form of civil society. The world of public ceremony was being eroded from above by hollow aristocratic forms imposed by the Medici, and from below by newly sponsored plebeian organizations.[78] The Medicean regime initially tried to suppress the midsummer biblical pageant wagons in an assault on traditional citizen culture,

[75] The basic source is Vasari's *Life of Rustici*: Vasari (1996) 11.524–30. Cummings (2004) 106 deciphers the foundation myth. Mozzati (2008) analyses the development of the Company. The idea of digging up a mandrake root correlates happily with the name of the society.

[76] See Bryce (1995) 94–6, Petrini (1996) 11, 21.

[77] Weissman (1982) 163; Trexler (1980) 252–6 on traditional confraternities, 384–6 on adolescent confraternities and theatre. Mozzati (2008) 213–14 argues that the Medicean Company of the Magi was the model.

[78] Trexler (1980) 411ff.

with a Roman-style triumph mounted in 1514 to echo Lorenzo's celebration of Aemilius Paulus.[79] Machiavelli stood on a historical cusp, analysing constitutional and military structures that could in theory preserve the old collectivism of the republican city-state, while unable to identify peaceful cultural formations that might consolidate a communal identity. He could not reconcile his sexual libertarianism with the austere ideals of Roman republicanism, nor could he reconcile his taste for pagan antiquity with the Christian ethics and customs that had long supported a corporate civic ethos.

Whilst the intelligentsia at the Orti were obsessed by language, the Cazzuola thrived on visual creativity. Two celebrated artists took charge of scenery for *Mandragola*: the painter Andrea del Sarto and his friend the architect Bastiano da Sangallo, who was Italy's greatest expert in perspectival scenography, and had pioneered the use of mobile flats.[80] The Pope in 1520 wanted to see the décor used in the original production, for the emergence of neoclassical comedy was bound up with perspectival art, both striving to provide a mirror of the spectator's world. The text of *Mandragola* assumes practicable doors for the two houses at either side, and does not require a doorway to the church at the vanishing point in the centre. Later in the century, perspective would be constructed by means of receding flats set in relation to the seat of the principal aristocratic spectator, and this magical evocation of infinity lent itself to the neoplatonist tendencies of ducal courts, but back in the 1520s the audience still sat within the same space as the actors, and the painted scene was a flat backdrop shared by both. The politics of vision were not apparent as they would be later in the century.[81] The trompe l'oeil image of Florence offered to Machiavelli's audience had a double force, celebrating the city which the audience knew and loved, but at the same time reminding the audience of their separation from the real streets of the city. Enactments and processions in the street were once the staple of republican celebrations, but in the post-republican world an artistic and social elite retreated from the public world to form its bonds of sodality in private houses.[82]

---

[79] Trexler (1980) 516, 506–8. Vasari, our principal source, gives 1512 as the foundation year, and the patronal feast day points to November, when the Medici were setting up the aristocratic Diamante and Broncone Companies, on which see Shearman (1962) and Cummings (2004).
[80] Vasari (1996) ii.431–2; Zorzi and Sperenzi (2001) 92–3.
[81] Cf. Scamozzi's reworking of Palladio's republican stage façade in the Teatro Olimpico: see Avagnina (2005). For the historical evolution of perspective, see Molinari (1964) and Klein and Zerner (1964).
[82] Zorzi and Sperenzi (2001) explore the process of privatization. Wiles (2003) 214–19 discusses the staging principles.

THE SUNFLOWER IN A POLITICIAN'S GARDEN

The Cazzuola possessed Machiavelli's adaptation of Plautus' *Aulularia*, and Vasari tells us that their performances included *La Clizia* ('The Sunflower'),[83] so the Society was almost certainly responsible for staging *La Clizia*, Machiavelli's last play, during the carnival season of 1525. A prominent politician, known as 'Il Fornaciaio' after the kiln in his famous garden, had been banned from the city for five years, and the play was written for a performance in his garden to celebrate his political come-back.[84] Machiavelli was a regular guest at Fornaciaio's banquets, and decided at short notice that a new play would be better than a revival of *Mandragola*. This was to be a flamboyant party, and a friend of Machiavelli commented that 'such things are usually done only for princes'.[85] The guest list included Ippolito de' Medici, bastard son of the Giuliano to whom Machiavelli once dedicated *The Prince*. It was only a few months since Giuliano's brother, Pope Clement, had sent the thirteen-year-old Ippolito, chaperoned by a cardinal, to occupy the Medici palace and function as ruler of Florence, against the advice of some, like Machiavelli's close friend Vettori, who thought it better if the citizens of Florence ruled themselves.[86]

Machiavelli's play is an adaptation of Plautus' *Casina*, which was in turn adapted from a Greek play named after its central scene where lots are drawn from urns. In Florentine republicanism offices were allocated on the basis of lots drawn from pouches, and two such pouches are used in *La Clizia* to determine which man gets the girl. Machiavelli makes an issue of who will draw the lots, and it is proposed that a boy should do so, though there is none such on stage. This is a clear occasion for audience participation, easy enough since young men sat on the stage on benches:

– Come here, boy [*fanciullo*].
– Properly it should be a virgin.
– Virgin or none, there have I never handled you. Draw a lot from this pouch, once I have said a few prayers.[87]

The adolescent boy incorporated in the action of the play echoes the role of young Ippolito, tasked with the appointment of republican officers.

The Plautine plot of *La Clizia* is essentially Oedipal. An old man loves his ward, but is the rival of his son and both employ servants as cover for

[83] *Life of Rustici*: Vasari (1996) II.530.   [84] Mozzati (2008) 220, n.195, finds the inference secure.
[85] Letter by Nerli: Atkinson and Sices (1996) 354.
[86] Vettori cited in Ridolfi (1963) 315. See further Jones (1972) 163–6.   [87] *La Clizia* III.vii.

their amours. In the climax, the old man beds his manservant thinking him the girl, and ends up being sodomized by him. The overt setting of Machiavelli's play is the season of Florentine carnival, and direct address secures an ever-increasing level of audience complicity in the carnivalesque mood. In the finale the audience are not shown the bedding sequence, but are invited to picture the servant standing naked and erect on the bed. Dinners with Fornaciaio had helped Machiavelli conduct his liaison with Barbera, whose songs between the acts would be a crucial part of this event. The name of the old man, Nicomaco, alludes to the foolish love of old **Nic**colò **Mac**hiavelli. The audience, as in Plautus, are denied any sight of the beautiful heroine, but what they saw instead was Barbera in the guise of a nymph with her chorus of four doting shepherds. The name 'Clizia' is taken from Ovid, where it belongs to a naked lovelorn nymph transformed into the turning sunflower.[88] The sequence of sexual frustrations narrated in the play is counterpointed by the promise of sexual fulfilment offered by a nymph-courtesan who is present in the flesh. On Ash Wednesday, Machiavelli's friend Nerli wrote to Machiavelli's brother-in-law reporting complaints that had reached him daily during the carnival period. But for political turmoil, Nerli is certain that people would be talking of nothing but Machiavelli, seeing that 'a paterfamilias of such character is playing the groom, I will not say who with, and has written a comedy that, from what I have heard, has some fine things in it'. Nerli wants the brother-in-law to put matters right, perhaps because Machiavelli as paterfamilias was in the process of arranging his daughter's wedding, and he doubts that sobriety will return with the coming of Lent. Nerli is more concerned by Machiavelli's indiscretion than by his immorality, and is keen to secure for himself a manuscript of the licentious play.[89]

In his prologue Machiavelli restates the classical principle that comedies were invented to combine usefulness with delight, and he lists moral dangers as if they were the Christian deadly sins: the avarice of the old, the fury of the lover, the trickery of the servant, the gluttony of the parasite, the indigence of the poor, the ambition of the rich and the deceits of the whore. The action of the play makes nonsense of such language, assailing the cornerstone of Roman morality, the *paterfamilias* who enjoyed powers of life and death over his children and slaves,[90] and at the end of the comedy, when Barbera directs the words of her final madrigal to the audience, morality collapses into irony:

---

[88] Ovid *Metamorphoses* iv.206–70.
[89] Atkinson and Sices (1996) 542. Translation adapted.   [90] Mozzati (2008) 267.

You, who so intent and silent,
excellent souls, have harkened to this humble and proper exemplar,
this wise and noble accounting of our human life,
and through it perceive
what things to shun and what pursue
to go the straight way to heaven,
and beneath a fine veil
something rather more, that takes too long to tell:
from this pray such fruits befall you
as your great courtesy deserves.

The language is Christian, but the singer is a nymph alluding to a pagan heaven, and is herself the wearer of a thin veil concealing her fruitful paradise.

Plautus was more fashionable than Terence in the early sixteenth century, seen as more essentially Roman.[91] One of Machiavelli's colleagues at the Orti offers a characteristic view of how the ancient world declined: 'The Greeks first corrupted their upright, ancient, and laudable practices, indulging in theatrical performances, scenes, and choruses, through which they would excite the ears and spirit with various sentiments. Then this pernicious effeminacy was exported to Rome, which broke the rigour of its ancient seriousness.'[92] There is no trace of sentiment or effeminacy in *Casina* and *La Clizia*. Plautus wrote a generation earlier than Terence, when Rome was still a gigantic fighting machine, before the influx of Greek wealth. In plays like *Casina*, Plautus resisted Greekness, pointing up the Roman qualities of his adaptation. Obscenity and a slave's-eye view of the world combined to subvert the Greek original. There was no exploration of the finer emotions, and extended singing prevented the Roman spectator from seeing the action as a mirror of Athenian life.[93] Plautus invited male complicity at the end of his play, promising that whoever claps 'will unbeknownst to his wife always bed the whore he desires',[94] and Machiavelli found in Plautus a satisfactory antithesis to the feminized world of Greece, opposing Roman republican values to the decadence of democracy. As his hero declares: 'Whoever likened lover to soldier truly told the truth!'[95] Machiavelli constructed his virile utopia in *The Art of War*, and *La Clizia* was a theatrical surrogate with women as objects of conquest. Castiglione was attentive to the honour of women in a court dominated by the duchess, and his courtier does not make them blush

[91] Poliziano (1973) 25 cites Quintilian X.i.99 on the Romanity of Plautus' language.
[92] Brucioli cited in Cummings (2004) 48. [93] Segal (1968) is the classic account.
[94] Plautus *Casina* 1016. [95] Machiavelli *La Clizia* I.ii.

through blasphemy or obscenity,[96] but Machiavelli and Fornaciaio were no such courtiers. At the end of his prologue Machiavelli declares that in order to win laughter and insult no-one, he must tell of 'the hazards of love. So should there be anything indecent, it will be said in such a way that these ladies may listen without blushing.' The public exposure of women in the auditorium to immodesty was part of the pleasure that Machiavelli purveyed for men. Bakhtin famously demonstrated that an aesthetics of the grotesque emphasizes human equality, while an aesthetics of classical beauty suits an elite,[97] but the politics of class do not tie up comfortably here with the politics of gender.

When Nicomaco's wife looks back to her husband's ordered citizen life divided between family, business, conversation with friends and religious observances,[98] we perceive a gap between two definitions of the citizen. On the one hand, there is the Roman citizen-warrior involved in the defence and government of his own city-state; on the other, there is the Florentine bourgeois, with no overt interest in political governance, and characterized by an ethics of sober self-governance. Machiavelli hankers vainly for the first definition and resists the second. His comic writing is plainly born from his sense of loss of the public sphere where men were once responsible for their own collective destiny.

In Nicomaco's normative bourgeois life, part of his day is spent educating his son, through ancient or modern examples teaching him how to live, but what Machiavelli demonstrates in *La Clizia* is the fraudulent basis of any educational theory of comedy. He observed that the sermons of Savonarola had no effect on the morals of the general population, and knew that republics cannot be built through moralizing.[99] When his comedies expose the sham of private morality, that exposure is incidental to their main purpose, which is to weld an audience through laughter into a collective body. Rejecting Cicero's view that humans have a natural propensity to support each other, he had to reject also the theory that humans imitate each other, and he needed to find other ways to weld individuals into a civic unity that would act in its collective self-interest.

What Machiavelli created in *La Clizia* was not a text with inherent ethical meaning but the scenario for a socio-political event. We hear of some insolent young men at the performance who forcibly admitted their friends and took control of their auditorium, showing no respect to old and honourable citizens. There was a confrontation when an elderly citizen

---

[96] Castiglione (1976) 145, 175.   [97] Bakhtin (1968).
[98] Machiavelli *La Clizia* II.iv.   [99] Machiavelli *Discourses* iii.30.

clambered onto the stage, expecting one of the youths to give up a place on his bench on the stage, but no place was yielded and eventually a servant of Fornaciaio had to find an extra stool.[100] Spectators were thus also performers on stage, acting out a battle for authority between age and youth that mirrors the action of the play. Trexler has shown how generational conflict was central to the politics of the day, and two years later such young men, hitherto excluded from public office, would rise up against the Medici and fight for a new republic.[101] The second anecdote tells how Ippolito de' Medici reacted when assigned a seat that he did not consider the obvious place of honour – and we must bear in mind of course that a traditional seat of honour in the front was not necessarily the best point from which to view a huge perspectival painting of Florence.[102]

When he was placed in his seat by the mace-holder, he looked well all around and everywhere; and seeing places much more befitting to one of his rank, he did not summon the man who allocated seats but the master of the house, saying to him: 'Sir, this is a fine perspective, and I must thank you kindly that you have done me the great favour of inviting me to see it, but I remain even more obliged to you for having given me the most honourable seat there is, for I see many others superior to me who have been placed in worse and more unworthy seats. Therefore with great courtesy I thank you.' All knew that his seat had become the best, because he who merited it had occupied it.[103]

Again we see the theatre functioning as a space of social performance. The unpopular youth whose rule had been imposed on Florence was not given the traditional seat of honour. The boy responded with aplomb by asserting his status in a manner that all could see and hear. *La Clizia* does not read like a political text, but its performance was a political event. As in Cicero's Rome, theatre became once more a site for the negotiation of power.

CODA: GOLDONI, AYCKBOURN AND THE COMIC GENRE

Machiavelli's plays became different things on different occasions: a courtly entertainment affirming the superiority of courtier over citizen, a carnivalesque event revelling in the common baseness of humanity, a celebration of local Florentine identity, a site of confrontation between age and youth, a commodity circulating in a free-market environment. It is pointless to seek any essential meaning of the text behind these manifestations which relate

---

[100] Giannotti *Repubblica fiorentina*, cited in Mozzati (2008) 267.
[101] Trexler (1980) 387–99, 491–547.
[102] Cf. Orrell (1988) 126 on a similar incident in England.
[103] *Primo libro delle sentenze dette da' fiorentini*, cited in Mozzati (2008) 267.

in such different ways to the central problem which preoccupied Machiavelli in his political writings: how to unite self-interested individuals to form a citizen body.

When Guicciardini invited Machiavelli to Faenza, he was preoccupied with the Habsburg threat that would culminate in the sack of Rome, but thought the production of *Mandragola* worthwhile 'because at least it is something which is within our power, so that one is not wasting one's time thinking about it'.[104] In the closed world of a theatre performance, disempowered spectators regain a kind of control, whether to predict plot outcomes or to bestow approval on the actors. By virtue of its separation from the Florence painted onto the stagecloth, and assisted by the contagious effect of laughter, an audience might experience its own collective identity as a republic in miniature, just as Machiavelli, when deprived of his role in public life, found in the confraternal world of the Cazzuola a surrogate republic where men could bond with men as social equals. While ancient comedy gathered in the theatre auditorium the kernel of the political community, comedy in the renaissance began to create substitute communities. Machiavelli's mimetic Florence was his surrogate for active citizenship, but it generated nevertheless a public space, with audience seats on stage maintaining the interplay between perspectival distance and live social encounter.

The versatility of comedy ensured its survival as a cultural form. The idea and reality of the citizen have always lain in the background, as a reference point for the comic genre, and I shall conclude this chapter by looking at two later examples that indicate how the citizen/comedy relationship evolved in comedy, one from the Enlightenment and one from the modern period.

Goldoni's *Le baruffe chiozzotte* ('Brawls at Chioggia') in 1762 marks a notable attempt to reunite comedy with an ideal of republican citizenship. The play portrayed a fishing community, and laid before its audience, as an authentic slice of Venetian life, a world that had hitherto seemed marginal sociologically, linguistically and geographically. Though the aristocrat Carlo Gozzi, whose *Turandot* appeared before the Venetian public a few weeks earlier, feared that Goldoni's play would foment intolerance in the 'people' towards their necessary yoke of subordination,[105] the bourgeois Goldoni claimed that in republican Venice more diverse spectators attended the theatre than in Paris, including shopkeepers, servants and fishermen, and he needed to create characters adapted to their intelligence,

---

[104] Ridolfi (1963) 222.
[105] Lunari and Pedretti (1978) 35. On the wider context see Zorzi (1977) 266–79.

where they could recognize their own faults and virtues.[106] The audience's encounter with the fishing community was mediated by a reincarnation of Goldoni's youthful self as a lawyer on the island. Like the author manipulating his text, the Goldoni-figure dispenses justice after the brawl and facilitates a trio of marriages, but also appears as a substitute for an absent magistrate, for on Goldoni's stage there could be no engagement between the people and the real agents of state power. The fisherfolk are citizens in that they are now recognized to be equal human beings, but they have not become empowered citizens in a fossilized Venetian republic.

When Goethe came to Venice in 1786 he was delighted to find the play still in the repertory at the San Luca theatre, where he loved to see how 'the spectators join in action, and the crowd merges with the stage to make a single whole'. It was a new experience for him to observe 'the pleasure the people expressed at seeing themselves and their families represented so naturally', and he understood that an author can only write this way through 'direct contact with one's own vivacious people', though as an aside he regretted how censorship prevented an appearance of the magistrate.[107] Goethe relished the transpersonal sense of belonging which Venetian comedy provided for its audience, but that belonging stemmed more from a sense of culture and ethnicity than from a sense of citizenship. Goldoni's play is best known today on account of its 1964 production by Giorgio Strehler, who sought to create an authentic portrayal of working-class life, a life which pointedly excludes the bourgeois lawyer.[108] Marxism has never comfortably reconciled itself to theories of citizenship that imply a transcendence of economic divides, and Strehler's staging encouraged a Brechtian mode of viewing based on an aesthetics of detachment. Neither emotionally active nor intellectually active spectatorship maps easily onto Machiavelli's ideal of active citizenship.

My modern example of the comic genre is *Ten Times Table*, with which Alan Ayckbourn opened his new theatre-in-the-round in Scarborough in 1978.[109] In Ayckbourn, the formulaic comic plot is no longer the boy-meets-girl story, but in a tradition we can trace back to Feydeau it deals with adultery and the problem of sustaining bourgeois life. Ayckbourn regularly structures his plays around a party or similar mode of celebration, so the audience's passive experience in the theatre becomes a substitute for active

---

[106] Preface to *Le baruffe chiozzotte*: Lunari and Pedretti (1978) 100–1.
[107] Goethe (1994) 66, 79–80.
[108] See Lunari and Pedretti (1978) 70–4; Aslan (1989) 126–7, 133–9.
[109] Comprehensive documentation on www.alanayckbourn.net. On the spatial ideal, see Joseph (1967). Text in Ayckbourn (1979).

participation in festival. In *Ten Times Table*, inspired by the committee work needed to secure his premises, Ayckbourn demonstrated the poverty both of provincial civil society and of the modern street festival. The folk festival imagined in the play re-enacts the massacre of eighteenth-century agrarian rioters in the town, and the would-be communitarian event is destroyed by the real class antagonisms of the 1970s, an era marked by dire industrial relations. The implication is clear, that Ayckbourn's theatre offers a safe place within a polarized society where people can see their middle-class apoliticism affirmed, with no threat of forced participation. The Scarborough audience were given mock festival programmes so they could at least toy with the feeling of integration in a lost communal world. Ayckbourn's device of performance-in-the-round creates the illusion of incorporation and social levelling, as though the audience are back in democratic Athens, but at the same time breeds self-consciousness and makes it impossible for spectators to respond as a collective body. The price of intimacy is individualization.

Both *Le baruffe* and *Ten Times Table* attest to a human desire for bondedness. In the centuries since Machiavelli, that desire has normally crystallized around nation or class, but Machiavelli wrote at a time when class, ethnicity, nation, place and citizenship all dissolved into the concept of the *cittadino*, and within the framework of the city-state it was still possible to conceive of *homo politicus*. Machiavelli craved for life in the public sphere where he could realize himself as *homo politicus*, not *paterfamilias* or *homo socialis*, and he wrote with such intensity because active republican citizenship was both a fresh memory and a future possibility. In *Le baruffe* we see the young bourgeois lawyer yearning for a lost communal life, and in *Ten Times Table* we see that a theatre of the streets where citizens live their civic identities is an unrealizable dream. When Jean-Luc Nancy finds loss to be constitutive of community, he points to a recurrent truth about theatre, that spectators are bonded by the shared sense of what they all lack. Comedy in the renaissance tradition defined itself as an authentic mimesis of social life, reducing the spectator to a passive onlooker gazing into a mirror of the world from which he or she has been separated, yet to look in that mirror is to see also one's fellows in the auditorium. This is the paradox of comedy. It may pretend to divert, or moralize or scandalize, but its function in society is almost always to build a surrogate community.

CHAPTER 4

From Coventry to London

CHRISTIAN FRATERNITY

I observed in the last chapter that Machiavelli had no interest in the Christian traditions that cemented medieval bonds of citizenship, and it is time now to examine that Christian conception of citizenship. In his letter to the Christians of Rome, St Paul set out a theory of society at odds with Roman traditions of citizenship. Though his assertion that 'there is no difference between the Jew and the Greek' was not in itself shocking to Roman ears, given Rome's tradition of ethnic inclusiveness, the idea that true circumcision is of the heart was entirely foreign, and this emphasis on inwardness was consolidated by the formula that 'a man is justified by faith without the deeds of the law'. Protestants later latched onto the idea that moral justification is ultimately based on inner faith rather than external works, and many of them also responded to Paul's notion that God has an 'elect' on the model of the Jewish people,[1] but the medieval Catholic tradition was more interested in Paul's proposition that we are all members of one corporate body, a theory which implies inequality of office alongside unity of membership. 'For as we have many members in one body, and all members have not the same office: so we, being many, are one body in Christ, and every one members one of another.'[2]

Paul the Jew addresses his Roman co-religionists as his 'brethren', though naming almost as many women as men at the end of his letter. 'Liberté, égalité, fraternité!' is often assumed to be the watchword of the French Revolution, but the 1789 *Declaration of the Rights of Man and of the Citizen* ignored brotherhood or *fraternité* and referred only to men born 'free and equal in respect of their rights'.[3] Liberty and equality of rights were the traditional slogans of classical republicanism which had inspired both democratic Athens and the Roman Republic. For the revolutionaries of

[1] Romans x.12; ii.29; xi.5. Authorized version of 1611.
[2] Romans v.4–5.   [3] Cahn (1997) 663.

1789 the Christian connotations of the word 'fraternity' were too strong, and it was only in the 1848 revolution that fraternity joined 'liberty' and 'equality' in a triad symbolizing French republican values.[4] A republicanism which holds that debate must take place in the openness of the public sphere necessarily resists closed communities where fraternal obligations may transcend loyalty to the republic as a whole. We saw in the last chapter how the fraternal Society of the Trowel epitomized a Medicean Florence. It was a secret society, unlike the religious confraternities responsible for sacred performances in the fifteenth century.

Early Christianity was not sympathetic to theatre. When Rome was sacked by foreign invaders and its political authority seemed transitory, Augustine wrote his *Civitas Dei*, which is better translated 'Citizenship of God' than the familiar 'City of God' for its emphasis is on membership rather than place. Resisting any accusation that Christianity had weakened Rome's civic spirit, Augustine made the theatre central to his assault on all that was wrong with the earthly city, inspired by Plato's eviction of the poets from his utopia. His Cicero was not the humanist admired by the Italian renaissance but the sponsor of prostitutes disporting themselves on a theatrical stage in honour of the goddess Flora. Although Augustine conceded that tragic and comic texts might have a valid place in education, he saw theatrical performance as a sexualized pagan rite rather than a mimesis of human behaviour, and he made much of the contradiction whereby Rome denied citizenship to actors while demanding their participation in ritual.[5] In one of his most powerful metaphors, cited at length by Artaud, Augustine picked on Livy's story that theatre was introduced by the Romans as a preventative against plague, and interpreted theatre as an inner plague that enters through the ears.[6] His best approximation on earth to the celestial city was not Rome but Jerusalem, founded by David whose psalms bred civic harmony, like the music performed in Plato's republic.[7] Augustine attacked not only the theatre and religion of Rome, but also its civic mythology. He condemned Romans for admiring Lucrece's suicide, an act which triggered the ousting of monarchy, because her concern was with honour in the eyes of human beings, and only God could tell whether in her inmost heart she enjoyed being raped. Brutus, the consul who killed his sons in order to preserve the rule of law with impartiality, was celebrated by Virgil as an exemplary patriot, but for Augustine such patriotism stemmed from a thirst for human praise, and this love of 'freedom' failed

---

[4] Ozouf (1992).   [5] Augustine *Civitas Dei* ii.27; ii.8; ii.13.
[6] Augustine *Civitas Dei* i.31–2; cf. Artaud (1970) 17; Livy vii.3.   [7] Augustine *Civitas Dei* xvii.14.

to recognize that true freedom is found in the afterlife.[8] Citizenship, conceived as an ethical force impelling human beings to put the interests of their political community before the interests of self and family, was fatally undermined by the demolition of civic myths such as these.

The Christian cities of medieval Europe were held together not by the Roman ideal of citizenship but by 'fraternity', with companies, fellowships, confraternities and guilds forming the fabric of the social system, and the necessary interpersonal bonds of brotherhood were sealed by eating, drinking and other forms of celebration. Ruling city councils were fraternities which drew their members from lesser fraternities. Fraternities normally elected on an annual basis a master, who presided not as a monarch but as Christ presided over his disciples at the last supper. Many cities like Florence drew their ruling councils from the structure of guilds, and often as in Florence these guilds retained only loose links to specific trades. In other cities like Coventry and London, aldermen were elected from wards, territorial divisions of the city, while the guilds retained a closer relationship to crafts and trades. These craft and trade guilds enforced social discipline, shaped civic ceremony, and through the system of apprenticeship provided the portal through which immigrants became 'free' of the city, citizens in the fullest sense with the right to vote, to manufacture and to sell.[9] Craft and trade guilds broke down any meaningful distinction between a private sphere and a public sphere, for a man's home was his workplace, and events like marriage and burial took place in the bosom of the guild. Divisions of rich and poor were attenuated when guildsmen fraternized as equals. English craft and trade guilds before the Reformation doubled as religious confraternities with their own patron saint and chapel, so domestic, political and religious spheres were all interlocked. The exclusion of women apart from widows from guild membership can be explained by the desire for stability. If a weaver's daughter learned her father's trade and then married a dyer, she might transmit her skills and her loom to one whose office in the corporate body of the city was different.

Perhaps the most important difference between the classical tradition and the Christian tradition lay in the dignity which Christianity gave to labour. Christ grew up as a carpenter, recruited fishermen and was metaphorically represented as a shepherd, while Paul made tents. For Aristotle and Cicero, citizenship was a practice in which a man could engage only when liberated

---

[8] Augustine *Civitas Dei* i.18; v.18.
[9] Black (2003) is the fundamental source for my discussion of guilds and citizenship. On 'freedom' see also Rappaport (1989) 23ff., and on guilds Epstein (1991) and Barron (2004) esp. 206.

from labour, but Christianity assumed that citizenship was a product of labour. In the Roman tradition theatre belonged to *otium* ('leisure') not *negotium* ('business'), but in medieval cities plays staged by confraternities were an extension of the citizen's basic activity, working.

In theory, Florence was an autonomous city-state, while English cities were components of a kingdom, but in practice Florence was subject to constant political threat or interference, notably from the Pope in the period of Machiavelli, whereas English cities, granted their 'liberties' by the crown in the fourteenth century, enjoyed a high level of autonomy, subject always to taxation and the fear of having those liberties removed, the most important being the right to control regional trade. Cities were demarcated by their walls, and their independence like that of Florence rested on having a strong militia. Without deploying the language of classical republicanism, English cities functioned nevertheless as miniature republics or 'commonwealths'; to be a citizen was not just to enjoy a privileged economic status and place of residence, but to embrace a set of ethical values related to the commonweal, the collective well-being of the corporate body.

My focus in this chapter will be upon England, and specifically upon the two well-documented cities of London and Coventry. In his *Survey of London*, John Stow described London as he saw it in 1598 from his perspective as a retired member of the Guild of Tailors, looking back nostalgically to the pre-Reformation era, and devoting barely a line to the new phenomenon of the Elizabethan playhouse, which a man of his class and generation would not think to frequent. He appended to his survey a short essay in urban theory written by an anonymous lawyer some twenty years earlier, which provides us with a convenient glimpse of how Elizabethans thought about citizenship at the start of the Shakespearean period, fusing Christian and classical conceptions of citizenship. The essay sets out ten arguments in favour of urban life.

1. The Ciceronian ideal of *humanitas*, for civilized manners are preferable to barbarism.
2. Religious discipline, for doctrine can be better imparted when people live in proximity.
3. Moral discipline, for people behave better when living in the gaze of others.
4. Good will between individuals, bred by companies and corporate bodies.
5. Intellectual enlightenment, a product of the liberal arts.
6. Prosperity, since crafts and trade thrive best in cities.

7. Charity, since poor relief is best administered in cities.
8. Local security, since the militia protect against both foreign invasion and internal rebellion.
9. National security, since the city is a pool for recruiting an army.
10. Political freedom.

The last argument is worth citing in full: 'Furthermore, even as these societies and assemblies of men in cities and great towns are a continual bridle against tyranny, which was the cause that Tarquin, Nero, Dionysius and such others have always sought to weaken them, so being well tempered they are a strong fort and bulwark not only in the aristocracy but also in the lawful kingdom or just royalty.' There is a republican undercurrent to this assertion that cities save the country when kings turn into tyrants, a tradition of thought and feeling that would culminate in the regicide of the 1640s. The essay concludes in a Catholic vein with the statement that 'this civil life approacheth nearest to that mystical body whereof Christ is the head, and men be the members' – though the instance given has a puritan flavour: Moses as the model 'head' of government 'in the commonwealth of the Israelites'. Stow was a conservative figure, and his *Survey* was widely read. His choice of theoretical text, with its unstable mix of Catholic, puritan and classical republican sentiment, suggests how complicated was the thinking of educated Elizabethan Londoners.[10]

Prior to the Reformation, the mystical body of Christ had been celebrated with ever-growing enthusiasm in the feast of Corpus Christi. The sanctified bread, which in the mass was supposed to transubstantiate itself into the authentic body of Christ, was paraded through the town under a canopy, and the town processed before and behind it as an analogous *body* politic. In the visually oriented culture of the late medieval period, the sight of the host had enormous impact. A sarcastic puritan account tells how a canopy protected the bread from bird droppings while

> The people flat on faces fall, their hands held up on high,
> Believing that they see their God, and sovereign majesty.

And associated with the procession, the poet tells us, 'Christ's passion here derided is, with sundry masques and plays', and in addition to the passion play he enumerates plays about saints.[11] In English towns and cities in the

---

[10] 'An Apology of the City of London' in Stow (1908) ii.196–9. On Stow, see essays by Archer and Manley in Smith, Strier and Bevington (1995). Spelling and punctuation here and elsewhere in this chapter have been modernized.
[11] Kirchmeyer (1570) 53–4. Duffy (2005) evokes the power of seeing the host. For an overview of the festival, see Hutton (1996) 304–10.

fifteenth century, tableaux on wagons were often constructed by craft guilds and incorporated in the procession that accompanied the host, and in several famous instances these wagons became stages for enacting a drama centred on the story of Christ's body. I shall draw my case study from one of the most prestigious of these Corpus Christi plays, that of Coventry, a Midlands city centred on the manufacture of wool.

In London, there was no tradition of a collective Corpus Christi play for a variety of reasons. The monarch resided in Westminster, so the creative energies of the city were required to support royal entries and other forms of state pageantry. The city was dominated by mercantile livery companies, whose members often had only a loose connection to a specific trade, while common craftsmen were relegated to the margins of an oligarchic city government. And the city was too big, with too many guilds to support a single act of mass self-representation. The Company of Skinners, dedicated as a religious fraternity to Corpus Christi, was rich enough to mount processions on a scale similar to many independent towns.[12] Midsummer was the time when London, like Florence, preferred to display itself as a totality with the parading of tableaus, but in the age of Henry VIII it was judged that such processions, which involved marching through the night, were a danger to public order.[13]

THE WEAVERS' PAGEANT IN COVENTRY

I shall examine Coventry from the point of view of a weaver performing or supporting the pageant mounted by his guild or 'craft'.[14] A theorist like Hannah Arendt, wedded to the classical distinction between work and political action, would have to regard sceptically the proposition that the weaver's involvement in the Corpus Christi play was an active expression of his citizenship. The classical republican perspective seeks to balance the weaver's individual *liberty* to participate in an important public ceremony against the *equality* that gives him a right to do so, while giving little weight to *fraternity* and the goal of a happy community free of conflict.[15] Modern individualism has even greater difficulties with the *fraternal* ideal.

[12] On London, see Stow (1908) 1.93; James (1983) 23–4; Rubin (1991) 229, 276; Barron (2000) 407–11; Barron (2004) 22. On the London Passion plays at Skinner's Well (Clerkenwell), see Lancashire (2002) 54–62.
[13] See Hutton (1996) 315, Barron (2000) 408, Davidson (2007) 38–42.
[14] Only one craft organization in Coventry was formally a 'guild', but I have used the word in its familiar generic sense in this chapter. 'Craft', 'Company' and 'Fellowship' are the terms used of the weavers' organization.
[15] See Ozouf (1992) 597.

To understand medieval thinking, we must put these difficulties aside and think of citizenship as a function of the urban organism rather than a function of the individual, although individual relations of amity are a necessary condition of success. A classical vocabulary can deal neither with the political values of the medieval city, nor with the aesthetic values of its theatre.

In 1494 the aldermen of Coventry concluded that the Corpus Christi play benefited the city as a whole, but that the individual guilds which had traditionally mounted plays were now too poor to support the burden on their own on account of the declining wool trade, and so called for mergers.

Forasmuch as the unity, concord and amity of all cities and commonalties is principally attained and continued by due ministration of justice and politic guiding of the same, foreseeing that no person be oppressed nor put to further charge than he conveniently may bear, and that every person without favour be contributory, after his substance and faculties that he useth, to every charge, had and growing, for the wealth and worship of the whole body... therefore it is ordained... that the Mayor and eight of his Council have authority to call all the said crafts... to adjoin to such crafts as be overcharged with the foresaid pageants.[16]

Coventry is construed as a 'body'. The plays contribute to the 'wealth' of this body by drawing in spectators, to the reputation or 'worship' of this body by their excellence, and to the unity, concord and amity of the corporate membership through the process of mounting the plays. Against the background principle of mutuality, we observe the imposition of top-down control, with performance seeming less an honour for the guild than a financial burden, and artificial partnerships imposed in the name of equity that do not correspond with natural divisions of the labour process. These tensions were not altogether new. Back in 1444 we hear of quarrels when four small disparate guilds were yoked together for the purposes of presenting a pageant, and disgruntled members were obviously seeking to act in other pageants.[17]

In a seminal account of the Corpus Christi play, Mervyn James in 1983 saw the body as a key both to the performance and to the medieval city. The bodily metaphor implies a dialectic of 'social wholeness and social differentiation'. The medieval city was never a stable structure, and James argues that the Corpus Christi play provided a mechanism 'by which the tensions implicit in the diachronic rise and fall of occupational communities could be confronted and worked out'. The play was a means by which 'status, and the honour which went with status, could be distributed and redistributed with a minimum of conflict resulting', and its essence was competition. When James suggests that conflict is 'the dark side of the moon of unity' and 'without conflict, no social wholeness either',[18] he echoes Machiavelli, who believed that conflict was the sign of a healthy body politic.

James' bodily focus can be challenged on the grounds that on Corpus Christi day the story of a saint was just as likely to be staged as a passion play about the body of Christ, and the quasi-pagan festival of midsummer was just as likely a moment for the city to present itself as a corporate body. This reservation does not invalidate James' central claim that civic drama provided a mechanism for competition, and Athens offers a good analogue for the principle that competition breeds solidarity. In 1991 James was criticized for endorsing a Turnerian ideal of 'communitas' by Miri Rubin, who was herself swayed by Heather Swanson's Marxist-leaning account of York artisans, which pictured a fundamental class divide between artisans who worked with their hands and merchants who controlled trade. The guilds on this analysis were essentially a means of keeping powerful workers under control, and the language of fraternity was an ideological cover for hard economic realities.[19] Our historical sources foreground the misleading language of officialdom.[20] As Swanson saw the past through a lens coloured by the suppression of trade union power in the 1980s, so the present book is necessarily informed by a twenty-first-century recognition of the interdependence of society and the inadequacy of mere economics to account for the distinctions of a multicultural society.

There is no question but that the Mercers who sold cloth had more prestige and economic power than the Weavers who manufactured that cloth. The Mercers marched last among the guilds in the Corpus Christi procession, thus nearest to Christ's body, while the Craft of Weavers marched in the middle of the procession, reflecting their middling status. The Weavers were nevertheless one of only ten guilds to have the honour of mounting a play,[21] and there was no systematic correlation between the narrative importance of a guild and its socio-political importance. The final pageant of Doomsday, performed by the high-status Drapers, did not in practice enjoy a prestige position, for the queen was unable to witness their pageant

---

[18] James (1983) 8, 18.
[19] Rubin (1991) 266. She also argues on p. 271 that *pace* James it is time to decentre the social body. Cf. Swanson (1989) esp. 38. Rubin's critique is echoed in Beckwith (1994) and Weissengruber (1997).
[20] See Swanson (1988).   [21] Ingram (1981) 16–17 prints the 1445 order of procession.

owing to nightfall when she visited Coventry in 1457.[22] Processional dramas disrupted the rigid hierarchy that governed the great civic processions on the morning of Corpus Christi and on Midsummer Night. As in democratic Athens, wealth in the face-to-face medieval city was valued in large measure for the civic honour that it brought, and if we measure wealth in units of symbolic capital rather than silver or gold, then drama had a redistributive role to play.

There was enough fluidity in the political system to ensure a basic consensus. The guild of Corpus Christi, responsible for coordinating the festival, was a fraternity that brought together aspirants for civic office drawn from a variety of guilds, though dominated always by merchants,[23] and a weaver rose to be mayor in 1526,[24] while another craftsman mayor led a major anti-enclosure riot in 1525.[25] The enclosure of city lands was an ongoing faultline, which did not simply divide the rich from the poor, for the enclosure of common lands to grow crops helped the poor in time of famine, while rights of common grazing benefited butchers and workers in leather more than, say, vintners or dyers.[26] Taxation was another faultline, and a verse pinned to the church door in 1495 in connection with new tolls or 'customs' illustrates an aspect of popular feeling:

> Be it known and understood
> This city should be free and now is bound
> Dame Good Eve made it free
> And now the custom for wool and drapery.

A citizen was said to be 'free' of his city, and the repeated word 'free' here has both economic and republican connotations. The city had its own local mythology based around Lady Godiva, defining its moral identity as a place that once freed itself from aristocratic oppression. A year later the language on the church door became more threatening:

> Cherish the commonalty and see they have their right
> For dread of a worse chance by day or by night.[27]

Yet it was never clear quite who constituted the commonalty. In respect of master weavers, journeymen were the commonalty, possessing their own fraternity or 'fellowship', and allocated at Corpus Christ the menial role of hauling the pageant wagon.[28] Merchant guilds often supported the rights

---

[22] Ingram (1981) 37.   [23] Phythian-Adams (1979) 120.   [24] Hulton (1987) 7.
[25] Rose (1969) 203.   [26] Rose (1969) 202–3.
[27] Harris (1911) 205–9. On Godiva, see Bolton (1969b) 242, 247.
[28] Phythian-Adams (1979) 113; Ingram (1981) 26–7.

of journeymen, in order to keep artisan guilds in check.[29] By such means, power was continuously renegotiated, so that riots were exceptional.[30] As James argues, the pageants thanks to their public prominence were integral to the rebalancing process that ensured stability.

The extant records tell of ten plays, which evidently told the New Testament story from the nativity to Doomsday, and it is likely that the ten plays once mapped onto the ten wards of the city, with each play performed in each ward.[31] The Corpus Christi festival was of particular importance in Coventry because it initiated an eight-day fair crucial to the economy of the city when traders from around the country converged and bales of the city's prestigious blue cloth were sold.[32] The pageants helped Coventry justify its status as the natural trading hub for the Midlands, operating under privileged economic conditions. To be a free citizen of Coventry meant above all being free to sell at the fair.

The text of the Weavers' pageant today is a palimpsest, revealing through its layers how the play changed in response to historical conditions. We see in the first instance how two stories have been stitched together: the presentation of baby Jesus in the temple, and the disputation between the boy Jesus and learned doctors, each with its own prologue delivered by Old Testament prophets. We infer that there were formerly more plays in the cycle with more guilds involved. The particular reason for yoking these two plays together is clearly their use of the same set, a wagon with two levels representing the temple of Jerusalem. An important part of the action in the first part involves decorating the temple before the eyes of the audience, and the raison d'être of the text was in a sense to bring to life this glorious physical structure, created by the skill of Coventry craftsmen and preserved from year to year. One magnificent temple was a better advertisement for the city than two modest and competing temples. It is easy to see through the extant text the bones of its twin predecessors. The core narrative was once played in simple quatrains rhyming *abab*, but that earlier text has been fleshed out by an eight-line stanza rhyming *aaabcccb*, and this later form, with its possibilities of playful and deferred repetition, provides a vehicle for comedy and characterization. The dramaturgy became more ambitious with time, the demands on the actor much greater.

The text that we have is the version of 1531, modified after the break with Rome. By chance a couple of leaves survive from a fifteenth-century

---

[29] Bolton (1969a) 210.   [30] Phythian-Adams (1979) 71.
[31] King and Davidson (2000) 10. Only two of the ten pageants are extant.
[32] See Harris (1911) 252; Bolton (1969a) 212.

manuscript, and alongside stylistic and theological adjustments we notice a striking depoliticization. In the first stanza of the earlier text Christ is interpreted as a star over Israel and 'among us', but in the later version 'Israel' becomes an abstract 'Hill of Woes'. In the earlier text Simeon (represented as a bishop) asks God to remember 'thy daughter Zion' and to spare Israel and Judaea from danger, while Anna (represented as an aged nun) hopes that God will rescue Israel and Judaea 'from dreadful bond unto liberty'.[33] The context of Israel as a nation enslaved by Rome vanishes in the later text, where the emphasis shifts to the personal emotions of Simeon and Anna. The Corpus Christi play places Coventry as an analogue of Jerusalem, the ideal city on earth, its temple constructed anew by the Company of Weavers, and we observe that the audience are no longer invited to think of their city in terms of external tyranny. By 1531, Coventry felt less like an autonomous republic threatened by the outside world, and more like part of a centralized Tudor state. In the context of the Reformation, to position Rome as the external enemy of Coventry/Israel would have been divisive.

The Weavers could not find enough talent amongst fifty-odd masters, their apprentices and their journeymen to meet the demands of the expanded and amalgamated text, but a tradition of 'love brethren' allowed them to swell the numbers of their fraternity for ceremonial purposes, and members of other guilds performing in the Weavers' pageant paid a small fee for honorary membership.[34] Actors were paid, but historians have not found it easy to explain why Simeon was paid more than Joseph, who had a longer part. Simeon is a figure of authority, and was probably played by someone with status in the world outside the play, while Joseph is a comic figure, and may have been played by an actor of lower status. This was a complex and unequal world, but it aspired also to be a fraternal world. Money invested in bread, meat and ale for the players was crucial to the building of appropriate personal relationships.[35]

In the text, actors address the audience gathered around the wagon as 'friends' or 'this company', and the final farewell is addressed to 'you, the commonalty', while Joseph asks the men in the audience to speak up and support him in an argument with his demanding young wife.[36] The performance itself was a means of creating companionship amongst the assembled spectators. In metatheatrical fashion, the action of the play, which represents two country people visiting the great city of Jerusalem,

---

[33] Text in Craig (1957) with appendix on 119–22. See esp. ll. 7, 209–11, 232, 237–8 in the appendix.
[34] Ingram (1981) 121, 562–3; King and Davidson (2000) 21.
[35] Ingram (1981) e.g. 156.   [36] In Craig (1957) ll. 463ff.

reproduced the experience of many of the audience, and in the second
part of the pageant Mary and Joseph refer three times to 'our festival day'.
Joseph's reaction to Jerusalem reflects the reaction of Coventry spectators
to the pageant wagon:

> Mary, my spirits be ravished clean
> And clearly cast out of all woe
> With these solemn sights that we have seen
> In yonder temple that we came fro'.[37]

Joseph is a comic figure, but his fear at engaging with doctors dressed in
fur, the symbol of rank and the uniform of liverymen, called for audience
sympathy,[38] while Jesus' exposition of Mosaic law without aid of books
had an anti-authoritarian appeal. As the physical wagon testified to the
achievement of labour, so the narrative attested to the value of the labourer.
For men characteristically working fourteen hours a day six days a week,
citizenship could not take the form that it did in the privileged slave society
of Athens.

Acting in the Weavers' pageant may be regarded in medieval terms as an
act of citizenship. Firstly, it was a contribution to public education. With
the Bible only available in Latin and guarded by the clergy, exposition of
the biblical narrative performed a public service to the laity in a city that
never forgot how it had secured its freedom from the rule of a powerful
Benedictine priory. Secondly, it was a means of presenting the city to
the outside world, and fostering trade. Thirdly, it established bonds of
fellowship within the Fellowship of Weavers. And finally, it created bonds
of mutual interdependence with other guilds that together made up the
social fabric of the city. Though a certain equality among guildsmen was
established by the performances at Corpus Christi, notions of personal
'freedom' and 'rights' were of little relevance to medieval citizenship. To
be 'free' of the city was a condition of performing, certainly, but such
freedom was not freedom to act as an individual, make political choices or
demonstrate one's unique civic *virtù*.

The decline of the Corpus Christi play can be explained in two different
ways. One story, which takes religion and ideas to be the driver of human
behaviour, maintains that the plays did not decline but were terminated
abruptly because protestant belief was incompatible with visual representations of the biblical story and with the playing of Christ by ordinary
human beings. An addendum to this story notes that, when chantries were

[37] In Craig (1957) ll. 815–18; cf. 757, 810, 1187.	[38] In Craig (1957) l. 1040.

abolished at the Reformation, guilds ceased to double as spiritual organizations concerned with the fate of their members in the afterlife, and were transformed into associations of a purely economic nature. The second story, identifying religion as ideology or false consciousness, emphasizes the economic decline of the autonomous guild-based city. Charles Phythian-Adams has in this light painted a vivid picture of the 'desolation' endured by Coventry when the wool trade failed at the end of the fifteenth century and the population shrank, with many emigrating to London.[39] Though economic decline explains why there was reluctance among the rich to take civic office and support the cost of pageantry, we might equally comment on the remarkable endurance of the plays during this period, and think how the plays provided moral sustenance in difficult times. To examine changing practices of citizenship is a way of drawing these two narratives together. The language of classical republicanism was not widely available in England, leaving the way clear for a puritan Christianity to root its civic ethics in the twin principles of personal discipline and charity towards the poor. Citizens came to define themselves less as components of a corporate body, more as autonomous moral and economic agents.

A unique feature of the 'decline' in Coventry was an experiment in 1584, when the city staged a full-scale alternative pageant play, using the old wagons to tell the story of the 'Destruction of Jerusalem'. It is clear from the accounts of one of the guilds that the play was based on Josephus' description of Israel in AD 66–70, when the Zealots seized control of the temple and attacked Jewish aristocrats.[40] Factional in-fighting resulted in a massacre, and the Romans were able to destroy the Jewish nation. The Weaver's wagon would clearly have been central to this drama with its representation of the temple, but how the narrative was divided up among the guilds remains unclear. The subject matter is fascinating once we read the holy city of Jerusalem as a metaphor for Coventry. Puritan attempts to gain control of the church were a threat to collective survival, and the Parisian massacre on St Bartholomew's Eve 1572 stood as a dire warning of what could happen in a divided city. If we had the text of this play we would be able to see how the city tried collectively to engage with the religious divisions that threatened its cohesion. In May 1591 the play was mentioned again in a resolution by the Council:

---

[39] Phythian-Adams (1979). Gardiner (1946) argued for the primacy of religious explanations.
[40] Sharp (1825) 42 identified the subject matter and its source in Josephus iv, but the play has occasioned little critical discussion. The Smiths' accounts are in Ingram (1981) 307–9.

It is also agreed by the whole consent of this house that the Conquest of Jerusalem, the Conquest of the Danes, or the History of King Edward IV, at the request of the commons of this city, shall be played on the pageants on Midsummer Day and St Peter's day next in this city, and none other plays. And that all the maypoles that now are standing in this city shall be taken down before Whitsunday next, none hereafter to be set up in this city.[41]

There is no evidence that resources were found to support a revival of this epic drama about Jerusalem. We know nothing of *Edward IV*, but 'the Conquest of the Danes' relates to the Hock Tuesday folk play reinstated at the request of the queen in 1576, like Lady Godiva an instance of the local mythologies that underpinned local identity.[42] Performance is no longer to be at Corpus Christi, but to be linked to the militarized Midsummer procession. The oligarchs of the Council are seeking in this edict to strike a bargain, in response to pressure from 'the commons', conceding a dramatic performance as quid pro quo for the definitive suppression of maypoles. When the butchers in 1559 drew their cleavers to protect the cross in the marketplace from destruction,[43] they saw themselves as the voice of the commons asserting their rights over the civic *forum*. Performance was no longer aimed at the 'wealth and worship of the whole body', but was now merely part of an internal power struggle.

SHAKESPEARE, HEYWOOD AND LONDON

Shakespeare probably came from nearby Stratford to see the Weavers perform their pageant before the plays were suppressed in 1580. He was a typical emigrant from the Midlands, perceiving better opportunities in London, where rapid urban growth accompanied centralization of power by the Tudor regime. It was in the interests of that regime to unify the nation so that people should think of themselves as English in the first instance, and citizens of their local community in the second. Though London had burst beyond its jurisdictional boundaries, the livery companies continued to provide it with a formal and effective organizational structure. Freedom of the city was opened up to migrants in a manner that would have been inconceivable in Coventry.[44]

---

[41] Ingram (1981) 332.
[42] For the Hock Tuesday play, see Robert Laneham's letter printed in Ingram (1981) 272–5, with commentary on xx and 581. *Edward IV* is unlikely to be a reference to Heywood's later play of that name, as this is centred on London rather than Coventry.
[43] Bolton (1969a) 218.   [44] Porter (1996) 62.

Elizabethan theatre was a marginal phenomenon.[45] As has often been remarked, its buildings were sited physically outside the wards of the city, or in former monastic property over which the crown retained rights.[46] Actors had an ambivalent social position, servants of the aristocracy permitted to build theatres thanks to courtly patrons, but at the same time capitalist entrepreneurs, often retaining a fraternalistic approach to the running of their enterprises. Wills tell us something of how actors conceived themselves. Only in the 1580s and then again in the 1630s do we find actors defining themselves in the first instance as servants of the monarch; the majority adopt the unverifiable title of 'gentleman', but a substantial minority name themselves 'citizen and x', where 'x' = saddler, goldsmith, grocer or some other title of a livery company.[47] Guild membership was useful in creating a legal framework for taking on apprentices to play female roles,[48] but there was clearly also an affective dimension: some men felt that they belonged to London, some did not.

Different stories can be told about the government of Elizabethan London. It can be portrayed as a repressive oligarchy, imposing the will of the few who ran the great livery companies. In this narrative, the Lord Mayor's show, a grandiose and scripted spectacle replacing the participatory festivals of the Catholic era, symbolizes the dead hand of power. Stow pointedly ignored this, the city's greatest modern celebration, just as he ignored the theatre, looking back to an age when citizens enjoyed a rich variety of Christiano-pagan festivals. For modern devotees of Shakespearean theatre, it is almost inevitable that the city government should be cast in the role of villain. Shakespeare is our greatest cultural heirloom, yet in its blindness the city government apparently sought to suppress Elizabethan theatre, unable to distinguish great poetry from the adjacent bawdry, bowling and bear-baiting. Recent historians of London, however, have given the 'judicious stewardship' of the 'city fathers' a much better press, remarking on how effective that government was in preserving social cohesion under intense pressure, taking over from monasteries the job of relieving the poor, preventing riots against foreign immigrants and physical conflict between religious groupings, and preserving economic stability in time of epidemics.[49] Just as historians of Athens have only recently

---

[45] For the concept, see Dawson and Yachnin (2001) 5–6.
[46] Mullaney (1988) is an influential account.
[47] Wills collected in Honigmann and Brock (1993). For the interplay of terms, see Hill (2004) 23–8. The link to crafts was usually nominal.
[48] Kathman (2004).
[49] Porter (1996) 66. Other major studies include Rappaport (1989), Archer (1991) and Barron (2004).

recognized the importance of democracy at the level of the deme, so London historians have recently recognized how office-holding at ward and parish level maintained the fabric of urban life within which huge numbers functioned as active citizens.[50]

The public playhouse was a new phenomenon, and in the early unregulated days it was easy for the city government to think like St Augustine. Asked by the queen to take measures against plague, the mayor in 1580 protested to Burghley that 'some things have double peril, both naturally in spreading the infection, and otherwise in drawing God's wrath and plague upon us, as the erecting and frequenting of houses very infamous for incontinent rule'.[51] By the end of the century, the city had found a *modus vivendi* with the new institution. The number of companies approved by the Privy Council was restricted to two or three, there were few Sunday performances to distract impressionable apprentices and many freemen of London were involved in this profitable new enterprise.[52] Beneath the surface tensions, city and crown enjoyed a symbiotic relationship, the crown providing protection in return for city finance. It remained, however, almost impossible to conceptualize the social function of the playhouse in terms of citizenship, and the task today is scarcely easier. Oliver Arnold in 2007 portrayed the Elizabethan theatre as a 'plebeian public sphere in which opinions might be shaped and political effects achieved', a radical democratic alternative to representative parliamentary government,[53] but an equal case can be made for seeing plays as adjuncts of royalist power.[54] New historicism has interested itself in the idea of 'self-fashioning', but has not found a methodology for describing collective self-fashioning, the process whereby people gathered up in an audience discover a group identity which transcends the individual.[55]

I shall address the question of how theatre built citizenship by looking at two contrasting texts, and seeking to reinstate them as performance events. As in renaissance Florence, so in England Rome was a tool that made thinking about citizenship possible, bypassing complications thrown up by Christian faith. I shall discuss Shakespeare's treatment of Caesar's assassination, when Brutus failed to resurrect the republic, allowing Octavius/

---

[50] Rappaport (1989) 182 estimates that one-tenth of male Londoners held a public office in any given year.
[51] Chambers (1923) IV.281.
[52] Wickham (2000) is the principal modern sourcebook.   [53] Arnold (2007) 43–4.
[54] Cf. Greenblatt (1981). On the theatricality of power, see Liu (1989) 723, with n.9, p.760.
[55] For a critique of the ideology enshrined in Greenblatt (1980) and followers, see Belsey (2007). Dawson touches on the collectivity of viewing in Dawson and Yachnin (2001) 93, 97.

Augustus to establish the imperial principle; and by way of comparison I shall examine Heywood's treatment of the rape of Lucrece, an event which resulted in the ousting of monarchy by a much earlier Brutus. The first of these great republican myths defines the death of the Republic, and the other its birth.[56] Republicanism, as Andrew Hadfield puts it, 'was a fund of stories and potent images ... as well as a collection of ideas and a political programme'.[57] Classical republicanism relied on its mythologies in the same way that Christian ethics relied upon the power of the biblical narrative to command the imagination.

There is no sign that Shakespeare developed any affective bonding with London. He invested his wealth in Stratford and acquired a coat of arms to certify his status as a gentleman, but there is no indication that he ever bought property in London or held public office there. His plays never flatter Londoners, and his utopias are always rural. His company was ambitious, foiled in its attempt to open the Blackfriars in the late 1590s as a theatre for the rich. Moving to the south bank of the Thames in 1599, where *Julius Caesar* may have been the first performance at the new Globe, the Chamberlain's Men were well placed to secure an audience arriving by water from Westminster and from the Inns of Court. Heywood like Shakespeare migrated to London as an actor/writer seeking to make his fortune, but his perception of the world was radicalized by a stronger classical education. He lived out his days in London in settled domestic fashion, and ended his career writing protestant pamphlets and serving as city chronologer tasked with scripting the Lord Mayor's pageant. His early plays, like *The Four Prentices of London* or *The Fair Maid of the Exchange*, celebrate civic identity, and his most famous play *A Woman Killed With Kindness* is a study of the puritan conscience. He wrote *The Rape of Lucrece* in 1607 for the new Red Bull playhouse, built north of the city where an audience of Londoners arrived by foot. His company, under the patronage of Prince Henry, was much less successful at this time in securing performances at court than Shakespeare's company under the patronage of the King.[58]

Shakespeare wrote *Julius Caesar* directly after completing his cycle of eight (or nine) English history plays. The cycle ended historically with the

---

[56] The Romans themselves did not periodize the *res publica* in quite this way; see forthcoming work by James Hankins.

[57] Hadfield (2005) 13.

[58] The standard biography for Shakespeare is Schoenbaum (1993); for Heywood, Clark (1931). On the implications of royal patronage at the start of the civil war, see Gurr (1996b) 77–80, Gurr (2004) esp. 176, 201.

birth of the Tudor regime, but in terms of conception and performance with *King Henry V*, portraying a model English king who welds men of diverse geographical origins into a single national army. Through exploring how the king is but a man, and ceremony but an idol, *Henry V* invited its audience to empathize with its royal hero. It was a logical corollary that Shakespeare, after exploring the violent history of English kingship, should turn to Rome and examine the necessity of kingship as an institution. The succession to Elizabeth was unresolved, and *Henry V* alludes to the quasi-regal role taken in Ireland by the Earl of Essex, who two years later would rise up in rebellion, wrongly believing that the city of London would support him.[59] Hadfield describes the last years of Elizabeth's reign as 'the republican moment' when the future of government was unpredictable.[60]

Like the antifeminism of *Taming of the Shrew* and the anti-Semitism of *Merchant of Venice*, the anti-plebeianism of *Julius Caesar* has proved an embarrassment to modern liberal assumptions. In this play, unlike *Coriolanus*, the mob of 'plebeians' is never dignified by the appellation of 'citizens', and citizens exist only as an absence, authors of concocted messages which spur Brutus into the false belief that he acts on behalf of the citizenry. *Julius Caesar* was interpreted as a republican play in England in the early eighteenth century, as also in the first century of US independence from British rule, but in twentieth-century England it became a staple of imperialist pedagogy,[61] so we must approach the text cautiously in search of a historicized reading. Educated Elizabethans were taught to admire the moral principles set out in Cicero's treatise *On Duties*, but were always reluctant to follow Cicero in his approval of Brutus which stems from those principles.[62] Brutus thus constituted a moral conundrum. A French text translated in 1598 told of 'Brutus amongst the Romans, who slew Julius Caesar to free the commonweal from tyranny, and to purchase the renown and reputation of a good citizen', but no English author put in print similar sentiments.[63]

Shakespeare's Rome was of course a figure for London. In the opening scene, the tribunes, whose function echoes that of elected London aldermen, seek to cancel the holiday which Caesar is going to exploit. Elizabeth's support of the Coventry Hock Tuesday play provides an early illustration

---

[59] Porter (1996) 67; cf. *Henry V* V.prologue.30–5. On Essex and Julius Caesar, see Rebhorn (1990) 100–6; Daniell (1998) 23–4, 29; Shapiro (2005) 144–5.

[60] Hadfield (2005) 205. For the background to English republican thought, see Peltonen (1995).

[61] See Ripley (1980), Spevack (2003), Royle (2006).

[62] Cox Jensen (2009) 79, 155–71. Cicero approves the assination in *De Officiis* III.iv.19, vi.32, xxx.82–3.

[63] From a commentary on Aristotle's *Politics* attributed to 'Louis Le Roy': cited in Cox Jensen (2009) 163.

of what Leah Marcus has called a royal 'politics of mirth', whereby the crown supported festivals that civic authorities wanted to suppress.[64] Stow's *Survey of London* is indicative of the popular feeling to which this strategy appealed. Shakespeare's tribunes apprehend two of the plebeians set on witnessing Caesar's triumphal procession:

Enter FLAVIUS, MURELLUS, *and certain* COMMONERS *over the stage*

FLAVIUS
   Hence! Home, you idle creatures get you home!
   Is this a holiday? What! know you not,
   Being mechanical, you ought not walk
   Upon a labouring day without the sign
   Of your profession? Speak, what trade art thou?
CARPENTER
   Why, sir, a carpenter.
MURELLUS
   Where is thy leather apron and thy rule?
   What dost thou with thy best apparel on?
   You, sir, what trade are you?
COBBLER
   Truly, sir, in respect of a fine workman, I am but, as you would say,
      a cobbler.
MURELLUS
   But what trade art thou? answer me directly.
COBBLER
   A trade, sir, that I hope I may use with a safe conscience; which is, indeed,
      sir, a mender of bad soles.
MURELLUS
   What trade, thou knave? thou naughty knave, what trade?[65]

In the guild-based city, the carpenter should be recognizable by the tool that is his badge, allowing the alderman to locate him, or his master if he is but a journeyman or apprentice, and ensure he is subject to civic discipline. The Carpenters of London were incorporated as a guild in 1477,[66] and this commoner would doubtless be in formal terms a 'citizen'. The cobbler, however, presents the tribune/alderman with a different problem, for cobbling was not strictly a 'trade'. In London in 1599, eighty-five cobblers were free of the Cordwainers, but there was a long-running dispute between the Cordwainers and the Curriers to control workers in leather. An influx of foreign workers catering for the luxury market at court resulted in a royal charter for a separate company of Cordwainers at Westminster, and

[64] Marcus (1986). Cf. Rose (1989), Wilson (2002).
[65] *Julius Caesar* I.i.1–17. Text cited from Spevack (2003).   [66] Unwin (1908) 163.

this cobbler could also be a freelance worker based outside the walls, over whom the Cordwainers claimed right of quarterage.[67] The cobbler's jest that he is a 'mender of souls' hints that he may be a religious dissident. The task of enforcing civic discipline is not a straightforward one, in the conditions of 1599.

When the commoners have been dispersed, threatened with plague for offending the gods, Flavius tells his fellow tribune:

> Disrobe the images
> If you do find them decked with ceremonies.
>   MURELLUS
>   May we do so?
>   You know it is the feast of Lupercal.
>   FLAVIUS
>   It is no matter; let no images
>   Be hung with Caesar's trophies.

Disregard of an ancient religious festival is just what we would expect of Elizabethan aldermen, who suppressed the old calendar of Catholic festivals in favour of a sabbatarian regime with its regular working days, and helped to dispose of Catholic 'images'.[68] In the next scene an off-stage Antony exploits the performativity of a superstitious fertility game, while Brutus declares that he himself is 'not gamesome'. Caesar characterizes Brutus as one who 'reads much', but 'loves no plays, / As thou dost, Antony, he hears no music'.[69] In an English context, Brutus the republican is necessarily also Brutus the puritan, and there is no cultural space for him to be a Machiavelli, a humorist content to separate civic virtue from private immorality. Brutus' distaste for 'plays' implicates the Globe audience, out to enjoy being 'idle creatures' just as Coventry people once enjoyed their 'festival day'.

In the Elizabethan and Jacobean age, the success of monarchy relied on its theatricality, and in the Forum Antony wins the hearts of the plebeians for the monarchical principle because he outperforms Brutus. Gathered around the thrust stage, the spectators in the yard of the Globe became an extension of the plebeians, their emotions subject to the same power of rhetoric. Brutus fails not simply because his prose cannot match the rhythms of Antony's verse, but also because his political vocabulary does not connect. The senatorial conspirators are fired by the ideal of 'liberty', but the commoners with their six-day week of labour have no interest in escaping political bondage to win a theoretical freedom, for in a London

---

[67] Unwin (1908) 252–3; Archer (1991) 136–7.
[68] On 'images' in the play, see Dawson and Yachnin (2001) 169–71.   [69] *Julius Caesar* I.ii.28, 201–4.

context many if not most of these men would already be 'free' of their city. 'Rome' in the rhetoric of Brutus is an abstraction, embracing Philippi as much as the walled city of Rome, and Brutus' argument that Caesar's death gave everyone 'a place in the commonwealth' does not relate to the real world of poor urban artisans. Antony speaks of citizenship only when he reads Caesar's will:

> To every Roman citizen he gives,
> To every several man, seventy-five drachmaes.[70]

For Antony, to be a citizen is to be a 'several man', an individual severed from the collectivity of a 'commonwealth', and monarchy triumphs in the Forum because it offers rewards to passive recipients. When the city can no longer be experienced as a corporate body, the gulf between plebeian and senator is too large to bridge with the homogenizing word 'commonwealth'. The lynching of Cinna the poet in the next scene again implicates the Globe audience, who have paid to hear the work of a poet, separating them now from the rabble of cobblers and carpenters on stage.[71] In the final part of the play the setting shifts from city to empire, and Brutus is put before the audience as tragic hero, inviting sympathy for his lonely idealism. His republicanism is hopeless when the venality of Cassius is the norm, and the monarchical rule of Octavius, the future Augustus, proves the only possible future for a Rome that has burst its urban bounds.

In Heywood's *Rape of Lucrece*, monarchy is ousted, and a consular commonwealth established. Heywood took Shakespeare's courtly, voyeuristic poem of *Lucrece* and repoliticized it, showing how the rape begot a revolution.[72] His hero is a very different Brutus from Shakespeare's, a humorous senator who acts mad in order to conceal his political dissidence, and when Lucrece's wounds like those of Caesar are displayed in the Forum, there is no ambiguity about the popular support that Brutus enjoys, most importantly among the young men who form the urban militia. The Tarquin king is an absolutist, who rules without recourse to a constitutional Council and sends free citizens into exile without trial. In Livy's account the Tarquins were exiled, but in Heywood's uprising they are killed. Rome is identified unambiguously with the city of London, and the rape is set up in class terms as the rape of a citizen wife by an aristocrat.

The play was a successful one, and there were five printed editions before the revolution, while *Julius Caesar* only appeared in Shakespeare's complete

---

[70] *Julius Caesar* III.ii.36–7, 231–2.
[71] Cook (1981) raised questions about the social status of the Globe audience that remain unresolved.
[72] It is only in the prose argument to Shakespeare's poem (*c.* 1593) that any such link is made.

works. From the Restoration onwards, Shakespeare's play has been recognized as a masterpiece while Heywood's has been ignored, and there is a complex historical relationship here between aesthetic and political values. It is impossible to separate Heywood's radical politics from his populist and localist dramaturgy, a challenge to the modern reader who is likely to experience Shakespearean dramaturgy as part of her or his bloodstream. In a classic study of popular theatre, *A Good Night Out*, John McGrath set out nine criteria that seemed to him to separate popular working-class theatre from the bourgeois values of places like the Royal Court: directness, comedy, music, emotion, variety, effect, immediacy, localism and a sense of identity with the performer.[73] Heywood's play illustrates these features rather well.

Music is a striking feature, for the play is packed with popular songs sung or led by a single singer. Later editions added more songs, making it impossible to define the boundaries of the authentic authorial play.[74] Aesthetically, the songs reflect a taste for variety rather than narrative structure, and in performance we may guess that the audience participated in well-known refrains, so coming to feel that they were collective makers of the performance. The principle of variety relates to an epic structure packed with incident, moving so fast that narrative, character and emotion require absolute immediacy and directness. Moral scruples by the rapist supply narrative tension, but character development is of no concern: Brutus acts mad and suddenly becomes a heroic leader, while Lucrece is the comic caricature of a kill-joy puritan wife one moment, and tragic heroine the next. The audience are invited to empathize with her plight, but a song soon follows which relives her rape, taking the audience up and down her body in the imagination.[75] The localizing references to London were so strong that the 'Cries of London Town' could comfortably be added as one of the new songs. While *Julius Caesar* is set in a historicized Rome, and scattered anachronisms call no attention to themselves,[76] Heywood makes constant play of the jump between Rome and London. The Senate is referred to as 'parliament', the Capitol is the House of Lords and the union of two kingdoms mirrors that of England and Scotland. Though Heywood's play is not a republican manifesto, and ultimately condemns absolutist monarchy rather than power-sharing monarchy,[77] the difference

---

[73] McGrath (1996) 54–9. The book is based on seminars given in 1979.
[74] Holaday (1950) is the standard critical edition, though his early dating has found no critical support.
[75] Camino (1995) 103 expresses her 'revulsion' at this song.
[76] Apart perhaps from the striking clock: see Royle (2006) 212–14.
[77] Kewes (2002) offers a good political analysis, and discerns the influence of Machiavelli.

between the politics of *Lucrece* and of *Julius Caesar* could scarcely be greater. Just as Heywood's Brutus plays the merry madman to conceal his views, so his play uses the cover of Rome, comedy and folk music to bypass royal censorship. Admittedly, royal power was now more secure than it had been in 1599.

Shakespeare placed his spectators as citizens of a nation-state. In his cycle of English history plays these spectators saw their nation being formed, and in *Julius Caesar* they were not encouraged for long to identify with the fractious plebeians of the city. The name of the new theatre, the 'Globe', attests to universalizing aspirations, and its location beside the Thames allowed a socially diverse audience to converge. Heywood by contrast contemplated monarchy from the perspective of Londoners. The name of his north London theatre, the Red Bull, evokes the locality of a tavern, and the masculinist values that characterized Machiavelli's republicanism. Playing to an audience of whom most, like himself, must have been migrants to London rather than native Londoners, Heywood used the theatre to give his audience a sense of belonging, and his plays transformed the gathered crowd into a body of London citizens, filling a vacuum left by the decay of the corporate guild-based city. Because today we are likely to conceive our own citizenship in terms of a nation-state rather than a city, Shakespeare's flight from the local may easily escape our attention.

Around the time of *Lucrece*, Heywood also wrote his *Apology for Actors*, a unique manifesto emerging from the theatrical profession. Purporting to be a response to puritan extremists, the *Apology* reads more like a bid for court patronage. Heywood portrays the Elizabethan playhouse as a descendant of the Roman theatre, and Julius Caesar as a man inspired to great deeds by theatre, himself builder of a famous theatre modelled on the geometry of the universe.[78] He sets out the classical case for theatre as a source of moral instruction, alleging that: 'Plays are writ with this aim, and carried with this method, to teach the subjects obedience to their King, to show the people the untimely ends of such as have moved tumults, commotions, and insurrections, to present them with the flourishing estate of such as live in obedience, exhorting them to allegiance, dehorting them from all traitorous and felonious stratagems.'[79] In *Lucrece*, as we have seen, Heywood does precisely the opposite, portraying an insurrection that is both justified and triumphant. In his *Apology* Heywood interprets the fall of the Tarquins merely as a lesson about lust, while chaste women are 'extolled, and encouraged in their virtues' by the likes of Lucrece. Horatius,

---

[78] Heywood (1612) B3, D2v. Caesar is also said to be a playwright: E3v.   [79] Heywood (1612) F3v.

whose heroism saves the city in Heywood's play, simply provides a lesson in magnanimity.[80] In this rhetorical exercise, the politics of Heywood's play were entirely effaced. There was a huge gap between what could be written for patrons and what could be said and done before spectators at the Red Bull.

An anonymous response to Heywood's *Apology* drew on St Augustine, and turned Heywood's historiography back to front. The puritan polemicist refused to see playhouses as an architectural ornament to the metropolis, maintaining that 'the honourable City of London hath spewed them out from within her walls, and rejected them to take up their standing in the remotest part of the suburbs'.[81] While Heywood praised Caesar for building a theatre, his critic writes as a republican, regretting how the famous dictator 'reduceth the commonwealth into a monarchy. And thus, whilst theatres flourished and stage plays were presented in greatest pomp, is the most flourishing estate of the Roman commonwealth brought into a monarchy.'[82] Caesar's sponsorship of theatre was a mistake: perhaps Brutus and Cassius failed to divert their minds with plays, but it is 'more likely that from plays (which are stuffed full of such matters) they learned the cleanly conveyance of their treachery, and how, in what sort, with what secrecy, and by what means to effect their treason'.[83] Heywood's puritan opponent correlates the rise of theatre with the decline of the Roman Republic, whereas Heywood blames the suppression of theatre and the subsequent fall of Rome on the pagan Marcus Aurelius. As we have seen, Heywood as playwright held to a middle course, keeping his distance from the Caesars of his own day, and continuing as a classicist to believe in theatre's contribution to the commonwealth.

The populist musical format of *Lucrece* was immediately parodied at the 'private' Blackfriars playhouse. In Beaumont's *The Knight of the Burning Pestle*, the affluent Blackfriars audience was encouraged to laugh at the spectacle of a grocer, his wife and his apprentice straying into a theatre where they do not belong.[84] The citizen of London is construed in the play as other, and betrays this alterity through a taste for participation. The apprentice is sent to join the actors on stage, casting himself as the knight errant of a romance, and in an apotheosis he is transformed into a May Lord dancing upon a fountain in the Strand, a festive role which involves lording over unruly apprentices armed with guns, and which begets a second role as Captain of the Grocers' militia mustered at Mile End. The world of

[80] Heywood (1612) F4v–Gv.   [81] Green (1615) 6.   [82] Green (1615) 11.
[83] Green (1615) 25.   [84] Text in Hattaway (1969).

participatory civic ceremony and masculine combat evoked by Beaumont was actually fading or gone. When London was preparing to beat off a Spanish invasion in the 1580s, organization of the militia by guilds was replaced by a ward-based organization under central control.[85] We saw in the last chapter how Machiavelli believed in militias as the necessary foundation of republican citizenship, but the authorities in Florence as in Elizabethan London were wary of anarchy. Maypoles were suppressed in England perhaps less for their phallic symbolism than for the anarchic behaviour they unleashed in young men.[86] The Maying once tapped the energies and creative imagination of young Londoners low in the social hierarchy, allowing them to contribute through collective action to the honour of the city,[87] but these participatory impulses no longer had a ready outlet, and plays like *Lucrece* offered young Londoners a substitute. On Shrove Tuesday 1617 a carnival band of apprentices wrecked the new Cockpit theatre, angered by the threat that Heywood's company might move its centre of operations from the Red Bull to an indoor theatre they could not afford.[88] No doubt as theatre-goers they also did not wish to learn the rules of polite non-participatory behaviour.

Beaumont's May Lord embodies the spirit of choral dance, eliminated by the speech-based culture of Elizabethan protestantism and Elizabethan theatre. When theatre replaced festival, the logic of the marketplace determined that the social classes would fan out, making it increasingly difficult to experience theatre as an expression of corporate citizenship. For many, sermons provided a more attractive performance art than theatre.[89] Theatre could not or did not tangle with religion, except when parodying extreme puritan sects, and it could not therefore engage seriously with those who placed themselves as citizens before subjects. The citizen as Calvinist saint bound by ideals of civic virtue and self-discipline found no place on the London stage.[90] Although the marketplace encouraged some localism and celebration of London, as at the Red Bull, broadly speaking, as Louis Montrose argues, theatre in the Stuart period served to place the values of the centre above those of the local, and to aggrandize the dynastic nation-state.[91]

The participatory theatre of the medieval city collapsed because people started to conceive themselves as individuals first, members of a body

---

[85] Strype (1720) 5.451; on the history of musters, see Lancashire (2002) 157–70.
[86] On maypoles, see e.g. Berlin (1986) 19.
[87] On London Maying, see Lancashire (2002) 168; on youth culture, see Brigden (1997).
[88] Gurr (1991) 325.   [89] On sermons, see Collinson (1996) 47, Brigden (1997) 70–2.
[90] Peltonen (1995) 12; cf. Lupton (2005).   [91] Montrose (1995) 73.

politic second. Elizabethan theatre is famous for constructing the figure of the individual tragic hero, a Brutus or a Lucrece, who stands alone on the stage of the world, and audiences have long gained a sense of fellow-feeling from gazing at these isolated heroes. At the start of the seventeenth century London audiences consisted in the main of migrants who could not easily define their identity in terms of class or place, or know whether they were ultimately citizens, subjects, consumers or inhabitants of the City of God. Heywood did more than Shakespeare to turn the audience back into citizens. We may or may not regard this as an impoverishment of the person.

JOHN MILTON AND THE REVOLUTION

In the final section of this chapter, I shall focus on Britain's most famous citizen-artist, and his dream of creating a theatre for revolutionary citizens. Milton's skill with language and dedication to the republican cause allowed him to become the public voice of the revolution, justifying to other European nations the execution of a king. Milton had no interest in being a citizen of London, and wrote as a citizen of his nation, liberated from subservience to monarchs and bishops appointed by the monarch, and committed to the brotherhood of man. Milton was devoted to the classics, but was also committed to his puritan faith and could only conceive a republic in Christian terms. As in the modern project of building an Islamic republic, the seventeenth-century project of building a Christian commonwealth required the reconciliation of two value systems. The secular classical tradition with its twin ideals of theatre and citizenship had to be united to a Christianity which for centuries had abhorred the professional stage, and now also shunned the Catholic taste for visual images. Milton was in many respects, notably on divorce and freedom of publication, a libertarian, and he assumed that certain civil rights must accompany the inner freedom offered by Christianity. Appalled though he was at the sexual values of public theatre, he could not accept the indefinite suppression of the poet's public voice.

Milton visited the public theatre in his youth, experiencing the pleasurable pain of tragedy described by Aristotle, but distaste for student theatricals alienated him from fellow theological students at Cambridge.[92] His main foray into writing for performance came in 1634 when he wrote a

---

[92] *Elegia prima* [1626]: Milton (1931–8) i.i.170; *An apology against a pamphlet* [1642] Milton (1953–82) ii.887.

masque for the lord president of Wales, pushing the genre as far as he could away from spectacle towards language, and in an important formal innovation he provided a major speaking role for a female performer.[93] 'Comus' or *kōmos* is the Greek word for a Dionysiac revel, and the rapacious figure of Comus animates the masque as Satan would later animate *Paradise Lost*, accompanied by men and women in animal masks representing popular energies that threaten the social order of Wales. Milton shows no more liking for the mob than Shakespeare did in *Julius Caesar*, and for all his republicanism he was never a democrat. How far Milton identified with the demonic figure whom morally and intellectually he hated is a matter for psychoanalytic enquiry.

The logic of the masque form was in the end too strong for Milton to subvert. Masques were a mode of conspicuous consumption, displaying visions of an aristocratic ideal. Back in London, Charles I famously used the neoplatonist idealism of the masque to justify the absolute nature of his own rule.[94] To disentangle theatricality from kingship was not easy, for Charles secured his power through the way he performed his kingship. Analysing Charles' exemplary behaviour at his execution, Milton likened this tyrant to a masked actor on the Roman stage, still ambitious for applause at his final exit.[95] Milton's Charles was a man who sat in the theatre in order to fondle women's breasts, and who read Shakespeare in his closet.[96] Shakespeare portrayed tyrants like Richard III too sympathetically for Milton's taste, and the dramatist he admired most was Euripides. In his politicized reading of Greek tragedy, monarchs like Theseus, Creon, Oedipus and Pelasgus acknowledge the ultimate sovereignty of the people, Orestes is a prince put on trial by the people, and Haemon declares that *civitas* does not lie only in the hands of his royal father.[97] Greek tragedy engaged with issues of tyranny and freedom that concerned Milton, while the discipline of the Greek form, with its preference for off-stage physical action, appealed to his puritan sensibility. In the year of *Comus*, he purchased a critical edition of Euripides which is now in the Bodleian library. The frontispiece represents a version of the tree of knowledge with a warning not to reach too high, and we may imagine the future author of *Paradise Lost* regarding pagan theatre as some kind of dangerous forbidden fruit. Through his annotations, we

[93] On the politics of the masque, see McGuire (1983); Marcus (1986) 169–212. Text in Milton (1931–8) 1.1.85–123.
[94] See e.g. Orgel (1975).   [95] *First Defense* [1651]: Milton (1931–8) VII.16, 484.
[96] *First Defense* [1651]: Milton (1931–8) VII.236; *Eikonoklastes* [1650]: Milton (1953–82) III.361.
[97] *First Defense* [1651]: Milton (1931–8) VII.306ff, 350; *Eikonoklastes* [1650]: Milton (1953–82) III.362, 589.

can trace his close systematic readings of the Greek text, and see how his classical ear was honed to the rhythms of Greek iambic verse, though the dance metres of choral lyric eluded him.[98]

It seems clear that the possibility of writing a Christian tragedy in the Greek style became apparent to Milton when, passing through Paris en route to Italy for the grand tour, he visited the famous champion of Dutch republicanism and theorist of natural law, Hugo Grotius. Grotius had in his youth written lively tragedies of the Fall and of the Passion. The first became an important source for *Paradise Lost*,[99] while the second, written in a land subject to Spanish occupation, addressed the politics of occupation, keeping the crucifixion off-stage.[100] Grotius had recently returned to dramatic writing, and his Old Testament play about Joseph constructed an ideal puritan governor, far sighted in conserving food supplies and firm in his handling of food riots. This Joseph restores the broken bonds of brotherhood through his high morality, and his twelve brethren provide the structure for a future Jewish commonwealth.[101]

Seeing no place for himself in the church, and sensing a new Britain in the making, Milton imagined a role for himself as national poet. Like renaissance Italians who elected to write in Tuscan, he determined not to write in Latin like Grotius 'but to be an interpreter and relater of the best and sagest things among mine own citizens throughout this island in the mother dialect'. In a manifesto of 1642 he declared himself unsure whether to use the epic form 'or whether those dramatic constitutions wherein Sophocles and Euripides reign shall be found more doctrinal and exemplary to a nation'. The Bible, he argued, employed the mode of drama in the Song of Solomon and the book of Revelation. Although at present youth and gentry sucked in corruption from plays written by ignorant poetasters, and King James' *Book of Sports* encouraged drunkenness and lust, the new commonwealth could not simply rely on sermons delivered from pulpits. Milton wanted to see military festivals to strengthen the body, academies on the Italian model to foster the intellect, and finally 'wise and artful recitations ... instructing and bettering the nation at all opportunities'. These should take place at 'set and solemn panegyries, in theatres, porches, or what other place or way may win most upon the

[98] Edition published by Paulus Stephanus in Geneva in 1602: Bodleian Arch.A.d.36. On Milton's reading of Euripides, see Hale (1991).
[99] *Adamus Exul* [1601] translated in Kirkconnell (1952) 96–220. On the context of these plays, see Gellinek (1983); on the visit to Grotius, Milton (1953–82) VIII.122.
[100] *Christus Patiens* [1608] translated in Grotius (1640).
[101] *Sophompaneas* [1635] translated in Grotius (1652).

people to receive at once both recreation and instruction'. He maps out five distinct functions for this drama: to 'inbreed ... the seeds of virtue and public civility', to calm and tune the feelings (through catharsis), to hymn the praises of God, to celebrate Christian deeds done by individuals and nations and finally (through mimesis) to 'paint out and describe' both external shifts of fortune and the internal flux of thought.[102] It was clear to Milton that theatre had a necessary role to play in the new world that lay ahead.

In his commonplace book, which also records his reading of Machiavelli's *Discourses* on the advantages of republican government, Milton takes issue with the early fathers of the church on the grounds that 'although the corruptions in the theatre deservedly should be removed, it is by no means necessary for that reason that all practice of the dramatic arts should be completely done away with'.[103] His ambitions at the start of the 1640s are revealed in the Trinity manuscript, where he sketches outlines for possible tragedies, dealing with subjects both historical and biblical. Heywood's *Apology* praised English theatre for the historical education it provided, asking who now could be of such 'weak capacity that cannot discourse of any notable thing recorded even from William the Conqueror ... ?'[104] Milton countered Elizabethan historiography by mapping out a different history that would culminate in the tragic killing of British Harold by 'William the Norman'. He wanted to portray a freer Saxon Britain rooted in natural law, and subject to the vagaries of its appointed kings, but not to an absolutist Norman yoke backed by a landed aristocracy. A 'Britain of the north parts' was included in this reframing of national history.[105] In his biblical projects, Milton did not fight shy of sexual themes. Salome's seduction of Herod and the attempt to drag Lot into a temple of Venus are amongst the more developed ideas, but the most substantive outline is the one that eventually yielded Milton's great epic poem. Conceiving the story of *Paradise Lost* as a five-act drama, Milton kept paradise beyond the gaze of a fallen audience, and used the resources of the masque to provide a finale, so Adam and Eve could see a vision of allegorical figures embodying all the evils they had unleashed on the world, relieved by help from Faith, Hope and Charity. He first envisaged a spectacular prologue delivered by a transfigured Moses on a mountain, but then replaced Moses with Gabriel, who might need to enter from heaven. Satan had a central role, while the

---

[102] *Reason of church government* [1642] in Milton (1953–82) II.810–20.
[103] Milton (1953–82) I.414–15, 490–1.   [104] Heywood (1612) F3.
[105] Hill (1968); sequence of thirty-eight subjects for history plays in Milton (1953–82) VIII.569–85.

allegorical figure of Conscience, or Justice in a later draft, saved any need to bring God on stage. Although Milton pondered a stage representation of Christ, whose agony in the garden of Gethsemane 'may receive noble expressions',[106] the drift of his thinking was to replace the New Testament focus of medieval theatre with an Old Testament emphasis, precisely as he replaced the prevailing history with an older and more authentic national history. The Old Testament narrative is, fundamentally, about building a nation and a rule-bound way of life, while the New Testament discredits external rules and the idea of nation.

When royalist armies marched on London, Milton in a sonnet imagined himself as Euripides, trapped in Athens before the advance of the Spartans, hoping he would be spared on account of his special status as an artist. He was, however, soon caught up in pamphleteering and serving the Cromwellian government, too busy to write any of these dramas. Moreover, there was no theatre, and too few in the new government who shared his classically rooted perception that theatre was necessary for the building of citizenship. Milton quickly realized, like Plato, that the only way to build a perfect republic was through education. Reformed political structures only breed conflict and selfishness if the mind has not been reshaped. The scheme that Milton maps out in his treatise on education is a rigorous one, with pagan authors to be read in the daytime and scripture at night, intermingled with physical activities like wrestling and military drill. The student moves from wholesome ancient and Italian comedies to political tragedies. Memorizing and vocalizing ancient works is crucial to the educational process, and the means by which the student can acquire the 'spirit and vigour of Demosthenes or Cicero, Euripides or Sophocles'. Performing the words of great citizens of the past is the way to become a true citizen in the present. Having absorbed the dramas of the past, the student is then in a position to read Aristotle's *Poetics*, understand the 'despicable' nature of modern playwrights and as a potential writer envision 'what glorious and magnificent use might be made of Poetry, both in divine and human things'.[107] The authoritarian control of the playwright over the theatrical process echoes that of the patriarchal educator and the puritan preacher, and Marx's famous question 'who will educate the educators?' does not arise because the classics, like the Bible, stand as an unassailable source of cultural authority.[108]

---

[106] Milton (1953–82) VIII.554–60. For a passage of dramatic text incorporated in the poem, see Burbery (2007) 78–9.
[107] *Of Education* in Milton (1953–82) II.397–8.
[108] Framed as a question by Brecht, based on Marx's third thesis on Feuerbach.

Had the Cromwellian regime succeeded in embedding itself, English theatre might perhaps have evolved along such counter-Shakespearean lines, yielding some English equivalent to Racine, famously the product of a Jansenist education.[109] Events turned out differently, Milton survived reprisals at the Restoration, and couched his greatest work in the form of epic not tragedy. Nevertheless, at the end of his life he published an exemplary Euripidean tragedy, *Samson Agonistes*, alongside the poem *Paradise Regained*.[110] The poem provides a context for the play, and we are reminded of the gap between republican and democratic thinking when Christ dismisses popular approval

> And what the people but a herd confused,
> A miscellaneous rabble, who extol
> Things vulgar, and well weighed, scarce worth the praise?[111]

Rome represents the *vita activa* and theatres are part of its splendid civic architecture, but citizens emerge 'from the daily scene effeminate', and the stage is a force for enslaving the inner man. Athens, on the other hand, represents the *vita contemplativa*, and in this world of philosophers tragedians teach moral prudence as they describe high passions. Yet Christ resists this temptation also, declaring that philosophers ultimately arrogate glory to themselves and not to God. The Greeks learned their performance arts from the Psalms of the Hebrews sung in captivity, and the Hebrew prophets are better than classical orators at teaching the 'solid rules of civil government', and 'what makes a nation happy, and keeps it so'.[112]

In his preface to *Samson Agonistes*, Milton makes a strong case for the Christian credentials of tragedy, but states that his play was not intended for the stage. We should regard this disclaimer not as a statement that the play is somehow untheatrical, but rather as a protest against the nature of the royalist Restoration stage.[113] The rhythms are more irregular than those of the epic poems, reflecting attention to the distinctive qualities of dramatic speech.[114] The blind protagonist is plainly a figure for the blind Milton, raging against those who had destroyed the English Commonwealth, the new Jerusalem. The play is conceived as theatre about theatre, for the captive strongman is required to become an entertainer in a semi-circular theatre that may recall Wren's Roman-style Sheldonian theatre recently

---

[109] Cf. the speculations of Gary Taylor: Taylor (1991) 148–9, 379.
[110] There is no serious evidence for the argument in Parker and Campbell (1996) 313–21 that the play was conceived in 1647.
[111] Milton *Paradise Regained* iii.49–51.   [112] Milton *Paradise Regained* iv.142, 263–6, 334–8, 358, 362.
[113] See Jose (1984) 158, Sauer (1998) 202.
[114] For the modern stage history, see Burbery (2007) 154–63.

erected in Oxford.[115] Samson pulls down two columns that presumably frame the doorway of the *scaenae frons*, killing along with himself the entire Philistine ruling class who sit in the covered stage area, but sparing the vulgar who sit banked up in the open air. From the perspective of the early twenty-first century this tale, which is set in Gaza and has for its hero an Israelite suicide killer who claims religious sanction for a massacre, can only be a chilling one.[116] Milton's attempt to marry religion and citizenship seems in this context morally repellent, and a reminder of why since the Enlightenment citizenship has been an insistently secular concept. Arguably, however, the ideal of citizenship has in *Samson Agonistes* been swamped by nationalism. And we should recall Arendt's warning that in practice every revolution has referred to a transcendent source of authority.[117] In France Robespierre had to invoke the Supreme Being, and in Florence it was Savonarola not Machiavelli who possessed the cultural authority to implement a republican revolution.

Milton like Plato believed that minds had to be shaped in order to build a functional body politic, and unlike Plato he believed that tragedians had a part to play in this process. Like Plato he believed in the right of the spiritual Guardian to impose laws and education, seeing no choice but to repress the Dionysiac energies of Comus, the rabble, the vulgar, the many-headed multitude. The puritan recipe for citizenship was an unflinching one: personal discipline, and Milton qua educationalist understood that theatre was a means of imposing discipline upon a population. *Samson Agonistes*, however, was written as a protest play, not a tool of government, and we can only speculate upon what would have transpired if Milton had been able to realize his project of the early 1640s. Would Milton the revolutionary dramatist have helped to reinforce a new ideology, and build new practices of citizenship? Or would the dialectical nature of the theatrical medium, the carnivalesque energies that stem from embodiment, and the implications of staging Eve, Salome and the world of Sodom, have undermined the authoritarian tendencies of Milton the pedagogue and politician? We can but surmise.

[115] Jose (1984) 156–7.   [116] Cf. Mohamed (2005), Brooks (2008) 1–4.
[117] Arendt (1963) 184–5.

CHAPTER 5

Geneva: Rousseau versus Voltaire

GENEVA

Threatened by censorship and arrest in Paris, Voltaire settled in Geneva in 1754, announcing his high hopes in a verse epistle:

> Liberty! Liberty! Your throne is in this place;
> Greece where you were born has lost you for ever,
> Along with its sages and its gods.
> Rome, after Brutus, never saw you more.[1]

A history of Geneva written soon afterwards affirmed in a similar vein: 'If liberty is the natural state of man, then the history of even the smallest republic should be of interest to all'.[2] Unfortunately, in the supposedly free city of Geneva, the Calvinist oligarchy found this concept of natural freedom intolerable, and publication of this history was prohibited. Eighteenth-century theatre in Geneva is of interest because of the clash between a theocratic Miltonian concept of citizenship and a new Enlightenment concept. More particularly, the tiny Swiss republic matters because it became the battleground for two intellectual giants contesting the place of theatre in the life of a free citizen community. While Rousseau styled himself 'citizen of Geneva', Voltaire was an immigrant from France who believed in transcending national boundaries. Voltaire fought all his life for individual freedom of thought and freedom of expression, and used the theatre to explore the limits of what could be said in a public space, but Rousseau rejected the Enlightenment tenet that theatre was a civilizing force. Influenced by his Calvinist upbringing, he stood for a communitarian ideal of citizenship which demanded active participation as part of self-realization, and he rejected passive theatre spectatorship.

---

[1] *Epistle* 95, in Voltaire (1877–85) x.   [2] Rosenblatt (1997) 239.

The fight for theatrical liberty began in earnest in 1756 when Voltaire invited to his home in Geneva Jean d'Alembert, distinguished scientist and founding editor of the *Encyclopédie*. D'Alembert was to write the encyclopaedia article on Geneva. Though Rousseau was a Genevan by birth and had written on music and political economy for the *Encyclopédie*, d'Alembert undertook this project because the article was a manifesto. He explains that, although the *Encyclopédie* would not have allocated so much space to the largest of monarchies, it may be that 'only in the smallest states can one find the model of a perfect political system'. The motto on Geneva's coat of arms, *post tenebras lux*, 'light after darkness', placed it as the model 'Enlightenment' city.[3]

D'Alembert mixes the precise language of science, noting for example how Geneva stands at 46° 12' latitude, 23° 45' longitude, with the language of utopia. He starts his article with the strategic location between Italy, Germany and France that had allowed the small republic to remain independent and prosperous. He describes the arrival of the protestant faith, and Calvin's authorship of the constitution. He says nothing about the waves of protestant migration which brought families like the Rousseaus to the city and helped build its prosperity, but provides definitions of the different categories of citizen: the true born *citoyens*, few in number; the naturalized *bourgeois* with voting rights; the *natif* who is born in the city and has some minimal rights; and the *habitant* who merely resides in the city. He goes on to describe the structure of government, with a General Council of citizens and bourgeois appointing the government, i.e. a Council of 200 controlled by an executive of 25. Concerned to portray an exemplary political system, d'Alembert gives little indication of just how far the rights of the General Council had been eroded in his own century, commenting only that the intervention of French mediators had restored harmony after the troubles of 1736–8. He applauds Geneva for having no hereditary aristocracy, and for sumptuary legislation which restricts display and prevents social divisions being flaunted. Since his purpose is to idealize, there is no mention of just how far a small group of families had gained control of government, and loved to ape the French aristocracy.[4] Nor is there any comment on how the prohibition of theatre was bound up with the sumptuary laws that banned the display of jewellery, carriages and other forms of luxury characteristic of theatre-goers.

[3] Text in Rousseau (2003) 203–13; see 213, 204.
[4] See e.g. Cranston (1983) 21, Launay (1989) 44–6, Kirk (1998).

In respect of religion, d'Alembert contrasts the firm morality of Geneva's Calvinism with a theology so liberal that many pastors no longer actually believe in a Christian God as distinct from an abstract Supreme Being. D'Alembert admires the moral drive of Calvinist sermons, but his aesthetic sensibilities rebel against unaccompanied hymn-singing and whitewashed walls that allow no place for art. He praises the tolerance of this city that allowed Voltaire to attack the founder of the constitution, Calvin, for having sent a heretic to the stake. In respect of theatre, d'Alembert displays his cultural partiality when describing how the French find Geneva a melancholy place to stay in, and he urges that the city should house 'honest pleasures' alongside freedom and philosophy. Through theatre-going citizens would acquire taste, tact and delicacy of feeling – terms which then as now have class associations. D'Alembert centres the controversy not on texts but on actors, whom barbarous prejudice presents as libertines and corrupters of youth, and he hopes that actors, excommunicated in Catholic France, might in free Geneva be treated with the same respect as other citizens. The traditional moral discipline of Geneva should in principle control actors, and thus create a model environment in which theatre could flourish.

D'Alembert paints a picture of the perfect liberal society. Welfare provision is good, tolerance broadly prevails and there is an appropriate balance of power between rich and poor. As a political system, Geneva replicates the mixed constitution of republican Rome, with its citizen militia a distinctively Roman feature. When it comes to theatre, d'Alembert urges that Geneva should unite the *sagesse* (good sense) of Sparta to the *politesse* (manners) of Athens, home of theatre. The broad utopian vision in this article was harnessed to a particular campaign. The French intervention of 1737 had required as part of the political settlement that a theatre should be established, and a tennis court within the city was duly converted, with *Tartuffe*, Molière's celebrated attack on religious hypocrisy, included amongst the repertoire of French classics. The opposition of the pastors and General Council caused the theatre's licence to be revoked once the French army had gone home.[5] Voltaire wanted to be seen as the Sophocles of contemporary theatre, but he had been prohibited from staging plays at his leasehold villa within Geneva. It was above all the wealthy elite who had flocked to see him in 1755, delighted that the greatest dramatist of Europe had come to live in their small town, and eager to use their wealth

[5] Long des Clavières (1920) 81, Chaponnière in Société d'Histoire et d'Archéologie de Genève (1951) 490, Kunz-Aubert (1963) 15–20.

to buy into the European aristocratic lifestyle.[6] Voltaire decorated his villa with erotic art and named it 'The Delights', in a provocation to puritan sensibilities.[7]

Rousseau was tipped off by Diderot, principal editor of the *Encyclopédie*, that d'Alembert's article was in the press, so he was poised to respond the moment outrage erupted in Geneva. A year after the article appeared, Rousseau, naming himself Citizen of Geneva on the title page, published his *Lettre à d'Alembert*, a passionate if rambling treatise now recognized as a classic of dramatic theory.[8] Rousseau's title and sobriquet '*citoyen de Genève*' is actually less demotic than it appears, since only some 1,500 men could lay formal claim to this hereditary title. Rousseau sets out cogent practical and philosophical reasons why good theatre is incompatible with good citizenship in an ideal republic. Before examining this anti-theatrical manifesto, which is pivotal to the argument of this book, I need to trace the intellectual and theatrical background that lay behind it.

ROUSSEAU

Rousseau had a complex cultural identity. His mother, who died in child-birth, came from the upper town where the elite resided, while his father was a working man from the lower town, so he knew Geneva to be a divided place. In the *Confessions*, Rousseau paints a vivid picture of how, while his father was at work making clocks, the young Rousseau read to him from Plutarch's *Lives*.

It was these absorbing readings, and the discussions they provoked between my father and myself, that formed my free and republican spirit, my indomitable and proud character impatient with any yoke of servitude, which has tormented me throughout my life, in conditions that have allowed it least scope to develop. Constantly preoccupied with Rome and Athens, living so to say with their great men, myself born the Citizen of a Republic and the son of a father whose patriotism was his strongest passion, I took fire by his example; I believed myself Greek or Roman; I became the character whose life I read.[9]

A clockmaker's son in Paris would never have enjoyed the same level of classical and political education. Reference to antiquity and particularly

---

[6] Gargett (1994) 116.   [7] On décor, see Maynard (1867) 11.234.
[8] *J.-J. Rousseau Citoyen de Genève à M. d'Alembert de l'Académie Française [etc] sur son article GENEVE dans le VIIe volume de l'Encyclopédie, et particulièrement sur le projet d'établir un théâtre de comédie en cette ville* (Amsterdam, 1758). Edition cited is Rousseau (2003).
[9] Rousseau (1959) 9.

republican Rome was the norm in Genevan political debate,[10] and Rousseau drew from Plutarch the two key terms 'liberty' and 'patriotism'. The patriots of the lower town sought through such language to protect the rights granted them by Calvin's constitution, and resist the Frenchifying ways of the upper town.

Rousseau's father decamped from Geneva after a brawl, masculine pugnacity being another unspoken value inseparably linked to patriotism and liberty. The parentless Rousseau progressed to an apprenticeship which he fled, seeking his fortune in France, where he embraced Parisian values wholeheartedly. The Parisian way of life incorporated formal Catholicism, music, theatre, opera and salons where one debated radical ideas and acquired mistresses. Writing plays and operettas was an expected part of Rousseau's activity as a man of letters. While serving as secretary to the French ambassador in Venice, he experienced the Italian affinity for music and, sensing that the roots of language lay in song, he questioned the logocentricity of French culture.[11] Thanks in some measure to his Calvinist upbringing, Rousseau fell out of love with a luxurious socialite world and sought to reinstate himself as a citizen of Geneva. He was taken back into the Calvinist church, a necessary condition of citizen membership, and experimented briefly with living in Geneva before taking up the life of a permanent exile, moving from one retreat to another. His roots were in Geneva, he knew the allure of Paris and he dreamed of a utopia where he might one day belong and be able to settle.

Rousseau made his name as a Parisian intellectual in 1750 with his 'Discourse' addressing a question posed by the Dijon Academy: whether the arts and sciences have contributed to refining *les moeurs*? The term *moeurs* embracing both morals and manners does not translate well into English. Rousseau prised these two aspects apart, arguing that there is an inverse relationship between true morality and mannered cultural forms like theatre. Rousseau idealizes Sparta, whose only monument was the memory of heroic actions, over against Athens with its monuments of marble and its cultural *politesse*. In republican Rome the appearance of Ennius and Terence, writers of tragedy and comedy, marked the moment of decline, when a militarized culture yielded to decadence. Rousseau endorses the rhetoric of an imagined Roman traditionalist: 'What are these effeminate *moeurs*? What do these statues, paintings and buildings mean?

---

[10] See e.g. the introduction to Touchefeu (1999).
[11] See Rousseau's *Essay on the Origin of Languages*: Rousseau (1995) 410, and his *Letter on French music* [1753]: *ibid.* 291–328.

Madmen, what have you done? You the masters of nations, you have made yourselves slaves of the trivial men you have conquered... Make haste, Romans, and hurl down these amphitheatres, smash these marbles, burn these paintings, drive out these slaves who have overwhelmed you, and whose baleful arts have corrupted you.'[12] Turning from Rome to the present, Rousseau cites the example of Voltaire who has succumbed to the tyranny of women in society and compromised his work. Voltaire's complaint about the pressure to introduce romantic love into his tragedy of *Brutus* provided ammunition for Rousseau's claim that Voltaire had sacrificed powerful male beauties to the false delicacy of the present,[13] and now it is only in corners of the countryside that one can find true 'citizens'.[14] In a supplementary essay he underlines the point that a critique of the arts cannot be separated from a critique of luxury.[15]

In his second 'Discourse' addressing the origins of inequality among men, Rousseau idealizes the figure of the natural savage, living in splendid pre-social solitude before the invention of private property. Once humans began to group their cabins together, Rousseau imagines a primal scene around a huge tree, where song and dance, 'the true children of love and leisure', occupied the company. From the desire to be seen by others springs the desire to compete as best singer, best speaker, most beautiful or most skilled, and thus did inequality emerge.[16] In his unpublished essay on the origin of languages, written as part of the same project, Rousseau paints a more lyrical picture of the primal festival. In a prelinguistic world, the first cake to be eaten is the 'communion of the human race'. At the well dug by shared effort, boys and girls meet beneath ancient oaks, where their feet spring to life in dance, gesture proves inadequate and the voice becomes expressive of feeling, so that flames of love rise from the pure crystalline spring here at the cradle of humankind.[17] The idea that song and dance have primacy over analytic language was fundamental to Rousseau's thinking about theatre and performance.

As a maker of theatre, Rousseau's big success was a short opera which portrays the love of a shepherd and shepherdess and culminates in a dance under the elms. The originality of *The Village Soothsayer* lay not in its narrative, which indicates how lovers should not be tempted to love outside their own class, but in its music. Rousseau drew inspiration from Italian

[12] Rousseau (1992) 39.
[13] Rousseau (1992) 45; cf. preface to *Brutus* [1730] in Voltaire (1877–85) II.322–4.
[14] Rousseau (1992) 50. [15] *Last Reply* [1752]: Rousseau (1992) 108.
[16] *Discourse on the origin and foundations of inequality amongst men* [1754]: Rousseau (1992) 228.
[17] *Origin of languages*: Rousseau (1995) 398, 406.

operettas that had recently been brought to Paris, and created a score that put melody before harmony to create a natural language of the heart. The political radicalism of the piece lay in its implication that true love can exist more authentically among natural shepherds than among refined courtiers. The politics of the opera were complicated by questions of nationalism when Rousseau argued for the superiority of spontaneous Italian music over the classical harmonic tradition of French music. All Paris, Rousseau maintains, became so engrossed in this question of culture that a simmering political revolt was averted.[18] In this opera written by an avowed republican, the contradictions are manifold. We hear of the king singing the songs of the shepherdess in a vile voice, while his mistress played on stage the role of the shepherd. Rousseau was able to observe the inverse relationship between the content of a play and its reception, when the royals transgressed boundaries of gender, class and national loyalty, driven by their passion for the music.[19]

Rousseau describes his emotions at the court performance in Fontainebleau. He presented himself unshaven and boorishly dressed to signal his non-compliance with aristocratic values, in a desire to be authentically himself. Finding himself placed at the front of a box, close to the stage and surrounded by beautifully adorned women, Rousseau explains how the voluptuousness of sex overwhelmed the vanity of the author. He had expected the mood of the audience to mock him, not caress him, so he trembled like a child, ravished by the murmuring of the women in his box. When he and they wept at the weeping of the stage shepherdess, the emotion generated by making lovely women weep compounded his own tears, and he yearned to mop up their tears with kisses. He explains how effect created its own effect so an utter, sweet and touching drunkenness took over the whole assembly,[20] vividly evoking the collective nature of theatrical experience. It is ironic but significant that he found himself before the public gaze playing the role of a rustic, but unlike the stage shepherd he was unable to resist the attractions of women from a higher social class. Rousseau writes as the child of Calvinism in finding not just beautiful women but performance itself to be a dangerous sexual experience.

Rousseau's success with *The Village Soothsayer* helped him secure an anonymous showing at the Comédie Française for his Italian-style comedy about Narcissus. The audience listened and applauded, but Rousseau found

[18] Text of *Le Devin du village* [1752] in Rousseau (1961) 1099–114; *The Confessions* provides an account of the *querelle des bouffons*: Rousseau (1959) 383–5. Cf. Cranston (1983) 275–89.
[19] Rousseau (1959) 380, 386.   [20] Rousseau (1959) 378–9.

himself so alienated from the whole experience that he went to the café after the second performance, proclaimed himself the author and publicly rubbished the play. In so doing he articulated 'what everyone thought', in other words he voiced the real feelings of spectators so self-conscious they could only present socially approved views. His account in the *Confessions* is inflected more by religion than sex: he utters his *peccavi*, and finds in his public confession some compensation for the vanity of which he was guilty in becoming a playwright.[21] The story of Narcissus is about self-love, triggered by a reflected image of self, seen not in water but in a work of art. In the *Confessions* we see how the play conceived as a moral education for the spectator turns itself around to become a lesson for the would-be teacher.

Although Rousseau regarded *Narcissus* as frigid in performance, he still believed it worth the reading, and in the wake of his first *Discourse* he wanted to justify his own status as a writer of plays. The language he adopts when introducing his text is the language of paternity, representing the play as an illegitimate offspring whom he loves despite embarrassment. He portrays his dramatic writing as a kind of homeopathy, using the ill to cure the ill, in the same way that you find the antidote in the venom of the insect that has bitten you. In a corrupt society, theatre is a useful device for control, and when there are no *moeurs*, one necessarily resorts to '*la police*', a word which combines notions of literary polish with policing. A better society is built on secure national customs, as in Rome where the militarized regime of Romulus was harnessed to the ritual regime of Numa to provide the foundation for a lasting republic. The rationalist eighteenth century, Rousseau alleges, heaps nothing but 'scorn on the duties of man and of citizen',[22] and a moralizing theatre rests on nothing but enlightened self-interest.

In 1754, a year after writing this preface, Rousseau made one final attempt at a full-length play.[23] He had by now taken up residence in Geneva, and we learn in the *Confessions* that he thought out the play while walking beside the lake, conceiving a local history at the same time. Like Heywood, he chose to represent Livy's story of the rape of Lucrece, a subject which he thought unplayable on any French stage as it offended the pseudo-morality of French neoclassicism.[24] The hero of the play, Lucius Junius Brutus, was

[21] Rousseau (1959) 387–8. [22] Preface to *Narcissus* [1753]: Rousseau (1961) 959–74.
[23] Rousseau's last dramatic experiment was the monologue *Pygmalion* (1762), where drama becomes a vehicle for exploring private experience.
[24] Rousseau (1959) 394. Text of *La Mort de Lucrèce* in Rousseau (1961) 1023–46. Cf. Rousseau's remarks in the *Last reply* about the false morality of Molière's audience: Rousseau (1992) 101, n.2.

also the hero of Voltaire's tragedy *Brutus*, which Rousseau would have seen in Paris, witnessing the stoicism of the consul who allows his sons to die for their support of a royalist counter-revolution.[25] Having declined a pension from the French king to avoid dependency, and having put his own children out for adoption on account of poverty, Rousseau probably did not find it hard to identify with a Roman who put public service before paternity, and he wrote some passionate lines in 1753 about this Brutus who 'revolts our century', but would himself have deserved to die for treachery had he put family before country.[26] In tackling a tragedy about Brutus, Rousseau competed with Voltaire on his own ground. This Genevan tragedy would be a republican manifesto, and escape the decadence of the French stage. Rousseau's Lucrece would display the virtues of a man (Plate 1).

The play was an attempt to write an engaged and efficacious piece of political theatre. Lucrece's father is a committed republican who has married his daughter to a member of the bourgeoisie, but the spurned Tarquin prince through an ingenious piece of sexual blackmail manages to bed her. Brutus seems a straightforward political firebrand, but the other characters demonstrate Rousseau's concern for the complexity of human emotions. The bourgeois husband is concerned for his career and argues that republicanism cannot work in practice, the Tarquin prince responds to Lucrece's virtue and understands the evil he is doing despite himself, and Lucrece represses her own love for the prince in favour of a dutiful bourgeois marriage. Rousseau projects onto Lucrece his own suppressed infatuation with Parisian life. Brutus' insistence that reversion to the old constitution will bring stability not anarchy to Rome echoes the conviction of most Genevans in the lower town that Calvin's constitution had been eroded.

A politics of form lies behind Rousseau's decision to write this tragedy in prose. While Voltaire likened a prose tragedy to a pencil sketch amid oil paintings,[27] Rousseau's prose, artfully rhetorical though it is, transforms the relation between fiction and reality. The political language of the play replicates the language of debate in Geneva, and the gap is reduced between actor and role. Rousseau frames a critique of French neoclassicism in *Julie*, where his Parisian theatre-goer laments that he always perceives on stage not the Emperor Augustus but the actor called Baron. Everything is as it were expressed on stage in the third person ('one feels...'), not in

[25] J. Scherer in Rousseau (1961) 1870.   [26] *Last reply*: Rousseau (1992) 117–18.
[27] Prefaces to *Oedipus* and *Brutus*: Voltaire (1877–85) II.53–8, 343. On experiments in prose tragedy, see Goulbourne (2000).

Plate 1. The death of Lucrece, while Brutus swears revenge. Engraving of 1742
illustrating Livy i.58.

the first person ('I feel...'), as if the words were written by logicians of
Port-Royal.[28] Rousseau's immersive aesthetic is quite different from that of
David Hume, Rousseau's host in England, who held that when we weep
for the tragic hero we comfort ourselves that the play is but a fiction,[29] and
he is closer to Diderot, who argued for prose tragedy, and yearned to write
a moral tragedy about the death of Socrates. Diderot wanted his Socrates
to be a complex characterization, bringing at every moment a smile to the
lips of the spectator and a tear to the eye, causing spectators who respond
to the magic of this illusion to feel morally troubled, as if in the presence
of an earthquake that makes their homes shake. When Lucrece praises the
virtues of bourgeois family life, the audience do not know of her love for
the aristocrat, and the confidante has her own back-story of love for the
villain. Prose opens up possibilities of subtext, requiring the actress to find
some way of signifying repressed and conflicting emotions.

We are not told why Rousseau abandoned this fascinating project,
whether it was the generic contradiction between a bourgeois *drame* and a
neoclassical tragedy that left him with no acceptable dramatic language for
private emotion, or whether he recognized that no theatre in the environs
of Geneva would ever stage this piece. Perhaps time simply moved on and
he saw no future for himself in a Geneva that was so unlike his dream born
of childhood memory. Or perhaps, pursuing the logic of his own philosophy, he concluded that writing theatre for citizens was a contradiction
in terms. At all events, his departure from Geneva coincided with abandonment of the project. The emotional predicament of Lucrece, bourgeois
in her moral commitment but not in her heart, was transposed to the
heroine of his great novel, written in the quasi-dramatic form of letters. In
the preface to his novel Rousseau explains that the language of dramas and
romances is not the restrained language in which people really express emotion, and intimate scenes in the novel would not be performable on stage.
Writing for people of the world is a hopeless enterprise, for inhabitants of
busy cities are not receptive to thought, and therefore reforming private
moeurs is the prelude to reforming public *moeurs*.[30] Rousseau's retreat from
Geneva was a retreat from the *vita activa* into the *vita contemplativa*, and
when he published his novel, Rousseau declined to sign himself 'Citizen of
Geneva'.[31] Writing a Roman play for the public stage would have constituted an act of citizenship on Rousseau's part, but writing a novel was the
act of a private individual. The novel sets up Geneva as the good city to

---

[28] Rousseau (1961) 253–4.   [29] Hume, 'On tragedy' [1757] in Clark (1965) 195.
[30] *Julie, or the new Héloise* [1761]: Rousseau (1961) 18, 25, 24.   [31] Rousseau (1961) 27.

counterbalance Paris the negative city, but it warns of danger, for Genevan women are seeking to become like French women, and Genevan men are growing ashamed of their own nationality, as the imported taste for luxury threatens the ancient simplicity of an open-hearted people.[32]

In his novel, which he was working on when he wrote the *Letter to d'Alembert*, Rousseau reflects back on his own experience as a Parisian theatre-goer. Julie's tutor and lover Saint-Preux visits Paris, fortified like Rousseau by a reading of Plutarch, and his odyssey is a journey to corruption, leaving Julie behind on the shores of Lake Geneva to become her teacher's teacher. Saint-Preux experiences Paris as a society of masks, where he is forced to keep his heart under lock and key.[33] Of the three Parisian theatres, he finds most to value in the Comédie Française, where classic texts are performed, however superficially. Though modern plays merely reflect the desire of a social elite to see their own kind on stage, the French golden age was far from perfect, for Molière wanted to hold up a corrective mirror to the audience, reflecting the vices of the aristocracy with his stock figure of the comic Marquis, but succeeded only in encouraging the bourgeoisie to ape the manners of the aristocracy.[34] Rousseau portrays an inverse relation between the affluence of the stage and the poverty of the population at large, and in respect of gender the theatre is a place of double standards, for lone women host salons but going alone to the theatre is held to be a social taboo.[35] Rousseau's most biting critique is directed at the Opéra, the ultimate place of show, which for Saint-Preux purveys expensive boredom. Singers with bursting blood-vessels and heaving diaphragms force out high-pitched notes, losing all contact with reality, and the emotional engagement of the audience, as at a fairground stunt, lies in hoping the routine will be accomplished safely.[36] Saint-Preux contrasts the French audience in the pit, which clumsily lumbers about when it hears a dance tune, struggling to follow the first violin, with the Italian audience which listens in absolute stillness.[37] Engaged spectatorship is not the same as physically active spectatorship.

Parisian life is like drunkenness, reason and nature alike are silenced, and Saint-Preux's empty heart is inflated with hot air like a balloon, distorting the divine image of Julie which he guards within him.[38] Saint-Preux's immersion in Parisian life leads him ultimately to the brothel, and a painful repentance. The *vita contemplativa* is not a tenable course in the real world,

---

[32] Rousseau (1961) 658–62.   [33] Rousseau (1961) 236, 255.
[34] Rousseau (1961) 252–3. The Marquis was launched in *Les Précieuses ridicules* [1659].
[35] Rousseau (1961) 270.   [36] Rousseau (1961) 285.
[37] Rousseau (1961) 286.   [38] Rousseau (1961) 255–6.

for to spectate is to become complicit. Saint-Preux comes to the heart of the philosopher's problem when he concludes:

The man of the world sees all and has time to think of nothing . . . Nor can you see and think alternately, because the performance demands continuity of attention, which precludes reflection. A man who wanted to divide his time sequentially between the world and solitude would inhabit nowhere, discomposed in retreat and for ever a stranger back in the world. There is no alternative but to divide your way of life in two, one part for seeing, one for reflection. Yet even this is nigh impossible, for reason is not a piece of furniture you can pick up and put down at will, and whoever has lived ten years without thinking will never think in his life. I see also that it is madness to try and study the world as a mere spectator . . . In the school of the world as in the school of love, you must start by practicing what you seek to learn.[39]

This philosophy undermines the principle which we can trace from Horace to the Brechtian *Verfremdungseffekt*, that in theatre the two opposites of pleasure and instruction must somehow be yoked together. Good theatre for Rousseau was such an involving experience that he could not think of stepping back and breaking the spell with rational thought. To watch is perforce to participate with all one's emotions, and Saint-Preux learns the cost of participating in a society of masks.

THE *LETTER TO D'ALEMBERT*

In 1757 a French company established itself in the Savoyard village of Carouge, close to the gates of Geneva, and the city was as it were under siege.[40] In May 1758 a play at Carouge represented Geneva as Athens, and Rousseau was Diogenes the Cynic philosopher, allied to the priesthood in his opposition to the establishment of a theatre inside the city, whilst the Council of Areopagites wanted a theatre.[41] In October Rousseau joined the battle, publishing his *Letter to d'Alembert*. Formally the *Letter* addressed itself to all Genevans as a united body, but its main target was the disenfranchised *demos* of the lower town, not the Areopagites on the hill of the upper town, prompting Voltaire to remark sarcastically that Rousseau had written for his ironmonger and his cobbler.[42] Rousseau's rhetorical strategy in the *Letter* was to insist on Genevan tradition in order to appeal both to

---

[39] Rousseau (1961) 246.   [40] Gargett (1994) 140.

[41] Mercet de Mézières *Diogène à Carouge*. See Gargett (1994) 150. Named after their seat on the Crag of Ares, the Areopagites were stripped of power by the democracy, an event that was a context for Aeschylus' *Eumenides*.

[42] *Letter to d'Alembert* [1761]: Voltaire (1963–93) no. 6420.

common citizens and to the more traditionalist and religious amongst the oligarchy. The great originality of Rousseau's tract lies in its separation of the content of a dramatic text from its performance in a specific socio-political context. Plays are not good or bad in themselves but only in their effect, and different audiences respond to different things. Whilst Voltaire saw Sophocles as an eternal ideal, Rousseau recognized that 'on our stage the best play by Sophocles would fall flat. We have no means to put ourselves in the place of people quite unlike us.'[43] Dismissing the platitude that good theatre offers moral instruction, Rousseau argues that theatre is a vehicle for emotions not ideas, and political action stems not from transient emotion but from *moeurs*, acquired habits. Rousseau summarized his case in a note appended to the *Essay on the Origin of Languages*.

I have said elsewhere why feigned miseries affect us more than do genuine ones. There are people who sob at tragedies but never in their lives took pity on a single unhappy person. The invention of the theatre is marvellously suited to make our self-love feel proud of all the virtues we do not have.[44]

The argument about the feigned and the real is grounded in Plato, and Rousseau later published a synopsis of *Republic* Book 10. Aristotle's counter to Plato, that theatre involves a cathartic purging of emotion, did not tally with Rousseau's own observation of spectatorship.[45] What he observed in the auditorium was the reinforcement of feelings that already existed, and much self-satisfaction.

I shall focus on three of Rousseau's case studies of famous texts. Firstly, Rousseau makes no secret of the fact that he has 'never willingly fore-gone a performance of Molière', and he devotes much space to Molière's masterpiece, *Le Misanthrope*,[46] suggesting that Molière invested much of his own moral passion in the figure of Alceste, the 'misanthropist' who opposes the falsity of court values. If Alceste had not been set up for ridicule, he would have seemed to the audience a madman on account of his high moral principles, and Molière's play therefore settles for compromise organized around the hollow figure of the confidant or *raisonneur*, Philinte. Identifying himself as much as Molière with the views of Alceste, Rousseau imagines Philinte fully realized as a dramatic character in the form of an eighteenth-century *philosophe*, apparently a rationalist but in

[43] Rousseau (2003) 67.
[44] *Essay on the origin of languages*, Chapter 1. Translation cited from Rousseau (1997a) 250.
[45] *On theatrical imitation* in Rousseau (1995); Rousseau (2003) 68.
[46] Rousseau (2003) 188n., 83–95.

fact wholly self-interested. Though this would be a more instructive play, it would in the end fail because people do not laugh at things that discredit themselves.[47] Molière is doomed by his attempt to satisfy the public.

Voltaire's *Zaïre* (1732) centres on a Moslem slave betrothed to the Sultan of Jerusalem, who discovers that she is a Christian by birth and undergoes a crisis of identity when reunited with her French father. The Sultan, whose nobility of character recalls Othello, suspects infidelity and has her assassinated before killing himself. In theory, Rousseau argues, this play should be a moral warning about the dangers of excessive passion, but in practice it stimulates passion. Women flock to the play and draw men after them, finding passion that culminates in death more delicious than a controlled passion. Because hero and heroine are idealized, the spectators slip into thinking that any decent man should be in love, and that to be loved is proof of a woman's virtue,[48] so the effect is to soften the heart, not stiffen moral behaviour. We have an account of Rousseau later watching an English adaptation of this play at Drury Lane with Garrick in the role of father, where an eyewitness records how 'the recluse philosopher was so very anxious to display himself, and hung so far forward over the front of the box, that she [Mrs Garrick] was obliged to hold him by the skirt of his coat, that he might not fall over into the pit'.[49] While this English observer took the recluse philosopher for an impostor, putting on a social performance for the benefit of the king opposite and crowds below, we should rather see an example here of Rousseau's almost uncontrollable emotional engagement with theatre, as he wept at the performance despite being unable to understand English. The expectation of social performance was precisely what he could not endure in the theatre. When Rousseau attacked the feminized values of aristocratic culture, he was doubtless fighting his own passionate impulses and inability to live with the sexual mores of Geneva. He must also have known that many in the Genevan ruling council had wept at this play in Geneva in 1755, when Voltaire played alongside the great actor Lekain, and his middle-aged niece read the part of the youthful heroine. 'Never were Calvinists so tender!' Voltaire proclaimed triumphantly.[50] Tears flowed again when the play was performed in Lausanne in 1757, and people flocked there from thirty leagues around.[51]

---

[47] See Maslan (2005) 93ff. for a revolutionary attempt to rewrite the play.
[48] Rousseau (2003) 105–6.
[49] Cradock (1828) 1.205–6. Commentary in Edmonds and Eidinow (2006) 121–6.
[50] Voltaire (1963–93) nos. 4046, 4048.
[51] Letter of 3 March 1757: Voltaire (1963–93) no. 4712. See Pomeau and Mervaud (1991) 242–3.

While *Zaïre* offered a positive image of the Islamic world, *Fanaticism, or Mahomet the Prophet* (1741) cast the founder of Islam as an out-and-out villain, a citizen of Mecca who unseats the worthy sheik and forcibly installs himself as a prince. Mahomet brainwashes the sheik's son to carry out a kind of fatwah, whereby the son unwittingly kills his father. When first put on in Paris, the play was suppressed after three performances because it was taken as an attack on Christianity, whereupon Voltaire published the play prefaced by a bogus letter from the Pope, purporting to give the play his blessing as an attack on the infidel, and it was successfully revived in 1751.[52] In Geneva in the 1740s we hear of an illicit early performance staged by a dancing master who performed peasant dances in the interludes.[53] When Voltaire brought the play to his villa in 1760, he recast the heroine loved by Mahomet. Instead of an actress who played in the statuesque classical style, he now preferred one in the romantic style possessed of a siren voice, a sensitive heart and eyes that dissolve in tears.[54]

Rousseau's argument is that spectators will always admire the genius of the villain, suspending their normal moral judgements, and given the Oedipal nature of the plot, his argument could be supported by a psychoanalytic perspective. Although Rousseau admires the elegant dialectical balance between Mahomet and the sheik, he argues that fanaticism is an irrational condition so no man can be reasoned out of it, and forcible suppression is the only solution. In light of flawed twenty-first-century efforts to extirpate Islamic extremism by force, Rousseau's judgement is a worrying one, yet his argument about the inversionary nature of moral responses in the theatre is based on sure observation. In his concern for Geneva, Rousseau fails to notice the cultural issue that makes the play unperformable today. A public reading in the French town of Saint-Genis-Pouilly, in the wake of Danish cartoons caricaturing the prophet, caused a minor local riot in March 2006.[55] The original Paris performance was delayed because of the visit of a Turkish ambassador, causing Voltaire to remark sarcastically: 'It would not be decent to denigrate the Prophet when the Ambassador is being fed, and to mock his sect on our stage. We French respect the rights of persons, especially Turks.'[56] It was left to a broad-minded Genevan pastor to remonstrate, after the 1760 revival, that 'putting revered persons on stage, and seeking to vilify them . . . is to lack . . . the relations of civility that all nations and creeds owe each other'.[57]

---

[52] See Cronk in Voltaire (2002) 20–2.   [53] Gabarel (1856) 33.   [54] Voltaire (1963–93) no. 6260.
[55] *Wall Street Journal* cited in www.jihadwatch.org/dhimmiwatch/archives/010527.php
[56] Voltaire (1963–9 II.549, 19 January 1742.   [57] Jacob Vernet, in Gargett (1994) 316.

Voltaire falsified Islamic history in the interests of creating a polemical para-
ble, and the shift from French-style to oriental-style costuming in the 1750s
may have emphasized the cultural implications.[58] While Voltaire took an
archetypal liberal position, protesting his right as an individual to absolute
freedom of speech, Rousseau's position implies that personal identity is a
function of community membership.

Having worked through his case studies, Rousseau turns to the binary
distinction critical to his own identity: on the one hand the corrupt
metropolis of Paris, on the other the small city of Geneva with its close
links to the countryside. Theatre is acceptable in the city that is already
corrupted, he argues, but would be a source of corruption in Geneva.
Moeurs rather than formal laws bind a society together, and theatre would
undermine irrevocably the ancient Genevan way of life. Moreover, a small-
town theatre would only be of provincial artistic quality. He then develops
an economic line of argument, well aware that the French company resident in 1737–8 had been unable to pay its debts,[59] and claims that Geneva
could not support a theatre financially. Theatre, moreover, would be a
form of indirect taxation upon the poor, tempting them to spend beyond
their means.[60] While France is organized hierarchically as a monarchy, the
Genevan republic depends on a relatively egalitarian distribution of wealth
to survive as a political system. Rousseau saw, correctly, that Genevan
social cohesion was at breaking point, and a commercial theatre would
both emphasize and increase disparity of wealth.[61] The eighteenth century
knew no alternative to a theatre whose vertical stratification of space, with
pit, boxes and balconies, replicated social stratification.[62]

'It is irrelevant to a monarch whether he governs men or women, so
long as he be obeyed; but a Republic needs men.'[63] Gender is a recurrent
preoccupation for Rousseau, inextricable from the question of political
structures, and antifeminist prejudice is all too obvious in this championship of masculine values.[64] It is above all actresses, for example, who are
said to utter fine moral sentiments on stage and forget them once safely in
the wings. When Rousseau claims that women in the salons of Paris trap
men in the slavery of a metaphorical harem, the essence of his concern is to
re-establish a public sphere, and he condemns theatre for reducing life to
the intimate sphere of erotic relations: 'Love of humanity, love of country,

---

[58] Voltaire (2002) 15, 330; on costume, see Pomeau and Mervaud (1991) 303–4.
[59] Kunz-Aubert (1963) 20.
[60] Rousseau (2003) 169–70. Cf. arguments in Britain when a national lottery was first established.
[61] Rousseau (2003) 170f.   [62] Cf. Wiles (2003) 180, 197, etc.   [63] Rousseau (2003) 155.
[64] E.g. Rousseau (2003) 158 n. 2.

these are feelings whose portrayal most touches those already imbued with them; when these two passions have been extinguished, there remains only love in the literal sense to fill the gap.'[65] Yet Rousseau does argue for a version of equality, based on separation of the sexes. Following Plato, he judges Sparta, where robust women were free to practise athletics like men, a better society than Athens, and there is nothing overtly antifeminist in his description of how theatre boxes placed women and girls on display like goods in a shop window awaiting purchasers.[66]

The would-be author of a tragedy about Brutus did not lightly relinquish the ideal of an educational and political theatre. Rousseau considers the possibility of dramas centred on Genevan history and myth, an ideal he would later promote in respect of Poland, but fears that local stories will appear trivial when exposed to international comparisons. Yet Geneva had of course Voltaire as writer in residence, and Rousseau suggests that if Voltaire could but develop the republican, non-erotic drama he aimed at in his Roman tragedies about Brutus, articulating the simple virtues of citizen behaviour, then there might be a way forward. There is a caveat, however, for Voltaire needs not only to supply his genius but must in his own life live up to his plays.[67] Famous for embodying his own philosophy, Rousseau highlights the gap between Voltaire's aristocratic expatriate lifestyle and the high moral sentiment of his plays. Many would have sensed the force of this argument when Voltaire built a theatre in his villa outside Geneva, and drew audiences and amateur performers to fashionable occasions that did not just involve theatre: the tragedy was followed by a comic operetta, a dance, a dinner, more dancing and departure by carriage at dawn.[68] Rousseau had good grounds to argue that a play was not an aesthetic object, it was part of a way of life.

In formulating a viable alternative to theatre, Rousseau reverts to child-hood memory, when the spirit of community was like a 'drunkenness sweeter than wine'. He describes a drunken Dionysiac dance performed by the neighbourhood militia of St Gervais after their annual dinner, with some five hundred men in uniform joining hands and snaking to and fro around the fountain on which stood the musicians. The order and musicality are spontaneous but flawless, and the variety limitless. At the end of the dance, wives and children descend from their houses round the square and reabsorb their menfolk back into domestic life. Rousseau recalls his father quivering with emotion as he kissed his son. '"Jean-Jacques," he said,

---

[65] Rousseau (2003) 173. [66] Rousseau (2003) 158, 166. [67] Rousseau (2003) 178.
[68] Gargett (1994) 221–2, citing letters by Du Pan; cf. Carlson (1998) 124, citing Gibbon.

"love your country! You see these good Genevans. They are all friends, all
brothers. Joy and concord reign in their midst. You are Genevan. One
day you will see other peoples. But should you travel as much as your
father, you will never see their like." The two immediate conclusions that
Rousseau pulls from this lyrical narrative are closely linked. Firstly: 'This
performance, by which I was so moved, would have had no appeal for
a thousand others; you must have eyes made to see and a heart made to
feel.' And secondly: 'There is no pure joy but public joy, and Nature's true
emotions govern only the people.'[69] Public emotion has an authenticity
lacking in private emotion, and only lifelong membership of a particular
community can give access to that emotion.

   Writing for Calvinist Geneva, Rousseau draws on an anti-theatrical tradition that goes back to the early fathers of the church,[70] and his originality
lies in translating an argument about the Christian life into an argument
about citizenship. In idealizing festival, he breaks ranks with Calvinism
and draws on the inspiration of pagan antiquity. In Plutarch's *Life of
Lycurgus*, he had seen how Sparta was founded on music, laughter and a
rich pattern of collective rituals; from Plato's *Laws*, he took the principle
that gods gave men festivals as a release from labour, that choral dancing
is a natural communal activity and that alcohol may be a force for good;
and from Plato's *Republic*, besides a broad argument about representation,
he took the metaphor of the imprisoning cave, dubbing the theatre a dark
cavern, whereas festival takes place in the open air where nothing can
be concealed.[71] His classical sources directed him to a close link between
music, military service and republican citizenship.

   The major institutional alternative to theatre which Rousseau offers, in
defiance of Calvinist sensibilities, is the *cercle* or club, where men unen-
cumbered by women gather to drink, talk politics, exchange crude jokes,
set off for hunting trips and swimming expeditions, and perhaps gam-
ble too. Here, he argues, one can 'dare to be oneself' as men bond into
'friends, citizens, soldiers and thus all that is best suited to a free people',
while women meet in parallel groups in private houses, their gossip having
a positive social function as a means of collective moral surveillance and
control.[72] These traditional social bodies would be undermined if theatre
rose up in competition. Rousseau notes how the *cercle* replaced the culture
of the public tavern at the time of the troubles of 1736–8, when space

---

[69] Rousseau (2003) 192–3n.   [70] See Léoni (1998).   [71] Rousseau (2003) 182.
[72] Rousseau (2003) 160–1. On *cercles*, see Picot (1811) iii.294; Trachtenberg (1993) 179–93; and Gargett
(1994) 156–60.

was needed for serious debate.[73] Rousseau believed that the lure of theatre would bring an end to this the citizen's most important forum for debate. The citizen militia, whose dance Rousseau idealized, was likewise not a politically neutral institution, but as in Machiavelli's Florence and Stuart London it gave the citizens physical power to rebel. When the revolution of 1782 was suppressed, both the *cercles* and the militia were dissolved by the Genevan oligarchs and their French enforcers.[74]

Rousseau offers the courtship dance as another ceremony supportive of the good society. He imagines a public ball where unmarried youth perform as dancers under the eyes of parents, grandparents, other interested citizens and a presiding officer of the state. The principle again is that a citizen's life should be lived in the public eye, and family life is celebrated because it produces citizens for the republic. Unlike an aristocratic ball, this dance will secure social homogeneity because couples will meet and marry across class boundaries. Courtship in the public eye will increase the individual's sense of freedom both by the elimination of sexual guilt and by making it easier for young people to select their own life partners. A competition to become Queen of the Ball will be equivalent to sportive contests among men. As a spectacle, this dance would scarcely be of interest to foreigners, but Genevan émigrés will find memories of such unique events engraved on their hearts, drawing them home.[75]

The key to this courtship dance, like the dance of the militia, is the expressivity of the musical body, not mimetic representation.

What then are the objects of these performances? What will be shown? Nothing, if you want. Under liberty, wherever congregation prevails, there also well-being prevails. In the centre of a square set up a pole crowned with flowers, gather the people, and you will have a festival. Do better still: turn the spectators into the spectacle. Let them be the actors. Do it so each one sees himself and loves himself in others, so all become better united.[76]

While theatre generates passive spectatorship, festival generates participation, and in place of representation we have the experience of collectivity, generated by the mutual interplay of gazes. Whether one can ever truly escape representation is an unresolved question, and Derrida discerns here a prime example of the 'metaphysics of presence', a logically inadmissible escape from signification.[77] Signification is of course present here, for the maypole was traditionally understood, on the basis of classical antiquity,

[73] Rousseau (2003) 153.
[74] Jean-Pierre Ferrier in Société d'Histoire et d'Archéologie de Genève (1951) 476.
[75] Rousseau (2003) 184–90.   [76] Rousseau (2003) 182.   [77] Derrida (1997) 307–9.

as a phallic emblem, and Rousseau's minimal festive apparatus is a sure reminder of patriarchy. The pagan associations of the pole likewise offered a direct challenge to puritanism.[78] Rousseau's political agenda is never far beneath the surface of his seductive prose.

The *Letter* was well received by its target readership in Geneva but caused dismay amongst the intellectuals of Paris, who saw it as an attack on the principles of the Enlightenment. D'Alembert himself reacted calmly, helping secure publication in Paris, while restating in print the principles to which he held.[79] Theatre, he responded, did not deny emotion by functioning as an instrument of moral instruction, for this was an age of progress, and audiences were more sophisticated than they used to be. D'Alembert challenged the case studies. Molière's *Misanthrope* elicits a double response, for the spectator can laugh at Alceste whilst simultaneously approving, loving and pitying him. In *Zaïre*, tears of pity warn us about the perils of jealousy, teaching us to repress negative emotion. And in regard to *Mahomet*, D'Alembert can only wish that the play had appeared two hundred years earlier to forestall the famous St Bartholomew's Eve massacre of Huguenots, and his one regret is that the play appears to deal not with Christianity but with zealots adhering to the 'false religion' and does not more directly target the worse bigotry of Christians. D'Alembert remains blind to Rousseau's argument about the cultural and collective nature of an audience's response. His tragic spectator is an introspective figure whose feelings become more profound when he looks into the depths of his own soul, in a process that entails 'a painful reversion to the sorrow of the human condition, which almost always makes us cede our passions to our duties'. The model is Cartesian, assuming some centre of selfhood from which one's soul can be contemplated. D'Alembert rounds off with Rousseau's Achilles' heel, the question of gender. French female spectators are *citoyennes*, responsive to more than just love stories, and he accuses Rousseau of an animus against women stemming from his own disappointment in love.[80]

Voltaire came nearest to a formal response in a letter to his Italian translator, published with his tragedy *Tancred*. While Rousseau paraded his private subjecthood in works like the *Confessions*, Voltaire always preferred ironic masks, and in this letter his mask is the dutiful Catholic departing for

---

[78] On maypoles, see Hutton (1996) 233–7.
[79] *Lettre à M. Rousseau Citoyen de Genève* [1759]: Rousseau (2003) 215–29. On the reception of the *Letter*, see Cranston (1991) 135–40.
[80] Rousseau (2003) 223, 228. Rousseau's public break with Diderot, signalled in the preface to the *Letter*, was triggered by a disagreement about Rousseau's conduct of his love affair.

Midnight Mass. When he claims that his Terentian comedy *The Prodigal Child* cured at least six prodigal sons, it is hard to take the audience research seriously, but it is not just irony when Voltaire argues that theatre is the 'best education for all orders of citizens; it is almost the only means to gather men together to make them sociable'. Social bonding requires a softening of *moeurs*, a feminine ideal, not the hardening of *moeurs* with which Rousseau wants to create defenders of the republic. Voltaire was a reformist, not a revolutionary, anticlerical but not an opponent of Christian ethics. 'To be a good Christian, you must above all be a good subject, a good citizen. And to be such, you must not follow Jansen, or Molina, or any other faction; you must respect, love, serve your prince... Let us not be for Apollo, nor for Paul, but for God alone, and for the king whom God gave us.'[81] Voltaire like many Enlightenment thinkers clung to the idea that benevolent despotism was in practice the only way a society like France could be managed, and the only framework for citizenship. Respect for authority was linked to a respect for the classics, and he had no truck with Rousseau's preference for popular fairground theatre.[82] Voltaire gave ground to Rousseau, however, in one important respect. He agreed that theatre could not be a commercial product if it was to be taken seriously, and in the best traditions of French centralism he urged that it should be the duty of magistrates to stage public games, as in republican Rome.

THE BATTLE FOR A PUBLIC THEATRE

Voltaire fought his real battle not in print but on the ground, seeking ways to infiltrate Genevan social life with his plays. In Les Délices, his Genevan villa of 'delights', he tried staging an open rehearsal in 1760, but this loophole was promptly closed. Like a miniature monarch, in 1761 he built a properly equipped 300-seat private theatre in the grounds of his model estate at Ferney, just across the French border, and invited the Genevan elite as his guests, whereupon the pastors tried in vain to ban them from participating as amateur performers.[83] And for the rest of the population Voltaire helped set up a theatre at Châtelaine, down river on French soil, with a resident French company. The public flocked to the opening, despite agitation in the *cercles*.[84] An eyewitness, who yielded to temptation lured by the fame of the great Parisian actor Lekain, conveys the flavour of the first season:

---

[81] Letter to Capacelli, 23 November 1760: Voltaire (1963–93) no. 6393.   [82] Cf. Rousseau (2003) 180.
[83] Pomeau (1994a) 64–5.   [84] Chaponnière (1936) 156, Gabarel (1856) 37.

I benefitted from the company of M. Mussard, a former Syndic, who, like me, had put aside his patriotic opposition to comedy in favour of the actor concerned. I saw sublime things which surpassed the impression of this perfect actor already imparted by his fame. How the passions painted themselves upon his face! What magnificent declamation! What nuances of gesture! What brilliance in mime! Yet his technique is not so remarkable as those abrupt starts, that manic energy, that involuntary abandonment of self which denies the spectator time for examination, and criticism scope for cold analysis.[85]

Observation of skill yields to the total absorption envisaged by Rousseau, and not the moral double-take envisaged by d'Alembert. The presence of Voltaire himself seated by the wings, conducting rather in the manner of Tadeusz Kantor, exclaiming in delight, weeping at the sad bits and leaping up to embrace Lekain in complete defiance of theatrical illusion, served to heighten the emotional temperature rather than create a *Verfremdungseffekt*. The presence of two international celebrities gave a double charge to the event. Whatever his rhetoric about the moral force of theatre, and famous for the irony of his prose, Voltaire became a different creature in the theatre, and effectively gave his audience a lesson in how to surrender self to emotion. The Genevans in the pit, however, were not completely bereft of their political faculties, and hissed a comedy by Voltaire that they interpreted as an assault on republican values.[86]

Rousseau was dismayed by Voltaire's continuing appeal, and lamented in 1760 that d'Alembert had been right after all: the corruption of Geneva had advanced so far that theatre was now justified as a 'palliative'.[87] There was comfort to be had, however, in 1761. In the course of a day dedicated to military displays and regimental dinners, a group of 200 citizens, in order to pay tribute, decided to re-enact the dance around the St Gervais fountain which Rousseau had depicted in his *Letter*. Rousseau's informant described the emotions of the day as a whole: 'The contagion of public friendship had conquered all the individuals of society; it entered us with the air we breathed; this emotional softening [*doux attendrissement*] was universal. Thousands of souls made up but one.'[88] When we juxtapose these two accounts of theatre and of festival in 1761, we notice how in both cases the contagious effect of the crowd helps the individual lose a sense of self. Rousseau's correspondent pictures participants 'without distinction of rank or estate, melted together, citizens who know no livery but that

[85] Letter by Pierre Mouchon in Gabarel (1856) 38. On these performances, cf. Maynard (1867) II.284–5.
[86] Gabarel (1856) 39–40; Chaponnière (1936) 156.
[87] Letter to Moultou of 29 January 1760: Rousseau (1965–98) no. 933.
[88] Letter by Mollet of 10 May 1761: Rousseau (1965–98) no. 1429.

of the fatherland'. The visitor to Voltaire's performance was swept up by the 'general madness' and would have stood in the pit had it not already been packed. He views the play as a member of his class, conscious of who he sits next to, but not as a citizen. The setting of the theatre, outside the city walls like the Elizabethan Globe and Red Bull, helped the spectator divorce his citizen self from his morally more relaxed private self.

The Genevan oligarchy tolerated Rousseau as a patriot and famous scion of the city until 1762 when he published *Emile* and *The Social Contract*. The first was too radical in religious terms, the second called for popular participation in government, and both books were burned by the public executioner. Rousseau resigned his citizenship in protest,[89] and citizens had either to be for Rousseau or against him. Having reassured his Calvinist supporters by affirming publicly the Christian nature of his beliefs, Rousseau became a spokesman and consultant for citizens who wanted to regain their formal right to make 'representations' to the oligarchy. It became increasingly evident that *The Social Contract* was inspired by the Genevan constitution, and the breaking of that contract by the elite of the upper town. Voltaire opposed the burning of Rousseau's books on principle, but had no scruples in publishing under a false name an attack on Rousseau as a failed playwright, a man who had abandoned his children and who wanted the Genevans to cut their own throats.[90] Amid threats of a general strike, and a withdrawal by the General Council from constitutional participation, the oligarchy called in the French army to 'mediate' and prevent civil war. Voltaire seized his opportunity, and persuaded the French mediator to insist, as part of the settlement, that a theatre should be set up on Genevan soil. The ruling Council agreed despite strong opposition from the pastors. Hastily constructed in wood, a theatre on the standard European model with three tiers of boxes was erected just outside the gates in the summer of 1766. The Châtelaine operation closed down and a director from Lyon moved in to stage a Parisian repertoire dominated by light opera.[91]

Voltaire's feelings about Geneva at this time are articulated in a tragedy called *The Scythians*.[92] Voltaire presents himself as an old man who has retreated from Babylon to write, and to cultivate his garden. The pastoral 'Scythians' amongst whom he lives are the Genevans, proud of their liberty, equality and fraternity. They address each other as 'citizen' and like the

[89] See e.g. Rosenblatt (1997) 269–77.
[90] *Sentiment des citoyens* [1764] in Voltaire (1877–85) xxv.309ff.
[91] Long des Clavières (1920) 83–8, Kunz-Aubert (1963) 29–30, Société d'Histoire et d'Archéologie de Genève (1951) 491.
[92] Voltaire (1877–85) VI.261ff.

Genevans decline to dress in gold and silks, which would be an insult to the poor. The heroine has come with her father from Babylon to settle in a rustic cabin, and, in a plot that echoes Rousseau's *Julie*, she accepts a local marriage to please her father. Her Babylonian lover, in the shape of a Parisian marquis, arrives with his army and kills the Scythian bridegroom, but is then apprehended. At this point the pastoral idyll ends, and Voltaire turns the mood about: the Babylonian/Parisian lover will have to be sacrificed on the wedding altar, and the heroine is required to strike the fatal blow. Voltaire's hatred of Calvinism was almost obsessive,[93] and *The Scythians* showed how the egalitarian values of Genevan citizenship were entangled with an inhumane and repressive religion. Voltaire's tragedy was designed for his private stage at Ferney, complete with rustic ritual dancing to stimulate the ball that followed, but it would not have gone down well in the new public theatre.[94]

While Rousseau kept his distance, Voltaire threw himself into the political fray. In a pamphlet of 1765 entitled *Republican Ideas*, he argued for republicanism as the best form of government in a small society, closer than France to the condition of natural equality. He sought a libertarian republic of property owners that would abolish restrictions on dress, on publication and implicitly on theatre. In the years after 1765, he took particular interest in a fissure that had recently become an open wound in Genevan society. The citizens and bourgeoisie of the General Council made up a minority of the adult male population (36 per cent according to the census of 1781) and were outnumbered by the 'natives' (46 per cent) whose forebears had come to Geneva in successive waves of immigration.[95] Having secured the right to become masters in clockmaking and other trades during the troubles of 1736–8, the natives aligned themselves with the citizens and bourgeois who shared a common lifestyle conditioned by puritanism and manufacturing. The demand by the General Council for its power to be restored drew attention to the natives who were excluded from this Council, as from many other civic rights such as fishing. Voltaire adopted their cause with enthusiasm, and eventually created a model industrial estate at Ferney for some 100 families who could not find in Geneva the freedom to which they aspired.[96] Here lay the ultimate flaw in Rousseau's passionate writings about Geneva and the importance of community feeling: who was and was not a true Genevan? Rousseau's title 'Citizen of Geneva' placed him within

---

[93] Maynard (1867) 11.283; Voltaire (1963–93) 27 September 1760.
[94] Letter of 16 March 1767: Voltaire (1963–93) no. 10026; Long des Clavières (1920) 111–12.
[95] Guichonnet (1974) 240.   [96] Gay (1959) 227–33.

an elite. Then as now, migration was not an exception but a constant, and Rousseau's own paternal forebears had fled France after the Reformation.[97] Rousseau's research into the history of Geneva taught him that there was no distinction between citizen, bourgeois and native back in the fifteenth century,[98] though there were of course other hierarchies in the feudal era. Voltaire's support of the Genevan natives followed logically from his concern for individual human rights. For Voltaire, the rights of the citizen and the rights of man should be equated, as the French revolutionaries would later insist. Political freedom, economic freedom and artistic freedom were of a piece for Voltaire, but his reference point was the individual not the community.

Whatever the ambiguities about authentic Genevan identity, the company who brought theatre to Geneva were unambiguously French, and their victory was a pyrrhic one. Audiences were reluctant to visit what they dubbed the 'Grange des Étrangers', the foreigners' barn. The two major hits were locally sourced: Voltaire's new tragedy *Olympie*, and Grétry's operetta *Isabella and Gertrude*, adapted from a story by Voltaire.[99] When the company finished their season in the spring of 1767, it seemed politic to suspend operations. French troops were policing the border to impose a trade embargo, and the families of the wealthy were evacuating the city in fear of their lives. Then, in February 1768, the theatre burned down. The fire brigade arrived promptly at the scene, but declined to douse the flames despite risk of the fire spreading to other buildings. The French were convinced this was arson, while a counter-narrative blamed prostitutes who hung lights on the arcades to advertise themselves at night. Whatever the circumstances, the theatre had gone, and there had not been sufficient income to repay the builders.[100] Voltaire worked the story into a satirical poem. He portrays a grim Rousseau who laments that all is lost on account of the new theatre: 'Geneva has pleasure... The *moeurs* of Genevans are softening... they are improving, they are starting to love each other'. Thérèse Levasseur, Rousseau's uneducated partner, is transformed into a vile fury from Hell who gathers old Calvinist pamphlets from the privy and piles them outside the walls to make a bonfire, sending spectators running for their lives. The poem goes on to declare that theatre

[97] Cranston (1983) 15–16.   [98] 'Government of Geneva' [*c.* 1763]: Rousseau (1995) 511.
[99] Long des Clavières (1920) 84–7, 98; Kunz-Aubert (1963) 29.
[100] Société d'Histoire et d'Archéologie de Genève (1951) 447ff.; Desnoiresterres (1875) 105; Long des Clavières (1920) 100–1; Kunz-Aubert (1963) 33; letter by Le Sage in Pomeau (1994b) 314. The theatre was also known as the Grange de Broutenville (graze-in-town) after the unpopular French plenipotentiary Beauteville.

is better than any sermon at educating and bonding people, so after the fire desolate Genevans abandon their work and turn to violence.[101] The reality was somewhat different. The theatre had exacerbated tensions, and a month after the fire a concordat was reached, with the prohibition of theatre in the city one of the concessions won by the General Council.

Though Carouge had also burned down, the theatre at Châtelaine was back in business by 1770 to lure Genevans in their carriages. The year 1782 saw a major revolution, and the citizens of the lower town took control during three months of popular rule. Again the French army was summoned, and cannon were laid out in the grounds of Les Délices to quell the revolution. French officers insisted that their social life was intolerable without theatre, which again became the cultural arm of an invasion force. A theatre was rebuilt over the ashes of the 'foreigners' barn', but this time in stone, investors deeming wood too insecure.[102] Since Genevan politics were often interpreted in the light of republican Rome, we should note the symbolism. Long resisted by republicans, the building of a stone theatre by Pompey effectively marked the end of the republican era, and stone theatres became monuments to the enduring greatness of imperial builders.[103] So too in Geneva, a monumental theatre marked the end of city-state republicanism. The gates of the city were opened, Geneva was annexed to France and when the French Revolution unleashed a new era of international class politics, the question of national boundaries, culture and identity ceased to matter so desperately. By 1789, when Genevan republicans gathered in the theatre to watch a play freshly imported from Paris about the fall of the Bastille, theatre had lost its former connotations.[104] A French institution, which had long proclaimed its cosmopolitanism, was now accepted as universal.

CONCLUSION: TWO IDEALS

Both Voltaire and Rousseau fled France and admired the Genevan constitution, both translated their philosophy into political action, both responded to the intense emotional experience of theatre, and they were both committed to an ideal of good citizenship, yet they were polar opposites. The argument between them sits at the epicentre of what is still today a fundamental debate about the nature of citizenship. They lived at the intersection of three broad systems of thought: those of classical antiquity, of

---

[101] 'The civil war of Geneva' [1768] ed. John Renwick in Voltaire (1990) 1–152.
[102] Kunz-Aubert (1963) 39, Société d'Histoire et d'Archéologie de Genève (1951) 475–6, 491.
[103] Frézouls (1983).   [104] Kunz-Aubert (1963) 47.

Christianity and of a scientific Enlightenment that sought to bracket liberty with equality and nationhood with membership of the human race. Both Rousseau and Voltaire were riddled with internal contradiction, and their creative genius lay in the way they faced those contradictions.

'Adieu, *citoyen*! And yet, a hermit is a very singular citizen.'[105] When Diderot and Rousseau parted company, the cosmopolitan Diderot put his finger on a paradox to which he could not reconcile himself: Rousseau wrote of collectivity, yet loved rural solitude, because the socialized utopia of his dreams could never be found. *The Social Contract* postulates a 'general will' whereby

Each of us places his person and all his power in common under the supreme direction of the general will; and in return as a body we admit every member as an indivisible part of the whole. Immediately, in lieu of the particular person of each contractant, this act of association produces a moral and collective body, which comprises as many members as the assembly has voices, and which receives from this same act its unity, its common self, its life, and its will.[106]

The collective will which characterizes the plenary assembly replicates the collective response of a theatre audience, yet, as we learn in the *Confessions*, when the young Rousseau went to the opera in Venice and experienced quasi-religious bliss, he did so by virtue of hiding in a box on his own and escaping the social milieu of dining and conversation.[107] Rousseau's sense of an ideal collective was born from his horror of society as it was. In preparation for life in society, Emile must be educated completely alone because one must first realize one's natural self in order to obey the General Will. In the unpublished sequel to *Emile*, living in Paris and betrayed by his beloved, Emile finds himself in the pit of a theatre on a first night. The space becomes his purgatory, with bright lights, noise, conversation and no catharsis of the emotions, and in repressed anguish, like some Christian martyr, he clutches his chest until his fingers drip with blood.[108] Here is perhaps Rousseau's most extreme picture of the Parisian theatre environment, a place where one's private self cannot connect to one's public self. Theatre offered Rousseau no equivalent to the experience of communality recalled in his childhood memories of Geneva. As Starobinski has pointed out, the 'public joy' found in Rousseau's festival at the fountain is 'the lyrical aspect of the general will'.[109] Theatre, by contrast, is always mediated, setting up a gap between the subject and the object of experience,

---

[105] Diderot *Oeuvres complètes* XIX.439 cited in Wilson (1972) 257.
[106] *Social contract* i.6: Rousseau (1964) 361.   [107] *Confessions* vii (1743–4): Rousseau (1959) 314.
[108] *The solitaries*: Rousseau (1965–98) IV.893–4.   [109] Starobinski (1988) 96.

and making any surrender to the General Will impossible. *Emile* contains
a foundational text for modern Theatre in Education when young Emile
visits a fairground magician who moves toy ducks across a painted pond,
apparently by telepathy. The boy learns two lessons, a scientific lesson
about magnetism, and a moral lesson about the evil of wanting to perform
and show off before an audience.[110] If theatre is to be an educational
tool for the future citizen, then it must resist the emotions traditionally
caught up with theatricality. The fairground entertainer himself is an honest
craftsman, at a far remove from the urban actors whom Emile will later
encounter.

When François-Marie Arouet rechristened himself Monsieur de Voltaire,
he denied his roots and adopted a mask. The genre of tragedy allowed his
characters to articulate incompatible positions, for Voltaire was an apostle
of tolerance, but intolerant of religious faith. He was a republican in
Geneva, but a supporter of 'enlightened' monarchy in places like Sweden
and Russia. He believed in the progress of society, but was a conservative
in respect of dramatic form. He was a dry ironist in his prose tales, but
wept his way through roles he played on stage. He was regarded as the
Sophocles of his day, becoming the canonical modern playwright in the
later eighteenth century and first years of the nineteenth, yet today he has
vanished from the repertoire, and this last contradiction is perhaps the
most interesting.

René Pomeau voiced the conventional twentieth-century wisdom about
Voltaire: 'He thought he could write tragedy by superimposing the alexandrines of Corneille and Racine. When linguistic evolution caused the tragic
style of the *grand siècle* to fall into disuse, the language of Voltaire ceased to
ring true, and today, thanks to his stylistic pastiche, his plays have become
wholly unperformable.'[111] I do not find this view persuasive. The tension between powerful emotion and a restrictive dramatic form is basic to
Voltaire, as it is to Corneille and Racine, and relates to the recurrent theme
of neoclassical drama: public versus private obligation. Our difficulty with
Voltaire today is rooted less in his style than his subject matter. The ethical
imperative of these plays can be summed up in the word 'citizenship', an
ideal that has nothing to do with religion as in Greek tragedy, or honour
as in the baroque era, or ethnic nationalism as in the romantic era or
King Henry V, or self-realization as in naturalism. When Jürgen Habermas described the decline of a bourgeois public sphere in the nineteenth
century, he explained the disappearance of the value system which made

---

[110] Rousseau (1969) 437–41.   [111] Pomeau (1955) 60.

sense of Voltaire's plays, along with the cultural environment that sustained their performance.[112] Voltaire's characters are creatures of their passions and functions of familial relationships, but never display the unique selfhood trapped in existential loneliness that was so vividly articulated by Rousseau and by all the romantics and modernists who followed him. Voltaire disappeared from the modern repertoire because a bourgeois mode of public living proved irreconcilable with modern individualism. Voltaire is at once too close to us and too distant.

The argument between Rousseau and Voltaire about the theatre of Geneva has many resonances, and I shall sum up the key points of divergence.

theatre versus festival: For Voltaire the classical modes of comedy and tragedy are a timeless ideal, and the monumental public theatre of Athens remains a model. The major justification of theatre is ethical. It provides spectators with moral lessons, but more importantly, in a concept which Voltaire probably derived from Polybius, it socializes people by softening their *moeurs*.[113] Rousseau's ideal, on the other hand, is the participatory festival where participants surrender their individuality to a greater whole, thereby realizing their true identities, as they will likewise in the general political assembly. In his later advice to Polish nationalists, Rousseau relaxed the distinction between theatre and festival, opening the door to ideological manipulation. Condemning court theatre which isolates people and distracts them from patriotism, he advocated mass open-air spectacles modelled on antiquity, bracketing recitations of Homer and performances of the tragedians with athletic contests as festive events which once kindled emulation, manly courage and civic virtue.[114] Faced with the huge nation of Poland, Rousseau knew that an enlightened lawgiver would have to create spectacles for the people in order to build citizenship from scratch, and could not simply rely on traditional rituals like the dance at the St Gervais fountain.

language: For Rousseau language was not in its origin functional but expressive, communicating not some material need but core emotions like love and hate, fear and anger. Poetry was prior to philosophy, and speech was originally harnessed to song.[115] Drama thus began in the form of spontaneous praise-songs to gods and heroes, and the language of Greek

---

[112] Habermas (1989).
[113] Polybius iv.21 describes how music softens the *ēthē* (*moeurs*) of mountain-dwelling Arcadians; cf. Plutarch *Moralia* 156d on how Dionysus as wine softens the *ēthē* of strangers.
[114] *Observations on the government of Poland*: Rousseau (1969) 958.
[115] *Origin of languages*: Rousseau (1995) 380–1.

theatre retained a musicality lost in modern European languages.[116] In his early *Letter on Opera*, Rousseau urged that performers should not be experienced as vocalizing lines of text,[117] for he sought an unimpeded directness of human communication in which music had a privileged place. Voltaire, having no such dream of unmediated human communication, was happy to think of dramatic language as a covering, with ideas wrought into the form of couplets. 'There is no complete language, none that can express all our ideas and all our sensations . . . Men have never been able to express what they feel. . . The most complete languages are those of people who have most cultivated the arts and society.'[118] Whilst different languages have different strengths, Italian for example suiting opera, a genius for dialogue makes French the supreme language for tragedy and comedy.[119] Beneath Voltaire's rationalism lay a politics relevant to the situation of Geneva. The French language has become the common currency of Europe, he observes, not through military conquest but through the theatrical success of plays like *Cinna*, *Phèdre* and *Le Misanthrope*. English and Italian authors manage blank verse, but the supreme burden of the alexandrine has been borne by authors whose works will endure as long as the French nation.[120] This formalist account of language is related to an aesthetic of performance. When Lekain came to perform at Châtelaine, Voltaire warned him not to surrender to wigmakers' apprentices in the pit by sacrificing elocution and style.[121]

ethics: Rousseau distinguishes an instinctual 'love of self' (*amour de soi*), which is part of the search for true being that allows union with others, from a calculating 'self-love' (*amour-propre*) which echoes the deadly Christian sins of vanity and covetise.[122] Theatre is 'wonderful for making our self-love proud of virtues it does not have'.[123] Though Voltaire lacks the same spiritual orientation, and never identifies a satisfactory rational basis for personal ethics, a sense of natural law surfaces from his evasions and ironies, exemplified by the biological obligations of mothers, of sons or of adults to feed children.[124] There is a natural right to freedom of expression,[125] and a natural right to property. Rousseau's contention that the enclosure of property was the first act of theft caused outrage in a man who became a

---

[116] *Origin of melody*: Rousseau (1995) 334–5.   [117] *Letter on opera* [*c*. 1745]: Rousseau (1995) 250.
[118] 'Languages' [1756], in Voltaire (1877–85) xix.564–5.
[119] 'Languages' [1771], in Voltaire (1877–85) xix.558–60.
[120] 'Languages' [1756], in Voltaire (1877–85) xix.567; preface to *Mérope* in *ibid*. iv.185.
[121] Letter of 16 December 1760: Voltaire (1963–93) no. 6378.   [122] See Cranston (1983) 298–301.
[123] *Origin of languages*: Rousseau (1995) 378n.
[124] Note to *The A B C*: Voltaire (1994) 88; 'Man' *ibid*. 69.
[125] E.g. in *Republican ideas*: Voltaire (1994) 201.

rich landowner through his own efforts.[126] Given the premise that people can only exist in society, and that the good life is inseparable from advanced forms of society, Voltaire's tragedies work out the tension between natural justice and social obligation. For Rousseau the theatre in Geneva was a manifestation of luxury and self-love, but for Voltaire the burning of the theatre was an assault both on private property and the progress of civilization. Though both men were drawn to ideals of natural religion, the ethics of Rousseau are rooted in a Calvinism that found justification in personal faith, while Voltaire's ethics are rooted in a Jesuit preference for external works.

self. Rousseau explains in his autobiographical *Dialogues* that he loves solitude because authentic communication is impossible in cities, but he nevertheless relies on company: 'Our existence is sweetest when relative and collective, and our true self is not wholly within us. Such then is the constitution of man in this life that one can never manage quite to enjoy oneself except with concourse of the other.'[127] Rousseau's theory of the General Will assumes that selfhood is not contained by the boundaries of the human individual, and he found in festival an authenticity of experience that confirmed his sense of transpersonal selfhood. While he agrees with Plato's proposition that the soul/self is the body politic in microcosm,[128] he cannot accept Plato's privileging of reason over passion. Rousseau as the child of Calvinism holds to the notion of an immortal human soul, but Voltaire rejects conceptions of soul and self as unknowable, finding his conceptual anchor in the ideal of reason triumphant over emotion. Scorning Rousseau's noble savage, Voltaire writes of the degradation of man in a state of nature, and in his essay on Man he places at opposite poles the civilized performance of an opera and the warfare of savages in canoes.[129] Voltaire's resistance to personal introspection attracted him to the medium of theatre where all is appearance. In an interesting discussion of emotional memory, Voltaire describes how skilled actors can fix on a painful memory and then by a willed act of imagination bring tears to their eyes, a skill which helps many an actress deceive her husband in private life.[130] While Rousseau values tears as a sign of sincerity, a direct conduit to self, Voltaire relishes theatrical tears as the ultimate artifice. Both Rousseau

---

[126] 'Man': Voltaire (1994) 70.
[127] Rousseau (1959) 813. Cf. Knee (2005).   [128] Rousseau (1995) 1211.
[129] *Questions on the Encyclopaedia* [1771] in Voltaire (1994) 63–75; cf. 'On the soul' in *The A B C* [1768]: *ibid.* 101–5.
[130] 'Tears' (*Larmes*) in *Philosophical Dictionary* [1771]: Voltaire (1877–85) x.571–2.

and Voltaire operated in a pre-Kantian universe that did not recognize the absolute moral autonomy of the individual.

cultural identity. When Julie's cousin visits Geneva, she declares: 'The more I consider this tiny State, the more I realise how fine it is to have a fatherland [*patrie*], and God help all who think they have one, and yet only have a country [*pays*].'[131] Rousseau's possession of a *patrie* was crucial to his sense of self. In his advice to the Polish confederates, he lamented globalization:

There are no more Frenchmen, Germans, Spaniards, even Englishmen, nowadays, regardless of what people may say; there are only Europeans. All have the same tastes, the same passions, the same morals, because none has been given a national form by a distinctive institution. All will do the same things under the same circumstances; all will declare themselves disinterested and be cheats; all will speak of the public good and think only of themselves.[132]

To lose national identity is to surrender to self-love. Rousseau's moral case for nationalism rests on the proposition that we escape from self-centredness only through the institutions of citizenship, whereby we discover our true selves to be part of a greater whole. While Rousseau encouraged Polish nationalists to resist Russia, Voltaire lent his moral support to Russia in the person of Catherine the Great, whose enlightened patronage of the arts involved setting up a court theatre and writing her own plays.[133] In an essay on '*patrie*', Voltaire explores the selfishness of patriotism and its meaninglessness for the majority of human beings who relate only to their immediate milieu. It is a conundrum of the human condition that 'to wish your own country to be great is to wish your neighbours ill. The man who wanted his homeland never to be larger, or smaller, or richer or poorer would be a citizen of the world.'[134] In abandoning France for Geneva, Voltaire aspired to such world citizenship, and he saw his plays operating in an international arena. Dedicating *Zaïre* to an Englishman, he declared that 'those who love the arts are all *concitoyens*' ('fellow citizens'); and adapting *Mérope* from an Italian original, he declared: 'my love of *patrie* has never closed my eyes to the merits of foreigners; on the contrary, the better a citizen I am, the more I seek to enrich my country with treasures not born from its bosom'.[135]

[131] Rousseau (1961) 657.
[132] *Government of Poland*: Rousseau (1964) 960; translation cited from Rousseau (1997b) 184.
[133] On the relationship, see Gay (1959) 171–84.
[134] *Pocket philosophical dictionary* (1764–9): Voltaire (1994) 29.
[135] Preface [1733] to *Zaïre*: Voltaire (1877–85) II.537; preface [1742] to *Mérope*: ibid. IV.185.

religion: Often regarded as his masterpiece, Voltaire's *Zaïre* is a remark-able exploration of cultural identity. Brought up a Moslem, Zaïre discovers her natal identity when reunited with her brother and dying father. Having learned that the blood of Christian martyrs and of twenty kings runs in her veins, she makes the fatal admission: 'I am a Christian', and thereupon finds herself lost, having no notion of a personal self to fall back upon: 'Am I actually French, or Moslem? Daughter of Lusignan or wife of Orosmane? Am I lover, or Christian?...The universe has abandoned me.'[136] It is interesting to notice how Voltaire's horror at the Crusades was erased in the London adaptation.[137] Voltaire understood how completely religious and national identities were intertwined, and his aspiration to world citi-zenship was bound up with a militant secularism. Rousseau, on the other hand, acknowledged the life of the spirit. When he became a Frenchman, he converted to Catholicism, and when he returned to Geneva he could not legally take up his citizenship without being reaccepted into the Calvin-ist church, but he never found it easy to reconcile the twin aspects of a citizen's identity. When we look at Rousseau's advice to the Poles on build-ing citizenship through the lens of twentieth-century history, we notice how evasive he was in avoiding mention of Catholicism as a marker of non-Russian identity.

citizenship: For both Rousseau and Voltaire, citizenship is bound up with freedom, but for Voltaire this is pre-eminently a negative concept, freedom from interference so one may say what one thinks and live as one chooses, while for Rousseau freedom is a positive, and involves being an active part of the sovereign body that exercises power. Voltaire worked with a loose ethical notion of the *citoyen* derived from current French debate, while Rousseau's tighter constitutional concept was rooted in his experience of republican life. Within Geneva, the nature of 'freedom' was contested, the oligarchy trumpeting the negative freedoms for which the city was famous, while the citizens of the lower town demanded the positive freedom to partake of political power.[138] Two dramatic texts will help illustrate these competing understandings of citizenship.

In Rousseau's *Death of Lucrece*, Brutus uses standard republican rhetoric to sway Lucrece's self-centred husband.

We abhor our chains as deeply as can be; time now to break them. All of Rome exhorts you through my mouth: either we shall all perish, or we shall destroy the monster devouring us . . . Choose . . . with us to avenge your *patrie*, your wife, yourself, to be virtuous, and free, and be – to say all in a word – a worthy

---

[136] *Zaïre* II.iii, III.v.   [137] Hill (1736).   [138] See Launay (1989) 87–8.

husband of Lucrece, worthy son of a virtuous father, friend to Brutus, and citizen of Rome.[139]

Citizenship is bound up with patriotism, freedom from aristocratic rule, and a close network of social and familial relationships. Rousseau saw Geneva through the lens of republican Rome, devoting the final book of *The Social Contract* to Rome, and this historical model blinded him to the fine distinctions between 'citizen', 'bourgeois' and 'native' in Geneva. Though he had himself migrated to France, he could not recognize the inevitability of change and immigration which complicated his model of a stable organic society, nor would he recognize that the close involvement of the Genevan oligarchy in the French banking system had already made Geneva part of a larger structure of political power.[140]

In a celebrated scene in Voltaire's *Orphan of China*, a wife is asked by her husband, a loyal public servant, to give up their child and substitute it for the baby who is heir to the empire, and is now being hunted down by Genghis Khan:

> – You weep, poor man!
> – Oh! weep with me;
> And yet with me take heed to save your king.
> – And sacrifice my son!
> – Such is our woe:
> A citizen you are before a mother.
> – What! Nature has so little hold upon you!
> – All too much hold, but not as much as duty.[141]

Though Voltaire felt Lekain was too weak for the barbaric role of Genghis Khan, he relished the pathos with which Mlle Clairon handed over her child to its fate; indeed Clairon's rendition of the part is said to have restored him from illness.[142] For Voltaire the term 'citizen' implies serving as the loyal subject of a benevolent monarchy, and there is nothing paradoxical about the feminine form of the word *citoyenne*, though of course Voltaire

[139] Rousseau (1961) 1039.   [140] Guichonnet (1974) 233.
[141] *L'Orphélin de la Chine* [1755] II.iii.
> – *Vous pleurez, malheureux!*
> – *Ah! pleurez avec moi;*
> *Mais avec moi songez à sauver votre roi.*
> – *Que j'immole mon fils!*
> – *Telle est notre misère:*
> *Vous êtes citoyenne avant d'être mère.*
> – *Quoi! Sur toi nature a si peu de pouvoir!*
> – *Elle n'en a que trop, mais moins que mon devoir.*
[142] Pomeau (1991) 250; Carlson (1998) 132.

took it for granted that the bonds of nature touch women more closely. Voltaire's elite Genevan audience wept copiously at *Zaïre* in 1755, for they could identify with the plight of someone trapped by her inherited class and religion, but there were fewer tears for *Orphan of China*, although the play was a great success in Paris.[143] The correlation of citizenship with duty to a king was not compatible with republican instincts.

Voltaire claimed that his inspiration for this play lay in a fourteenth-century Chinese original, written under the Tartar dynasty descended from Genghis, and that it belonged to a dramatic tradition older than Athens. The flourishing of drama under Tartar rule demonstrated the triumph of genius and reason over barbarism.[144] Refused Chinese citizenship before the play begins, Genghis becomes in Voltaire's play a paradigm of enlightened despotism, and he saves the citizen child just as the Tartar dynasty preserved theatre. The Chinese source helps Voltaire situate his work as part of a continuous and global civilizing process.

gender. Voltaire celebrated the achievement of France in creating a language of conversation, proclaiming France the first nation 'where women have been free, and even sovereign, when elsewhere they have been slaves', adding that the art of the best French writers resembles that of French women, the most beautiful in the world not by nature but by virtue of their adornment.[145] Both Voltaire and Rousseau agree in identifying theatre as a feminized environment. From the perspective of a small city-state clinging to military independence, Rousseau like Machiavelli argued for a culture of masculinity, while Voltaire, from the perspective of a country where monarchs had long used the delights of court to subdue the warlike proclivities of provincial nobles, saw fewer charms in a male ethos. The softening process engendered by feminine emotion was for him a force for good, and like the Greeks of antiquity he placed the spectacle of female suffering at the centre of almost all his dramatic writing. While Rousseau's reference point is the clockmaker's workshop where sons are welcomed but daughters have no place, Voltaire's reference point is the aristocratic salon, and it is impossible to separate the politics of gender from the politics of class. Perhaps the greatest paradox is the fact that the feminine institution of theatre arrived in Geneva courtesy of French military muscle. French soldiers were heartened by the spectacle of female tears.

---

[143] Letter of 2 May 1755: Voltaire (1963–93) no. 4046; Carlson (1998) 98.
[144] Prefatory letter to the Duc de Richelieu.
[145] 'Languages' [1756]: Voltaire (1877–85) XIX.566–7; cf. preface [1736] to *Zaïre: ibid.* II.551.

In this chapter I have pitted the would-be citizen of Geneva against the would-be citizen of the world. Rousseau is backward-looking, seeking to recover a lost human innocence within a community rooted in its own history, while Voltaire is forward-looking, believing in the spread of a civilization which ripples out from Paris and other urban centres. Where Voltaire gives pride of place to the rational individual, Rousseau regards the community as prior to the individual. Both give some ground to the other. Voltaire concedes that commercial theatre panders to the love interest, while Rousseau concedes that in a less-than-ideal society theatre may have homeopathic benefits. Rousseau's ideal is the festival, where participants surrender their egos and their reason to the rhythm of the dance in order to experience themselves as part of a greater whole. Voltaire's ideal is the formal crafted play where the spectator's intense emotional response is triggered by the cognitive grasp of a complex moral dilemma.

Rousseau's organic bounded community is essentially mythic. Geneva had always been porous, and its component groups divided by birth and occupation had always had competing interests. Calvin's moral precepts never sat comfortably with an economy that purveyed luxury goods and financial services for the European aristocracy. Rousseau dreamed of a world that never was. On the other hand, Voltaire's claim that tragedy transcends national boundaries seems equally deluded. The theatre that he practised was part of a hegemonic French culture, and could never escape its Frenchness. Voltaire was a progressive landlord who improved the lot of his tenants, but the idea that culture trickles down from the elite to the masses becomes much less credible when we look at Catherine the Great's theatrical activities in St Petersburg. Calvinist Geneva in the mid eighteenth century was a much more equal and literate society than France or Russia. Personal liberty is not easily yoked to social equality and fraternity.

In 1842 the anonymous author of a pamphlet entitled 'On the theatre of Geneva' identified theatre as both the sole pleasure of the people, and an efficient way of circulating money. Fighting the residual puritanism of the municipal government, the pamphlet campaigns for public money to have the theatre equipped with stage machinery, heated, and redecorated in bright colours, with good-quality actors licensed to perform. 'The people values its pleasures quite as much as its rights. It knows its pleasures when it is deprived or restrained; it has a weak knowledge of the rights that could be won through the agitation of revolutionaries.'[146] Like bread and circuses in imperial Rome, theatre can be used judiciously by the ruling classes to

---

[146] Anon. (1842).

avert the threat of democracy and revolution. The Genevan *cercles* once constituted a public sphere within which a discourse of rights could be articulated, but have now been supplanted by theatre as the site of popular recreation. The legacy of both Rousseau and Voltaire was forgotten when Genevan theatre became a tool to build not citizenship but contentment of the masses.

CHAPTER 6

Paris and the French Revolution

During the French Revolution 'citizenship' as a moral ideal was pursued with a fervour and logical rigour that has never been equalled. *The Declaration of the Rights of Man and of the Citizen*, drawn up by the National Assembly in August 1789 and circulated on painted tablets that echoed the Ten Commandments, served as a reference point both for revolutionary debates and for all twentieth-century declarations of 'human rights'. The coalescence of the two terms 'Man' and 'Citizen' guided all aspects of revolutionary life, and shaped discussion about theatre. The Enlightenment had bequeathed a conviction that human beings are the product of their education, and that citizens are made not born. Though Rousseau in some respects paved the way for ethnic nationalism, he was also the author of *Emile*, a study in the art of moulding human nature, and of *The Social Contract*, which argued that the foundations of society are neither ethnic nor providential but contractual. For revolutionaries of all strands in the years after 1789, it was axiomatic that theatre should be a contribution to public education, and help to construct the figure of man-as-citizen. From Molière to Voltaire, the classic French theatre tradition had always insisted upon its social utility, and that article of faith was now put to the test.

The coalescence of 'Man' and 'Citizen' was never going to be comfortable. In the same month the *Declaration* was published, a month after the fall of the Bastille, the Parisian public saw exhibited in the Salon Jacques-Louis David's painting entitled: *J. Brutus, First Consul, returned to his house after having condemned his two sons who had allied themselves with the Tarquins and conspired against Roman liberty: the lictors return their bodies so that they may be given burial* (Plate 2). The painting captures the pain of Brutus, the paradigmatic citizen, celebrated by Rousseau for his decision to put public

Plate 2. *Brutus* by David.

duty and loyalty to Rome before his bond to family.[1] Brutus, in shadow on the left beside a statue of the goddess 'Rome', reveals his pent emotion, while light falls on the overt and expressive grief of his wife and daughters. The painting shows how the public world of the citizen has intruded on the home of the Man and brought him torment, posing the stark question: has Brutus denied the Man by acting as good Citizen?

David's painting owes much to the theatre. As Corneille's *Horace* lay behind David's *Oath of the Horatii*, so Voltaire's *Brutus* of 1730 lay behind this painting of 1789. The play was regarded as one of Voltaire's minor works, but David may have seen the production at the Comédie Française given in 1786, abruptly cancelled after a single performance, and more importantly in 1789 he was in close dialogue with Alfieri, who was working on an Italian adaptation.[2] The curtain pinned to the columns, which creates tension between a manly public space of Doric columns and a domestic female space, was a theatrical feature.[3] The painting has no vanishing

---

[1] See p. 118 above.
[2] Starobinski (1979) 72–3, Crow (1985) 250, Roberts (1989) 30, Alston (1993) 179. On the *Oath of the Horatii*, see further Dowd (1960) 4.
[3] Herbert (1973) 78.

point, and only the abandoned workbasket beneath the outstretched hand serves to unite the binary oppositions of male and female, public and private, rationality and sensibility, citizen and humankind. In Voltaire's play, one of the sons repents and gives his blessing to Brutus' unfatherly deed, thereby lending moral authority to Brutus' act of civic responsibility, but in David's painting the shallow picture plane offers no receding vista of infinity as the location of transcendent value, and so denies the viewer moral reassurance. The gods of pagan Rome have no power to validate the acts of rational human beings, who are forced into moral choice. The title of the painting points to David's ultimate and problematic human desideratum, 'liberty'.

Exploring the roots of the word 'revolution' in cyclicity, Hannah Arendt comments on how the French and American revolutions, like the English revolutions of 1642 and 1688, were seen as reversions to an earlier order, and thus acts of restoration.[4] The utopian world of the Roman Republic, and to a lesser extent Athens and Sparta, provided the French revolutionaries with moral legitimacy and a blueprint for what is humanly possible. David's rendering of the republican world, compiled with meticulous care for costume, hairstyle, furniture and architecture, and borrowing the features of Brutus from a bust that David had acquired in Rome, created the feel of a historic reality that could be reproduced not just on canvas but on the political stage of Paris.[5] We have seen in Italy and England how the Roman Republic was a symbolic site where the meaning of citizenship could be negotiated and contested. While Heywood at the Red Bull chose to recount the story of Junius Brutus, Shakespeare at the same period told the story of Coriolanus, a proud aristocrat spurned by the plebeians of a misguided republic. Louis XVI had commissioned David to paint Coriolanus as an appropriate public image for the Salon, but David reneged and chose to portray Junius Brutus, running the gauntlet of censorship before his image could be shown.[6]

The republican implications of David's subject matter are reinforced by his aesthetic. There is no hint in this painting of luxuriant aristocratic rococo, and austerity of line echoes the austerity of Brutus' ethics. Originally the hand of Brutus' wife reached out towards the heads of her two sons impaled on poles, but after the violent assault on the Bastille David decided to eliminate any possible celebration of violence in order to

[4] Arendt (1963) 34–41; cf. Corfield (2007) 97–8.
[5] See Lee (1999) 124–6. He did not reproduce republican funeral practice: Crow (1985) 255.
[6] Dowd (1948) 19, Herbert (1973) 54.

concentrate upon the consequences of moral choice.[7] He had learned from
his studies in Rome how to portray drapery in order to reveal without
gratuitous sensuality the expressive form of the human body. Plain classical
costume required that people be seen as functions of their humanity and
not of class. Immobile like ancient statues, David's figures reveal through
the configuration of the body universal emotions of loss. Classicism in his
hands became a democratizing idiom, exposing the common attributes of
humanity.

Painting was a performative art. This was not a private work for a patron,
but designed for the biannual Salon, where David was permitted to exhibit
because he had penetrated the privileged ranks of royal academicians. The
painting was a public statement, most readily interpreted in 1789 as a
call for Louis and his courtiers to put public responsibility before private
gratification, though when exhibited again in the Salon of 1791 it could be
read by some as a tribute to the destroyer of monarchy. In the course of the
Revolution, David worked from within to destroy the Academy with its
embedded structures of courtly patronage, and to substitute other modes
of training and of singling out talent. Later he found new ways of making
his paintings perform, and his two great paintings of republican martyrs
were hung beside the chair of the president of the Convention.[8]

David's painting was not only inspired by the stage, but gave impetus to
a decision to restage *Brutus* at the Comédie Française in November 1790,
whereupon the play became a canonical piece of revolutionary theatre. In
order to contextualize that production, I shall turn to the dramatist Jean-
François de la Harpe, a former protégé of Voltaire. In December 1790,
on behalf of a syndicate of writers determined to assert their rights over
a Comédie Française which controlled theatre as the Academy controlled
painting, La Harpe delivered a speech on theatrical freedom.

La Harpe began by setting out what the Revolution actually entailed for
human beings:

All our thoughts, all our deeds, all that till now formed the basis of our individual
life, must henceforth yield to that kind of public and social life which we owe to
liberty; at the least they become subordinated to it, or I might even say incorporated
such that one and the other are but one and the same thing. Woe to him who,
having the good fortune to be free, cannot apprehend that all titles of glory,
whatever they be, vanish before that great title of free man and citizen.[9]

---

[7] Herbert (1973) 51, Lee (1999) 124. The heads are visible in David's preliminary sketch now in the
National Museum of Stockholm.
[8] Lee (1999) 174.   [9] La Harpe (1790) 2.

The monopoly of the Comédie Française is a constraint on freedom, La Harpe argues, and their classical repertoire should be regarded as public property, for theatre is a fundamental force in the creation of public opinion.

Of all places where men gather, nowhere is the communication of feeling quicker, stronger, or more contagious. Since you go only to be moved, your soul filled with its want of emotion opens up on all sides to receive or bestow emotions. Through conjunction, these grow and exalt themselves, by dint of direct expression and expression by others: you lead or are drawn, and soon all voices make but one cry ... It is here, indeed it is here, that in all its power arises the dominating voice of opinion.[10]

La Harpe then uses the metaphor of multi-faceted mirrors to suggest how opinion is multiplied through a process of reflection, and the metaphor of a thermometer to suggest how different factions raise or lower the moral and political temperature. At the Feast of the Federation, when delegates came from all over France to mark the anniversary of the Bastille, La Harpe claims that the Comédie Française cooled the patriotic spirit through their choice of repertoire.[11] The popularity of David's painting explains why there was a call at the time of the Federation for Voltaire's little-known play, a call which the actors staunchly resisted.

La Harpe takes an optimistic view of the popular audience, impatient with protests by the Comédie Française actors that in Voltaire's play Louis XVI would be identified with Tarquin, the unseen tyrant.

Happily experience has shown that they know their public no better than they know their king. This public, whose discernment is rather finer than theirs, did not mark with applause whatever attacked monarchy in itself, but was content to greet with rapture all outbursts of liberty and patriotism. In a word, the performances of *Brutus* were a triumph of the public spirit, despite all efforts of the aristocracy to trouble or destroy the outcome. Did not one enemy of the revolution think he could call attention to himself by responding to a line that banished kings with cries of 'Long live the King!'? The whole assembly, with one united voice, by repeating 'Long live the King!' and adding to it 'Long live the Nation!', demonstrated that, even if the conquerors of the Bastille were equal in courage to the Romans, Paris did not think its revolution should resemble that of Rome, or that Louis XVI could resemble Tarquin.[12]

La Harpe is aware that the meaning of Voltaire's play is not inherent in the text but is made through the response of the audience. This audience

[10] La Harpe (1790) 4–5.
[11] La Harpe (1790) 2–6. On the Federation, see Schama (1989) 500–13.   [12] La Harpe (1790) 11.

is an 'assembly' which echoes the political assembly and makes known the opinion of the people of Paris. La Harpe emphasizes the consensual nature of the theatre audience, and the tendency of multiple voices to become one through processes of emotional contagion. He implies that the two cries of *vive le roi!* and *vive la nation!* were convergent, reflecting consensus that France needs a constitutional monarchy. Most other commentators disagreed and pointed out that aristocratic sympathizers were shouting for the king while revolutionaries who considered themselves 'patriots' were shouting for the nation, in this space that had been rechristened the 'Théâtre de la Nation'. Indeed spectators had to be relieved of their weapons at the door to ensure that expressions of feeling remained symbolic.[13] On the first night we hear that 'each party seized enthusiastically upon what flattered their own views, but the patriots of the pit always had the upper hand, as in the play'.[14] One member of the audience recalled: 'Never was illusion more complete: the spectators were as so many Romans; all believed they were participating in the action.'[15] Another tells how the 'patriots' identified with Brutus and Publicola, while their opponents identified with other characters.[16] The audience were at once engaged in a power struggle in the Parisian present and lost in a world of the imagination. Mirabeau was a conspicuous figure up in the fourth row of balconies, identified by some spectators as a contemporary Brutus, part of the wider drama that was playing itself out.[17]

It was not only in the auditorium that power was being contested. François Joseph Talma was a radically minded actor who had campaigned for a performance of *Brutus* at the time of the Federation, and had been expelled from the company and later readmitted by a mixture of public demand and political pressure. Confined to a minor role, he marked his presence by appearing in an authentic historical toga, to great applause from the 'patriots'. The politics of costume were important because actors had traditionally appeared in fashionable attire most often given them by aristocratic patrons, so that on stage actors were visibly an extension of the world of court.[18] Talma later remarked on how Racine and Corneille put poison in their tragedies, but costume was used as the antidote, removing the venom from their plays. When fellow actors accused Talma of looking in *Brutus* as if he had wet sheets over his shoulder, grotesque like an ancient statue, he responded by unrolling a sketch by David to attest the

[13] Renwick (1998) 95. Renwick gives a full account of audience responses.
[14] Lüsebrink (1992) 1874.   [15] Herbert (1973) 15.
[16] Gorson cited in Renwick (1998) 96.   [17] Renwick (1998) 96.   [18] Tarin (1998) 167.

authenticity of his garment.[19] To appear before the king in such a state of undress would have been an insult, and thus on stage it became a political statement: a rejection of courtly luxury and falsity, and at the same time an assertion that the Roman Republic had a real historical existence. What once could be, could be again. At the end of the first performance, in response to a call from the audience, the theatre's bust of Voltaire was brought on stage and crowned. A print of the crowning gives some idea of the semi-classical costume used in the 1790 production, with glorious ostrich plumes, renaissance doublets and a female costume that displays the sumptuousness of its fabric rather than the form of the body (Plate 3). The triumph of the production was the triumph of Voltaire's sombre story, not that of the actors.

Voltaire's text ends with Brutus learning in a public place that his son is dead, and declaring that Rome is free, so at the end of the second performance, a *tableau vivant* was appended, setting up the scene of David's painting, and this still image must have highlighted the discordance between revolutionary and theatrical costuming. At the third performance the Marquis de Villette, a former protégé of Voltaire and now a prominent revolutionary, climbed onto the stage to call for the transfer of Voltaire's remains to the Pantheon, which became the first of the great festivals of the Revolution. An actor representing Brutus greeted the vast cortège when it stopped outside the Comédie Française, and an image of Brutus was prominent on the huge chariot which bore Voltaire's remains.[20] The gap between painting, theatre and festival was a fluid one in the revolutionary period.

For most contemporaries, it was taken for granted that the ideas of the Enlightenment precipitated revolution. Condorcet spoke of how Voltaire's tragedies, over half a century, liberated youth from the charms of a servile education, allowing a nation to think. De Tocqueville, looking back, had no doubt that France was the most literary nation in Europe, and that writers were responsible for new habits of thought whereby peasants spoke of themselves as citizens, though Voltaire in exile failed to see how his own reformism had fallen behind public opinion.[21] Twentieth-century historiography was more reluctant to see ideas as the motor of history, and sought deeper causes in economics. Georges Lefebvre, for example, in his standard account of the Revolution first published in 1951, makes no mention

---

[19] Talma's recollections in Regnault-Warin (1904) 159–67. A number of secondary sources incorrectly attribute these events to 1789, including Collins' biography of Talma: Collins (1964) 44–5. On the politics of costume, see Frantz (1998) 111.
[20] See Dowd (1948) 50–1, Schama (1989) 561–6.   [21] Tocqueville (1998) 195–202, 215.

Plate 3. The crowning of Voltaire. From a contemporary revolutionary journal edited by Camille Desmoulins.

of theatre, which is implicitly dismissed as ideological superstructure.[22] Examination of audience behaviour in 1790 shows how limiting it is to conceive of thought, ideas or ideology in isolation from the human body, given the extent to which the individual was (in La Harpe's apposite term) 'incorporated' in public life. The partisans of Brutus created not just an 'imagined' Roman community, but an embodied and visceral community of jostling bodies, waving fists, piercing whistles and contagious emotions. Social reality was not reflected in the theatre but constituted by theatre.[23]

To understand the relationship between theatre and revolutionary citizenship, we must consider what it was to be a spectator. When Louis Sebastien Mercier, hostile to the power of actors at the Comédie Française, described playwrights in 1773 as the most useful of citizens, privileged to influence the *moeurs* of their fellow citizens, he took it for granted that the theatre of the Enlightenment required a kind of energized passivity. He identified the unique role of the theatre as a place where the voices of men can rise in concert, and argued that actors should learn from the audience as from a sounding instrument. Joined to others by the electricity of feeling, Mercier's spectator judges not as an individual but as a public man, mindful of the collective interest, and the 'people' usually proves an honest judge, particularly in the provinces far from Court. Mercier argues for bigger theatres with a broader social base, but does not question the ultimate authority of the writer who lifts hearts with the thread he holds in his hand.[24] Effectively he places the auditorium as the site of Rousseau's 'general will', but he cannot dispense with the writer as legislator.

Mercier wanted seats installed in the pit, since he saw no liberty in men packed like herrings in a barrel, but four years later, in his *Encyclopédie* entry on the *parterre* or 'pit', Marmontel argued for retention of the standing pit because of the electricity and emotional contagion that bonds a crowd together, even though 'a seated mind be wiser'. While boxes can only be the site of individual judgements, the pit allows public opinion to form, and a scattering of enlightened members has a positive influence on the mass. An intelligent pit will quickly discern the fakery of actors whose only concern is to play for applause. Seating, Marmontel claims, would have a negative effect on that body politic which is the theatre.

---

[22] Translated as Lefebvre (1964). Albert Soboul is the other dominant figure in the Marxist tradition. Furet (1981) put historiography in perspective. Hunt (1986) is an important study of the psychopolitical impact of symbol and ritual. Schama (1989) popularized a culturalist approach. On Ozouf see n. 79 below.

[23] Cf. Tarin (1998) 78. On imagined communities, see p. 8 above.

[24] Mercier (1773) 1–8, 200–4, 234, 347–8. On Mercier, see Boës (1982) 79–87.

[T]hat species of republic constituted by our performances would change its nature, and the democracy of the pit would degenerate into aristocracy: less licence and tumult, but also less liberty, straightforwardness, warmth, openness, and honesty. It is in the pit, and a free pit, that applause starts, and applause is the soul of emulation, an outburst of feeling, a public avowal of personal judgements, and as it were the sign from every soul to take enjoyment, and double up the interest on those joys through mutual and instant communication of their common emotion.[25]

The eighteenth-century auditorium, an encircling space where everyone could see everyone, is conceived by Marmontel as a political microcosm.[26] When the Comédie Française in 1759 abolished the seats on stage used by rich men to display themselves, there was a shift of gravity towards the pit.[27] The pit was an overtly democratic space inasmuch as it generated collective expressions of feeling, it was a space of independent males, and it was cheap to enter yet socially mixed, for some who could afford to pay more preferred its excitements. Women avoided it, but were conspicuous in the boxes, where men adopted an aristocratic persona through sartorial display, and through displaying themselves as part of exclusive friendship groups, family groups or liaisons, enclosed in modular units that functioned like private salons.[28] The auditorium did not simply mirror the social structure: it was the public space of encounter which allowed Parisian society to contemplate itself and align itself.

Seats were introduced in the new Comédie Française of 1782, and by 1788 fears were being expressed that this grand new theatre had 'deprived theatrical republicanism of its last refuge'.[29] Despite this apparent embourgeoisement of the performance space, the seated pit nevertheless, once the Revolution broke out, became a site of direct democratic expression through singing, heckling, the display of emblems and throwing of notes on stage for the actors to read aloud. It was impossible for a dramatist simply to pull the strings. The playwright Millin de Grandmaison reflected on the error of despots who fear the theatre as a place of assembly, since they have everything to learn from seeing the first storm-clouds arise when their yoke becomes intolerable. It is in the pit that spirits electrified by their

---

[25] Marmontel (1777).
[26] Cf. a letter of 1735 on the pit as 'sovereign legislator': Johnson (1995) 34. See also Ravel (1999) 193.
[27] On the abolition, see Howarth (1997) 587; on the debate, see e.g. Friedland (2002) 87.
[28] Ravel (1999) 19 sets out the limitations of earlier audience studies by Lough and Lagrave. Johnson (1995) offers the best overview. See also Lever (2001) 25–34, Wiles (2003) 222–5. Banu (1989) evokes the world of the *loge*.
[29] Restif de la Bretonne, cited in Melton (2001) 183.

friction will start to overturn an unjust rule. Millin mentions how, particularly before the play begins, men stand up in the seated pit to harangue the crowd, a crowd which is judicious enough to hoot down any motions that are ridiculous.[30] The Revolution generated a huge amount of theatrical energy, and if no playwright of that era has subsequently received critical acclaim, this may be because the playwright had such limited control of his or her medium.

The revolutionary constitution of 1791 set up a distinction between 'active' citizens, men who paid tax, and a substantive minority of 'passive' citizens, men who enjoyed rights qua human beings but not the right to elect political representatives. This proved unpalatable to the Jacobins, who insisted on the ethical dimension of citizenship as something which demanded the active involvement of all.[31] A theatre that placed spectators as passive receivers of enlightened ideas was incompatible with the great revolutionary ideal of the fully active citizen.

TRAGEDY AS A SCHOOL FOR CITIZENS: THE CAREER OF M.-J. CHÉNIER

I shall trace the progression of the Revolution, from its libertarian beginnings to the implosion of its communitarian aspirations, via the career of Marie-Joseph Chénier, a dramatist at the epicentre of the struggle to determine theatre's function in a society of citizens. The private man was so fully incorporated in the public man that it is impossible to tell whether with hindsight we should see Chénier as a power-hungry opportunist or a high-minded idealist, but whatever the motivation he was consistent in his dedication to the idea that theatre should be a school for citizens. He came to fame through his history play *Charles IX*, which the Comédie Française declined to stage in the aftermath of the attack on the Bastille, or to restage at the time of the Federation a year later. The rejection of his work by the Comédie Française made him feel, like Mercier and many others, the victim of an integrated regime of patronage.

In common with most of his fellow playwrights, Chénier was a devotee of Voltaire. Like Voltaire he saw freedom of speech as the greatest cause to be espoused, and like Voltaire his preferred medium was tragedy.

It is above all to his tragedies that M. de Voltaire owes his influence across all of Europe. A book, however good it is, can never act on the public mind in a manner so rapid, or so vigorous as a fine play in the theatre. Sensational scenes, luminous

---

[30] Millin (1790) esp. 43–5.   [31] Jaume (2003) 134–5, Magnette (2005) 120.

thoughts, and truths of feeling, expressed in graceful poetry, engrave themselves easily in the heads of most spectators. On the multitude detail is lost, and the linking thread of argument eludes it, but it retains the results. All our ideas stem from our feelings. An isolated man can only be moved in moderation, but the impressions made on men when gathered together are strong and durable. No-one, amongst the moderns, has understood so well as M. de Voltaire the electricity of theatre.[32]

In *Charles IX* Chénier told the story of the massacre of protestants on St Bartholomew's Eve in 1572, the worst act of religious fanaticism France had ever known, and his play pointed the finger of blame directly at the king, while presenting his heir, the future Henri IV, as a figure of tolerance and reconciliation. This was a story that Voltaire could only tell in a narrative poem, the *Henriade*, since censorship precluded its representation in the politically dangerous medium of theatre. Though flawed medieval kings were a staple of English Elizabethan theatre, the French neoclassical tradition never tolerated such representations of historical monarchs, so Chénier's play broke a taboo. The use of Voltaire's classical form, with its unities and strict alexandrine versification, underlined the radical nature of the content. When the play was finally performed in November 1789, the authenticity of the set design, which reproduced the Caryatid room in the Louvre, gained added resonance from the enforced residence of Louis XVI in the Tuileries Palace adjoining the Louvre.

The first phase of the Revolution was its libertarian phase, preoccupied with overthrowing structures of oppression, and Chénier sought a production of *Charles IX* on the grounds of his right to free expression. In a manifesto on theatrical freedom he declared that in states where all positions are obtained by graft, 'a good book, which is to say a useful book, is the only public action permitted a citizen who will not sink to humiliating steps', but freedom of the press is worthless if it does not extend to publication through the medium of performance. Feelings and ideas make more impact on crowds gathered in one place than on a multiplicity of individuals, and good Parisian plays are quickly reproduced in the provinces and other European capitals, so a state cannot be free without freedom in the domain that matters most. Chénier places himself in a line of radical writers – Machiavelli with *Mandragola*, Shakespeare who weighed up kings, peers and prelates in a spirit of liberty, Molière with his *Tartuffe*, Voltaire with plays like *Mahomet* – all of whom had attacked the Catholic Church, an institution tied to royal despotism.[33] Chénier's anticlericalism relates to

[32] *Charles IX: discours préliminaire* [1788]: Chénier (2002) 73.
[33] *De la liberté du théâtre en France* [June 1789]: Chénier (2002) 167–88.

a church hostile to actors, one that had famously denied normal burial to Molière, and still denied marriage to Talma.[34]

Charles IX came to be performed thanks to new structures of power which filled the vacuum left by the old order. The new Comédie Française of 1782 was sited in the Cordeliers district, where poor medieval streets were replaced by avenues focused on the new and sumptuous classical building. It was in the popular assembly of the Cordeliers district that Danton built his political power-base, an assembly based not on representation but on a participatory democracy where power fell to men who chose to become activists. The district assembly controlled the local unit of the National Guard which had responsibility for policing the streets around the theatre, and it sent its representatives to the municipal assembly. When the system of district assemblies was abolished in May 1790, and a more controllable structure of 'sections' was implemented, with the area now named after the theatre, Danton established in the old Cordeliers monastery across the road from the theatre the famous Cordeliers Club, originally called the 'Society of Friends of the Rights of Man and of the Citizen'. The Cordeliers district and subsequently the Cordeliers Club was a focus for radical activism, with the participation of many journalists including Marat and several dramatists. To gain a showing for *Charles IX* was a perfect cause for Danton, Desmoulins and their associates to adopt. Crowding the pit and rushing the stage on 19 August 1789, the Cordeliers 'patriots' staged a demonstration proclaiming that the theatre must henceforth belong to free Frenchmen and not be run any longer by Gentlemen of the Royal Bedchamber.[35] Marmontel's 'democracy of the pit' was pushed to a new extreme, and it is impossible now as then to say how far Danton represented the 'general will' of the local community. Chénier consolidated his relationship with the locality by donating the proceeds of a benefit performance to the poor of the Cordeliers district.[36]

Danton wielded power in his local community but failed to get himself elected as mayor of Paris. Bailly, the new mayor, was the heroic revolutionary figure whom David placed at the centre of his epic painting of the *Tennis Court Oath*, a painting he had to leave unfinished when Bailly eventually fell victim to the guillotine. For Chénier and the Cordeliers patriots,

---

[34] See Chénier's *Courtes réflexions sur l'état civil des comédiens* [September 1789]: Chénier (1824–6) IV.440–9. On Talma, see Collins (1964) 74.

[35] Brown (2002) 370–5 brings out the Cordeliers connection. On Danton, see Hampson (1978) 31–8. On the architecture of the new theatre, see Lever (2001) 101–3. The cause célèbre of *Charles IX* has been much recounted: see e.g. Bingham (1939) 8–30, Hamiche (1973) 39–143, Hemmings (1994) 50–3, 73–7, and Ambrus/Jacob in Chénier (2002) 10–24.

[36] Bingham (1939) 27, Brown (2002) 374–5.

it was clear that the municipality had to take from the Crown responsibility for the Comédie Française, but Bailly himself, as the man now responsible for maintaining public order in the month after the fall of the Bastille, was far from happy at the prospect of sanctioning *Charles IX*, and he made a note of his feelings after the demonstration. The play risked whipping up anti-royalist feeling, he thought, and so might divide the revolutionaries, while the wishes of the public expressed in the theatre were essentially the wishes of organized cabals. Theatre was in a special category and freedom of the press should not extend to it, for 'I think one must exclude from the theatre, where many men gather and electrify each other, all that might tend to corrupt morals or the spirit of government. Theatre [*le spectacle*] is part of public education, which cannot be left to just anyone, but must be overseen by the Administration.' We notice how the metaphor of electricity is now almost mandatory to describe the peculiar energies arising from encounters in the auditorium. Censorship of theatre, Bailly argued, is not a restraint on freedom but marks respect for the freedom and moral security of the majority. There is a ring of paternalism in his final note that the theatre should be a place where he can safely send his children.[37] In the event Bailly was overruled by the Parisian assembly, and the play went ahead.

In the short term Bailly's fears proved groundless and there were no riots at the performance, but Danton remained confident that just as Beaumarchais' *Marriage of Figaro* in 1784 had 'killed off nobility, so *Charles IX* would kill royalty'.[38] Beaumarchais himself was of Bailly's opinion. With the royal family under house arrest, he thought this was no moment to represent barbarism that might encourage the 'people' in their own excesses, alienating wise and moderate men. The recent lynching of a butcher showed up the risks of presenting assassination so vividly, and the situation called for plays of inspiration, not despair: 'We need rather to be consoled by a picture of our ancestors' virtues than terrified by our vices and our crimes.'[39] Hearing of the production across the Channel, Edmund Burke's reaction was more extreme:

It was but the other day that they caused this very massacre [of St Bartholomew's Eve] to be acted on the stage for the diversion of the descendants of those who committed it . . . Was this spectacle intended to make Parisians abhor persecution, and loathe the effusion of blood? – No; it was to teach them to persecute their own pastors . . . It was to stimulate their cannibal appetites (which one would think

---

[37] Chénier (1824–6) 1.367–70.   [38] Lieby (1901) 48.
[39] Letter of 9 November 1789: Welschinger (1880) 48.

Plate 4. The Cardinal of Lorraine blessing the daggers of the assassins.

had been gorged sufficiently) by variety and seasoning; and to quicken them to an alertness in new murders and massacres.[40]

The debate prompted by such accusations leads us to fundamental questions about theatre, and what theatre does to its audience. Let us focus that question on the most celebrated moment of the play, when the bell sounds, the nervous king calls for blood and the cardinal blesses the daggers of the aristocratic conspirators[41] (Plate 4).

For Chénier, the rationalist case was irrefutable. The play inspires a horror of fanaticism and civil war, crime is punished, and the rule of law is supported.[42] Against this classical argument from mimesis, whereby the audience learns from seeing an imitation of life, stands Bailly's counterargument that theatre is a social event which raises temperatures on the emotional thermometer, and creates energies which one may conceive as an interpersonal electricity. Against Voltaire's moral fervour to expose the perils of fanaticism we must set Rousseau's insight that spectators are always part of the spectacle. The argument from mimesis cuts two

[40] *Reflections on the Revolution in France* [1790] in Cahn (1997) 680.   [41] *Charles IX* IV.vi.
[42] *Discours préliminaire*: Chénier (2002) 80.

ways. To watch a king on stage acting as the enemy of his people is to conceive it possible that another king in time present may be no less an enemy of his people. The aesthetics of performance did much to shape the play's reception. Within the shell of the classical form, with its traditional hierarchical divide between high and low, noble and plebeian, heroic world and everyday world, Chénier inserted not myth but historical actuality. Authenticity of set and costume were tied to a new technique of acting. Talma took the role of Charles IX because his colleagues judged it invidious to play such a character, and his method was to subvert the traditional rhythms of declamation, playing classical alexandrines almost as if they were prose,[43] thus reinforcing the idea that this king was an ordinary man, a psychologically comprehensible and weak human being, led by a series of understandable steps to calling for the murder of his people. It was the memories carried by the classical form that made its use now so potent.

Following the turmoil over *Charles IX* and *Brutus*, and legislation ending the monopoly of the Comédie Française, in April 1791 Chénier and Talma set up their own company in the Palais-Royal complex on the Rue de Richelieu, closer to the Palace, Jacobin club and National Assembly. In a manifesto that Talma was prohibited from delivering at the Comédie Française, Chénier lamented that actors were still afraid to speak out as citizens. Since theatre was a school for morals and liberty, it must develop the talent of new writers to fill a stage aggrandized by revolution.[44] The new theatre on the Rue de Richelieu had been built as an opera house but, as Chénier explained to the Cordeliers assembly, it was not apparent how operatic ariettas and balletic *pas de deux* could create citizens. Frenchmen needed plays in order to learn liberty, patriotism and virtue from works acknowledged as masterpieces by public opinion.[45]

Chénier's first play written for the Richelieu theatre was *Jean Calas*, a tribute play to Voltaire, but he probably made more impact on the public with his song written for the great procession which carried Voltaire's remains to the Pantheon.[46] Two major works followed, *Caius Gracchus* and *Fénelon*, written concurrently at the end of 1791. It is helpful to see these as a diptych: one austerely classical, the other romantic, the one a product of artistic discipline, the other of inspiration, the one a tragedy portraying heroism in face of intractable obstacles, the other a tear-jerker designed to warm the heart. The king had been fatally weakened by his

---

[43] See Guibert (1986).　　[44] Chénier (1824–6) IV.457–60.
[45] *Rapport sur l'établissement de l'opéra* [April 1790]: Chénier (1824–6) IV.450–6.
[46] Bingham (1939) 47–8.

capture at Varennes after a crass attempt to escape from Paris, and in July a republican demonstration staged by the Cordeliers and other local Parisian groups was suppressed with much bloodshed in the 'massacre of the Champs-de-Mars', the Jacobin club split apart, and there followed a crackdown on the radical republican movement. The issue was no longer how to overthrow royal despotism but how to avoid bloodshed amongst revolutionaries and how to build a new political structure upon the ruins of the old. *The Declaration of the Rights of Man and of the Citizen* held that property was an inviolable right, but the poor of Paris were starving.

Caius Gracchus, which opened in February 1792, portrayed internecine conflict in the late Roman Republic. Caius Gracchus champions the 'people' in their demand for an egalitarian distribution of publicly owned spoils of conquest, and he is supported by his mother in this idealistic stance while his wife urges him to put family before public duty. In the finale, Gracchus commits suicide rather than remain as a rallying point to perpetuate fighting that will result in a mass slaughter of plebeians. The new tyrants of Rome, four hundred years after Brutus drove out monarchy, are the senators, who may be construed by the audience as the aristocracy of the old regime, but who may also be construed as property-owning citizens denying bread and a full republican constitution to the Parisian masses yearning for freedom. The play's success owed much to this ambiguity, appealing to both sides of the new divide.[47] Its most famous phrase, 'laws not blood', later printed as an epigraph, would eventually prompt public protest from a Robespierre supporter, and the play was withdrawn during the Terror.[48] The ambiguity of the drama on stage stimulated the drama of the pit, where we hear of sixty aristocrats arriving in disguise to form a cabal, happy to applaud lines like 'laws not blood', while patriots responded with a call to attack the king in the nearby Tuileries.[49]

Crucial to this production was a collaboration with David. Following the success of his two great paintings of the Roman Republic, the *Oath of the Horatii* and *Brutus*, David took this opportunity to translate his visual aesthetic into the medium of theatre, and there was much praise for his set and costumes. When analysing the art of acting, Talma explained how 'I became a painter in my own way',[50] and Chénier's text is best read as a framework for a series of painterly images: the oath sworn before the urn containing the ashes of Tiberius Gracchus, the defiance of the mother, Caius' surrender of his child to preserve the peace, grief around

---

47 See Bingham (1939) 56–60.   48 Estrée (1913) 393–4, Bingham (1939) 125–6.
49 Lieby (1901) 89, Bingham (1939) 56–61, Dowd (1948) 43–4.   50 Talma (2002) 37.

the hero's bloodstained corpse. David's classical paintings look remarkably like *tableaux vivants*, with intense emotions caught in statuesque stillness, and they reflect the quintessential skill of the neoclassical actor which lay in capturing and magnifying discrete emotions.[51] Although David's designs have vanished, forcing scholars today to encounter *Caius Gracchus* as a work by Chénier and not David, we can nevertheless find plenty of analogues in David's paintings: the heroic suicide of Socrates, the oath sworn by the Horatian brothers, the child held above the Roman crowd by his Sabine mother, the multiple emotions of women facing their combative menfolk. In a youthful reworking of Shakespeare's *Julius Caesar*, Chénier judged that a playwright who wants to work on behalf of the people must not represent the people, for to do so properly would repel the audience.[52] The situation had now changed and the great challenge for both painter and dramatist was to represent the Roman 'people' as a collective and positive entity. Their solution was to shift focus from stage to auditorium. When Gracchus, the Senator, and the corrupt Tribune spoke in turns from the rostrum, with an idealized city of Rome on the backdrop, the on-stage extras playing the 'people' were of small consequence. The pit in the Richelieu became the Roman Forum, and the Parisian crowd became the Roman crowd.

The only extant theatre image by David is a drawing apparently for a curtain design of 1794[53] (Plate 5). Beside the chariot of Liberty and Equality march figures evoking the three plays that were in August 1793 canonized by the Convention as prescribed works that taught civic virtue: *Caius Gracchus*, *Brutus* and *William Tell*.[54] The two brothers Gracchi with their mother are followed by Brutus waving a text from Voltaire's play that reads 'let my son be led to death', and by Tell with his son holding the apple. Following these exemplary parents willing to sacrifice their sons for liberty and equality come recent martyrs of the Revolution including Marat and Lepelletier, paintings of whom David had placed in the Assembly. The Gracchi are shown as children, so the drawing does not in any literal way capture the stage production, but we get some sense of mood, movement and costume. The people are figured symbolically by Hercules seated on a huge chariot, freeing David of the need to represent authentic plebeian faces.[55] By 1794 Chénier and David had diverged politically, with David an uncompromising supporter of Robespierre and Chénier a centrist, and

[51] See e.g. Jelgerhuis (1984), Roach (1985) 69–92.
[52] *Brutus et Cassius, les derniers romains: épitre dédicatoire à mon frère*: Chénier (1824–6) vi.193.
[53] Rosenberg (2002) no. 129.   [54] Lieby (1901) 115, Carlson (1966) 165, Johnson (1992) 63.
[55] Perhaps echoing David's Hercules at the Festival of Unity: see Schama (1989) 750–1.

Plate 5. *The Triumph of the French People*. Detail showing Cornelia with the child
Gracchi, followed by Brutus, William Tell, Marat and Lepelletier.

this divergence may reflect their respective media. David was in complete
control of his pen or brush when portraying the remorseless forward march
of revolution, but Chénier was always answerable to his audience, and his
words were the activating force for the drama of the pit, audible only
against the sounding board of a mixed audience.

Written concurrently but performed a year later, *Fénelon* portrays a celebrated reforming archbishop, admired by Voltaire for his sceptical theology
and his public criticism of Louis XIV.[56] In this play family life is not broken but restored. Mother and daughter are plucked from a convent, where
the mother has been incarcerated for contracting a marriage incompatible with the class structures of the *ancien régime*. Fénelon overrules the
abbess, and speaks for humanitarian values against loveless dogma, freeing
the plucky *ingénue* at the centre of the story to build a new future. The
revolutionary context had changed since the production of *Caius Gracchus*.
The overthrow of the monarchy on 10 August 1792 was followed by the
'September massacres' when prisoners were slaughtered by a mob whipped

[56] See Voltaire's *Siècle de Louis XIV* [1733] in Voltaire (1792) XXII.279–93 – a text annotated by Chénier's
collaborator Palissot.

up by Marat. Chénier was now a member of the National Assembly, but having failed miserably in his attempt to win votes from the radicalized people of Paris, he represented the provincials of Seine-et-Oise,[57] and he had cut his links with the Cordeliers when moving to a theatre north of the river. In *Fénelon* we see him moving from a politics of hate and confrontation in *Charles IX* to a politics of love, pacifism and compromise.

In a preface published soon after the opening, Chénier explained his intentions in staging *Fénelon*. Theatre should not just 'follow the march of the national spirit but determine its progress', and he wanted each of his works to be seen as an act of *civisme* or 'citizenship'. When he staged *Caius Gracchus*, covert royalists were in the ascendant, but now that whole political edifice has been swept away and a new constitution needs to be erected.

Yet this building will collapse if it is not built on the foundations of public morality. So it is this morality that must be created. This is the aim that should be set down by legislators, philosophers, poets, and orators, the true teachers of nations. It is this objective that I had in view when composing the tragedy of *Fénelon*, and I believed there could be no more suitable moment for its performance than when the two great works of the republican constitution and national education were about to be debated. I also thought that in these dark and stormy times, when bad citizens preach theft and murder with impunity while true republicans, those who accepted a need for the severest acts of national justice, weep still for public morality flouted by the crimes of September, it was more than time to hear in the theatre that voice of humanity which always resonates in the hearts of men gathered together.[58]

Chénier was now a member of the Committee for Public Instruction, charged not with public safety or the creation of laws, but with the long-term task of creating an educational system to build public morality. The severest act of 'national justice' was the guillotining of Louis XVI, to which Chénier had assented, and the archetypal bad citizen is plainly Marat.[59] Chénier offers his play to the audience as a lesson in public morality, and Fénelon is the model figure of authority, the epitome of toleration and humanity.

The setting of the central scenes in a torchlit dungeon where voices echo through a grill is far removed from the stark classicism of David. Chénier argued that his play was unambiguously a tragedy despite the happy ending because its aim was to draw tears,[60] but there is no moral ambiguity about

---

[57] Bingham (1939) 100–1; cf. on the city-country split Tulard (1989) 272.
[58] Chénier (2002) 251–3.   [59] Bingham (1939) 116–17, Ambrus and Jacob in Chénier (2002) 413.
[60] Chénier (2002) 250.

the horror of this convent prison, and nothing equivalent here to the moral uncertainty about whether Gracchus should indeed have surrendered his own child to save bloodshed. Chénier reverts in *Fénelon* to the sentimental norms of the 1770s, whereby audience tears are taken to be the sign of authentic humanity, very much in the spirit of Rousseau.[61] Susan Maslan describes a 'politics of pity' informing this style of revolutionary theatre, with the ideal of 'sympathy' crucial to a new brand of citizenship.[62] Whilst it is easy with hindsight to be sceptical about a bourgeois humanism that expresses itself through tears, we should not forget that in the face of a demagogic tyranny these humane tears were a political signal.[63]

Chénier was too busy with his political work to write more plays at this time, but he did manage a short entertainment for the Opéra, performed a few days after the king's execution.[64] In the past a blatantly aristocratic institution, the Opéra now needed a revolutionary repertoire. As dramatist, Chénier had always worked in the tradition of Voltaire, committed to the principle that spoken words are the medium of enlightenment, but his lyrics written for revolutionary festivals had helped him appreciate Rousseau's insight that music is prior to language and a stronger force for creating human bondedness. Whilst Rousseau seemed fundamentally wrong in his critique of representative democracy, he seemed right in his feel for the universality of song. Music inspired soldiers marching to war and was the essence of national festivals. As sacred music had supported the church, so patriotic music must support the splendour of a republic.[65] Chénier's operatic entertainment has a strong flavour of Rousseau, depicting citizen peasants who come to dance around the liberty tree in order to fraternize with soldiers camped on the border. The soldiers are inspired to win and, in the spectacular manner of opera, Liberty descends on a cloud from above and recounts her history. Chénier incorporated material from his hymn sung at the Federation on 14 July 1792, not to save himself labour but to play on the power of memory, carrying the emotions of a mass national festival into the confines of the opera house.

Dismissed from the Committee for Public Instruction in the autumn of 1793, and finding that both *Fénelon* and *Caius Gracchus* were no longer ideologically acceptable in the period of the Terror, Chénier nevertheless determined to write another play, *Timoleon*. A new and select 'Commission

[61] On sensibility in the 1770s, see Johnson (1995) 60–5.   [62] Maslan (2005) 107–8, 120–1.
[63] *Épître dédicatoire* [1802] in Chénier (2002) 264.
[64] *Le camp du Grand Pré*: Chénier (1824–6) II.
[65] *Rapport sur l'organisation de l'Institut National de Musique* [July 1795]: Chénier (1824–6) v.281–93; *Sur une édition des Oeuvres de J. J. Rousseau* [1801]: Chénier (1824–6) IV.277.

for Public Instruction' had been appointed to address the dilemma which theatre posed for the Jacobin government, at once uncontrollable and a cornerstone of education.[66] Whilst the old Comédie Française was stripped of its box divisions and painted in the colours of the tricolour in an attempt to create an egalitarian space based on the principle of the circle, with admission confined to uniformed patriots, the theatre on the Rue de la République remained nominally self-determining.[67] Despite warnings to desist, Chénier got halfway through an open dress-rehearsal before the play was interrupted, he was accused of being 'a counter-revolutionary in disguise', and forced into a public burning of his manuscript.[68] David is said to have remarked, after reading *Timoleon* as a member of the Committee for Public Safety: 'Chénier, a fine tragedy, impossible! To render freedom well did he ever feel it in his soul?'[69] Unlike the painter or the poet, the dramatist always faced the conundrum of sincerity: how could he demonstrate the authenticity of his own feelings when penning words to be spoken by others?

For *Timoleon*, as for *Caius Gracchus*, Chénier turned to one of Plutarch's inspirational narratives which told of public duty superseding the bond of blood. As in France at the end of 1793, so in the democratic republic of Corinth there has been success in war but instability at home. Timoleon returns from war to find his brother plotting to accept a royal crown, allegedly in the interests of firm government. The brother refuses to relent when his links with the King of Syracuse are exposed, and Timoleon gives the signal for an assassination in order to preserve democracy. On the face of it, this is a classic republican story on the model of *Brutus*, and the brother like Charles IX is a study in the psychological weakness that makes a tyrant, so Chénier could not create dramatic interest without making his tyrant comprehensible, and inviting sympathy for a monarchist laid him open to charges of moderatism. The unspoken issue, however, was the possibility that the brother who turns tyrant despite his robust republican parentage might be a metaphor for Robespierre. The text refers to the wielding of power through 'terror', but these unmistakable allusions were probably added at the point of publication. The Jacobin censors knew that the ultimate meaning of a play is not fixed by its author but determined by the context of performance, and it was open to the public to make this either a play supportive of Robespierre or a play condemning his dictatorship. The risk was too great.

---

[66] Estrée (1913) 38ff.   [67] Chevalley (1961) 60–3, Guibert and Razgonnikoff (1989) 247–8.
[68] Bingham (1939) 158–68.   [69] Reported by Vilate: Estrée (1913) 134.

Chénier's most interesting formal innovation lay in his treatment of the 'people'. His Grecian setting legitimated a return to the conventions of Greek tragedy, and the 'people' became a Greek-style chorus, able to articulate its collective voice through song, swearing a fraternal oath and celebrating nationhood.[70] Chénier's operatic experience had taught him how music allowed the masses to be represented with dignity, and not as a multiplicity of grotesques as in Shakespeare's *Julius Caesar*. In *Caius Gracchus*, the democratic rostrum was set stage centre so the audience in the pit could become the addressees, but in this play the rostrum was placed stage left so a more detached audience could contemplate direct democracy in action.[71] When Timoleon returns from war, he gives a full account of his generalship to the assembled people so they can judge how well he has served them, and at the end of the play they exonerate the assassination. Despite Chénier's efforts to tread a safe line, the dress-rehearsal was broken off on the grounds that the people should need no prompting in order to resist calls for monarchy.[72] Neoclassical theatre could not exist without heroes like Timoleon, but the Jacobins demanded absolute equality. Chénier decided to be a survivor not a hero when he burnt his text.

Service on the Committee for Public Instruction forced Chénier to consider in both theoretical and practical terms how true republican citizens might be formed. His principal efforts were directed at setting up a system of state primary education, to wrest the formation of young minds away from the Catholic priesthood, and he lamented that politicians were preoccupied by issues of security while education was overlooked. The fundamental importance of education was set out by Plato and Rousseau, and we have seen how Milton addressed the same questions. Chénier sought to be pragmatic, scornful of Robespierre's utopian schemes that were inspired by visions of Sparta and were incompatible with modernity. His ideas were crystallized in a report which the Convention approved and circulated in November 1793.[73]

Reason marches slower than armies, Chénier argues, but its results are more lasting, and in the forward march of the human spirit French republicans will one day influence Europe and the world. Instruction should fall into three categories: the teaching of skills, the gymnastic training of bodies to which vigour of the soul will cling, and moral education,

---

[70] Biet (1994) 117–24 traces the gradual emergence of the chorus in *Oedipus Rex* (later adapted by Chénier) as a figure for the people in neoclassical theatre.

[71] s.d. to Act II: Chénier (2002) 343.   [72] Julien de la Drôme cited in Bingham (1939) 166.

[73] *Discours sur l'instruction publique*: Chénier (1824–6) v.120–37.

which is to say the education of the heart. The teaching of *moeurs* ('moral habits') requires inspiration, and here the role of festivals is critical, drawing upon the inexhaustible treasures of the imagination in music, dance and poetry. When Chénier envisages seeding the year with memories, commemorating the great moments of the French Revolution, his model is the Christian festive cycle. On the debris of old superstition, Chénier wants to found a universal religion which brings peace not the sword and which forms citizens not subjects. In this secular religion, the creed will be equality, the oracles laws, the priests magistrates and the altar dedicated to the *patrie*. You have made laws, Chénier concludes; now you must make *moeurs*.

THE REVOLUTIONARY FESTIVAL

In the last chapter I contrasted Voltaire's idealization of theatre as a progressive force with Rousseau's idealization of festival, polarities which we can trace back to Aristotle and Plato. Starting as a playwright in the wake of Voltaire, Chénier came to recognize the revolutionary power of festival. Though plays could be reproduced in theatres across France, festivals could just as easily be replicated and offered more scope for building a new public morality. Plays written in the engaged tradition of Voltaire tended to generate controversy, while festivals tended to generate consensus, and within the Assembly there was certainly more consensus about the merits of festivals than the merits of theatre, always suspect as a class-based institution. Chénier's creative contributions to festivals won him acclaim, while his writing of plays exposed him to abuse, and *Timoleon* put his life at risk. In Milton's England, the protestant religion provided a secure ethical and celebratory framework which theatre could potentially complement, but Chénier was faced with a cultural tabula rasa. The relation between theatre and festival had to be rethought.

The greatest of the revolutionary festivals was the Festival of the Supreme Being. The celebration took place, in Paris and simultaneously across the country, seven weeks before the Thermidorean coup which brought Robespierre's power to an end. It was choreographed as usual by David and controlled by Robespierre. Robespierre had concluded that no public ethic could be based upon atheism, and he sought to harness old religious impulses in the revolutionary cause, so the chosen date of '20 Prairial' was in fact Whit Sunday under the Christian calendar as well as a day of rest under the new decimal calendar. The festival was conceived in response to the Festival of Liberty and Reason, which had been staged the previous

November inside Notre Dame in quasi-theatrical fashion using professional performers. The organizers were the Hébertists, Parisian radicals whom Robespierre had now crushed and condemned as atheists. David played no part, though Chénier's 'Hymn to Liberty' was a prominent feature.

Robespierre prepared the ground for the Festival of the Supreme Being in a major speech to the Convention, arguing that people could only escape egotism if they believed in the immortality of the soul, and the state needed therefore to develop a new religion whose sole priest is Nature.[74] His thinking is imbued with Rousseau, though he prefers to cite Voltaire as the precursor of revolutionary deism. He also draws on Chénier's report, arguing that public education is needed to create men who are citizens not *messieurs*, and that national festivals should bring the people together.

Gather men together, and you improve them, for men gathered together seek to please each other, and they can only please through acts that win them esteem. Bring to their encounter a great moral and political motive, and the love of honest things will enter their hearts pleasurably – for men cannot see each other without pleasure.

Man is the greatest thing there is in nature, and the most magnificent of all spectacles is that of a great people assembled. The national festivals of Greece are never spoken of without rapture: yet they scarce had any purpose except as games where bodily strength shone forth, or the skills, or at most talents, of poets and orators. But Greece was there. In the spectators themselves one saw a spectacle greater than the games.[75]

Like Rousseau, Robespierre saw Greek theatre as an exemplary mode of civic education, though he accorded little significance to the person of the dramatist. When he claims that on the basis of the year's achievements 'you can show the world the new spectacle of democracy set strong in a vast empire',[76] we notice that the word 'democracy', implying the direct sovereignty of the people, has entered republican discourse.[77] In the festival France will be performing itself, not just to create citizenship through natural processes of bonding, but also to offer an image of its collective self to the outside world.

Robespierre ended by proposing a decree which effectively substituted the old list of the 'rights of man and of the citizen' with a new statement about the positive obligations of the citizen.

---

[74] Speech of 7 May 1794 in Robespierre (1965) 243–86.   [75] Robespierre (1965) 276.
[76] Robespierre (1965) 249.   [77] See Arendt (1963) 117.

Article I. The French people recognizes the existence of the Supreme Being, and the immortality of the soul.
Article II. It recognizes that the best way of worshipping the Supreme Being is to do one's duties as a man.
Article III. It considers that the most important of these duties are: to detest bad faith and despotism, to punish tyrants and traitors, to assist the unfortunate, to respect the weak, to defend the oppressed, to do all the good one can to one's neighbour and to behave with justice towards all men.
Article IV. Festivals shall be instituted to remind men of the Deity, and of the dignity of their state.
Article V. These festivals shall be named after the glorious events of our revolution, the virtues which are most dear to men, and most useful, and the chief blessings of nature.[78]

A conception of citizenship which foregrounds rights is likely to find theatre an exemplary site where freedom of expression may be exercised, while a conception of Robespierre's kind which foregrounds duties is almost bound to chafe at the individualism of the playwright, the dialogism of the dramatic form and the hedonism or aggression of an unchecked audience.

The first part of the festival was staged in the Tuileries gardens, incorporating speeches by Robespierre, revolutionary songs and the pyrotechnic demolition of a statue of atheism. David's vision of the public was of an 'animated *parterre*', meaning by the word *parterre* not a theatrical pit but a flowerbed.[79] The people came clutching flowers, and it was noted how they left the royal flowerbeds unmolested, for these were now public property and belonged to the citizens themselves.[80] The *parterre* is an appropriate metaphor for the festive audience: colourful, diverse, organic, alive, but also carefully managed and harmonious.[81] A Hymn by Chénier was planned for the gardens, hailing the Supreme Being as 'the source of truth, outraged by imposture', and evoking the different divisions into which the republic was cast: warriors, mothers, old men, boys, wives and girls.[82] However, in a last-minute change of plan, Robespierre cancelled or relegated Chénier's

[78] Cited from Thompson (1968) 182.
[79] Aulard (1892) 308. Aulard remains the best source of primary documentation. For interpretation, see Ozouf (1988) 110–18. Published in French in 1976, Ozouf's synchronic structuralist analysis of the revolutionary festival has been deservedly influential. On the theatricality of festivals, see Starobinski (1987) 100–4.
[80] Aulard (1892) 324.
[81] On the metaphor of commonwealth as garden, cf. Shakespeare *Richard II* III.iv.
[82] Chénier (1824–6) III.364–7.

Hymn, and new words set to the same tune were sung in unison by members of all the forty-eight Paris sections. One explanation is a personalized one, seeing Chénier as a man who had fallen out of favour, but it is more likely that Robespierre found the words lacking in spirituality, and rejected the polished professionalism of a complex text sung by members of the National Institute of Music in favour of mass participation. Anything that smacked of the performative could be seen as inauthentic 'imposture' and alien to the purposes of the festival.[83]

In the great procession that led from the royal gardens to the Champs-de-Mars, the people were marshalled according to their residence in the forty-eight sections. Women marched in a column on the left, men on the right, with armed adolescents like classical ephebes in the centre, and the language of flowers was used to distinguish different age groups.[84] Whereas theatre audiences were always tiered with people paying to display their status, the festive participants are here organized on the basis of biology and geography, and class is made invisible. In the theatre auditorium, women functioned as feminine objects of male attention, but in this festival they appear as regenerative beings yielding a crop of farmers and warriors. The agrarian imagery of the Festival of the Supreme Being was in counterpoint not just to the guillotine but more importantly to war. Republican order had been secured by militarization, and the final image of *Timoleon* is symptomatic: Timoleon and the chorus march towards the vanishing point of the perspective where the fleet will take them back to war. Robespierre attempted to create an image of republican peace (Plate 6).

The Champs-de-Mars was the preferred space for republican celebration, levelled in July 1790 by the voluntary mass labour of Parisians to receive provincial delegates for the Festival of the Federation. A giant mountain, reminiscent of Calvary, now stood as the stage, and Robespierre led members of the Convention to the summit while the slopes were packed with revolutionary emblems and with singers: men to the right, girls and mothers to the left. The vast crowd joined in well-known refrains, and one participant recalled how verses by Chénier evoking the Federation 'produced a thrilling sensation of exhilaration and of religious awe impossible to express even after feeling it amid 500,000 spectators all seized by the

---

[83] Documentation in Bingham (1939) 171–3. Bingham adopts the personal interpretation. On Robespierre and the problem of sincerity, see Johnson (1992) 73 and Scurr (2006) 311.

[84] Aulard (1892) 317–19.

Plate 6. Festival of the Supreme Being on the Champ-de-Mars.

same emotion'.[85] To separate religious feeling from patriotic feeling had become an impossibility.[86] Robespierre was right in sensing that the mere act of gathering people together created its own dynamic, its own sense of a performance event, but it was also clear to immediate bystanders that many members of the Convention, dragooned into wearing David's costumes and mounting his revolutionary stage, resented the roles they were now being forced to play.[87]

Following the festival, offers were made to reproduce this great event in the theatre, just as the fall of the Bastille had once been represented.[88] Robespierre's Commission for Public Instruction responded with a lyricism that is worth reproducing at length.

What stage with its rocks, its cardboard trees, its skies made of rags, could claim to rival the magnificence of 20 Prairial, or wipe out its memory? The drums, the music, the boom of brass, the cries of joy hurled to the heavens, waves from a brotherhood of people, giant waves whose gentle and majestic swelling displayed both the power of intoxicated vision and the serene calm of public awareness! Those moist curtains, the clouds which playful zephyrs suspended above our heads, parted from time to time for rays of the Sun, as if seeking to make him witness to the finest moments of the festival! And then the Hymn of Victory, the people and its representatives united with arms raised and extended to the heavens as before the Sun they swore themselves to Virtue and to the Republic! There you have the Eternal, nature in all her glory, the whole of the feast of the Supreme Being.

It is only in these memories that one can recover the deep feelings which moved our hearts; to seek them elsewhere is to weaken them; to put this sublime spectacle on stage is to parody it. Thus, the first who thought to make a play of such festivals degraded their majesty, destroyed their effect, and held up the signal for federalism in the religion of the French people and of the human race. For were it permitted to cram popular festivals into a theatre, or deck them up on a stage, who cannot see but that these masquerades would become the festivals of choice for *fine company*, and offer certain persons the pleasure of isolation, and escape from the momentum of the nation. The festivals of the people are virtues, they are general, and can only be celebrated en masse.

What incense offered up to the Eternal might such bizarre products be, raucous anthems by a rabble of new-born authors never inspired by liberty! . . . The writer who provides in place of lessons only repetitions, in place of drama only dumb shows, in place of portraits only caricature, is of no use to literature, to morals, to the State, and Plato would have driven him from his republic.[89]

---

[85] Tissot in Bingham (1939) 173.
[86] On Robespierre and patriotism, see Hampson (1988) and Bell (2001) 165–7.
[87] Aulard (1892) 318–19.   [88] Cf. p. 136 above.
[89] Aulard (1892) 327–9. On the issues, see Johnson (1992) 72–3.

This conception of the festival as the expression of Rousseau's 'general will' leaves no space for theatre, or indeed artistic representation of any kind. Theatre is suspect because it involves repetition rather than spontaneity, generating not just intoxication but irony, not just immersion in the present but reflection about past and future; and it is suspect as an enclosed place where people regress to become convivial individuals in their boxes or form conspiratorial cliques in the pit. The auditorium models the nation as a multicultural federation, not as a unity under Jacobin legislators imbued with Platonic wisdom. The theatre is a space of artifice and masquerade, not of nature and truth.

After the fall of Robespierre, Chénier took up his duties again on the Committee for Public Instruction. Under the Directory, the Revolution had as it were a second chance. The Directors and Assembly, attached as they were to the right of private property, had somehow to reconcile the libertarian ideals of 1789 with the communitarian ideals of Robespierre and many in the local Paris sections. With the nation at war, patriotism became a stronger rallying call than republicanism.[90] In this context Chénier tried to hold the reins of two different horses, urging on both the ideal of a free theatre, where plays are the property of their author, and the ideal of the festival whereby the legislator effectively becomes the playwright and the public his actors on the stage of the nation.

Chénier put his major article of faith to the Assembly at the start of the Terror when artworks were being vandalized, urging that 'the representatives of the people cannot possibly doubt that it is to books that we owe the French revolution'; and he made the same point more poetically in his song that accompanied Voltaire's ashes to the Pantheon: 'From the proud accents of the two Brutuses, France conceived the need to be free!'[91] He condemned the censorship imposed by Robespierre's regime as barbaric, and misguided: power founded on violence must inevitably perish, for you can kill men but you cannot kill opinion, and crime begets crime; when public opinion grows malevolent, a wise government raises philosophers not armies.[92] Later, under Napoleonic censorship, he wrote that talent is silenced when writers become frightened of their own thoughts and write what is safest to say.[93] Whilst championing the freedom of the writer, Chénier realized also that deregulation of the theatre had led to anarchy and a decline in artistic standards. In 1797 he recommended that only the

[90] See Jones (2002) 520–1.   [91] Chénier (1824–6) III.348, v.160n.
[92] *Rapport sur les fêtes décadaires* [December 1794]: Chénier (1824–6) v.173.
[93] *Tableau historique de la littérature française*: Chénier (1824–6) VIII.350–1.

Comédie Française and Talma's theatre in the Rue de Richelieu should be allowed to perform spoken drama in Paris, while just one theatre should be allowed in provincial cities of less than 100,000 people, for the state had a legitimate right to oversee the dramatic arts.[94] Chénier knew that his own writing sat in a tradition stretching back via Racine to the Greeks, and came to the hard realization that this tradition was incompatible with a bourgeois free market.

Because of his role in public life, his dramaturgical skills were devoted at this time to festivals rather than plays in the theatre. He saw festivals as essential to the identity of a Republic, which would be but an empty name were its glorious moments not commemorated in annual festivals, and these moments had now to include the fall of Robespierre on 9 Thermidor. He looked back nostalgically to the spontaneous expressions of individuals in the 1790 Festival of the Federation, and saw no such spontaneity in the Festival of the Supreme Being. In the anti-Robespierre poem which he published with *Timoleon*, he lamented:

> Where are the solemn festivals
> Which, across France, amid swearing of oaths,
> Witnessed in a thousand embraces
> The uniting of a thousand cities?[95]

In plans for the tenth or decadary day of rest designed to replace the Christian Sabbath, he stressed the need to avoid military-style planning, and to allow the latitude demanded by the genius of the French people.[96] Woe to the legislator, he declared, who tries to move men like pieces on a chess board. The science of political leadership is the science of directing sensibilities in order to make better and happier people.[97]

Whilst one of the Directors, La Révellière-Lépeaux, had grandiose dreams of a permanent arena on the Champs-de-Mars where a crowd of 300,000 would be marshalled into four-part singing, Chénier was more pragmatic.[98] In a speech on the reawakening of the sciences, he pointed to the cost of the Jacobin festival of Republican Reunion, which commemorated the attack on the Tuileries Palace and left nothing behind it save rags and plaster, arguing that the money spent could have built thirty public sculptures and commissioned a hundred creative artists to write enduring

---

[94] *Motion d'ordre sur les théâtres* [November 1797]: Chénier (1824–6) v.409–13.
[95] *Ode sur la situation de la République Française durant la démagogie de Robespierre et de ses complices* [June 1794]: Chénier (1824–6) III.332.
[96] *Rapport sur les fêtes décadaires* [December 1794]: Chénier (1824–6) v.173.
[97] *Rapport sur l'organisation de l'Institut National de Musique* [July 1795]: Chénier (1824–6) v.285.
[98] Grange (1977).

masterpieces. Citing composers like Méhul (his collaborator on *Timoleon*), painters like David, and his own poetic works, he argued for the convergence of artist and festival. Playwrights had sunk into lethargy under the Terror, but gather them under the umbrella of national protection, he urged, and 'we shall have festivals and monuments worthy of the people; for genius needs liberty and liberty needs genius'.[99] In advocating state patronage of the arts, Chénier failed to address the problem that acknowledged men of genius like Racine and Voltaire had thrived under a despotic regime, their art born of contestation.

Chénier returned to writing for the oppositional medium of the stage when the Directory gave way to the Consulate. His work was censored, and all he could achieve was one performance of a play commissioned by Napoleon himself. Neither Napoleon nor the audience of the Comédie Française appreciated the mix of approval and admonition given to an enlightened despot, and the play closed ignominiously.[100] To salvage his republican credentials Chénier published a long 'Epistle to Voltaire', celebrating the luminaries of the Age of Reason and implicitly placing himself in that line, smoothing over the fracas between Voltaire and Rousseau as a personality clash in order to portray a century of steady progress towards enlightenment. Under Napoleon Voltaire's achievements have been reversed: 'We preserve the right to think in secret / But folly preaches and reason is silent.'[101]

The Platonist dream of a harmonious society, cemented by rhythms of song and dance in festivals that unite all its members into one body, was never to be realized. However fully Robespierre might live up to his nickname of 'the incorruptible', authoritarian rule by the guardian-philosopher-legislator could never find acceptance in a world of flawed mortals. Chénier sensed, though he lacked a theoretical language in which to articulate the point, that theatre had its place in building a messier and less purist form of citizenship, where the experience of self as part of a collective was conjoined with the experience of self as autonomous moral agent. It was not easy for him to let go of the utopian theory which construed the dramatist as teacher, vested with the authority of a republican legislator, for like Milton he had an interest in casting himself as the embodiment of genius and probity. Nevertheless, the Revolution taught him a certain modesty, for it was all too clear that the eighteenth-century theatre auditorium did not lend itself to the passive reception of

---

[99] *Rapport sur le réveil des sciences* [September 1794]: Chénier (1824–6) V.151–8.
[100] *Cyrus* was performed on 8 December 1804: see Lieby (1901) 215, Bingham (1963).
[101] Chénier (1824–6) III.85–102.

teaching. As in Cicero's Rome and Machiavelli's Florence, the theatre was a public space where political power was negotiated in time present.

DIDEROT AND BOURGEOIS REALISM

From the perspective of the present century, with its segmented audiences resistant to any form of expressivity, it is not easy to engage imaginatively with the public emotions exhibited in the eighteenth-century theatre. Our theatre is typically a privatized affair, where anonymous spectators come together and witness events from the darkness of the auditorium. In order to understand the transition from the world of the eighteenth-century citizen to the world of the private individual, I shall reverse chronology and step back a generation to Diderot, who seems to me the fundamental prophet of twentieth-century modernity, conceiving a route for theatre quite unlike those of Voltaire and Rousseau. Diderot did not foresee the Revolution, and posited his vision of the future upon the bourgeois who is preoccupied with private living, not the citizen preoccupied with public living.

Diderot remarks in his essay *On Dramatic Poetry* (1758) that different peoples excel in different genres, and 'tragedy seems to me more of the republican genius, while comedy, with its gaiety, has more of a monarchical character'. Whereas comedy in a hierarchical society like France offers a means of criticizing social superiors, Diderot's concept of republicanism is informed by an Athens whose theatre was once filled with images of men giving ritual expression to grief, or of the female who bares a breast to her son, scours her face, foams in prophecy or runs with maenads. Here lay a true theatrical poetry, he claimed, quite unplayable in the modern civilized world, where even the off-stage cries of a woman in childbirth demanded by Terence would be howled down by the pit as a breach of decorum.[102] Whilst Diderot is plainly attracted by this world of primal emotion, a return to the birth of civilization is not something he conceives or wants. His feeling for primitive antiquity echoes personal feelings about his long-haired and romantic youth, when he frequented Parisian theatres that were not yet controlled by armed guards.

Fifteen years ago our theatres were tumultuous places. The coolest heads grew hot as they entered, and men of sense were fairly carried away like madmen . . . You were stirred up, heaved and shoved, your soul was beside itself. And I know of no mood more favourable to the poet. The play was hard to get started, often interrupted, but what a fine place thereafter! The din was unbelievable, endless encores were demanded, all were infatuated by the actor and actress. Delirium

---

[102] Diderot (1936) 183–8. On the sentiment of loss, cf. Starobinski (1991) 45.

passed from pit to amphitheatre, and from the amphitheatre to the boxes. You arrived glowing, you left intoxicated, some visiting whores, others filtering into society. It was like a distant storm dispersing, its rumbles audible long after it had cleared away. That was pleasure! Today you arrive cold, listen cold, leave cold, and head I know not where.[103]

Diderot's description is at once nostalgic and ironic for this is not a theatre that anyone progressive would want to resurrect, and he argues instead for bigger theatres with better acoustics where a different actor-audience relationship may be possible.

In dialogues of the same year published to frame his play *The Natural Son*, Diderot hankers after a communitarian ancient world that sounds more Roman than Greek. This was a world of public spectacles, where the audience might number 80,000, and the sight of an eminent member of the Republic weeping had a huge effect on the crowd of fellow spectators. The contrast between then and now seems to him extreme: 'What difference between the amusement, on such and such a day at such and at such an hour in a small dark place, of a few hundred people, and securing the attention of a whole nation on its festive days!'[104] Though Diderot salutes the ancient ideal, he sees it as irrecoverable, and the classical apparatus of masking and declaimed verse, which were part and parcel of this large-scale public mode, have become a historical anomaly. In *The Natural Son* Diderot formulated by way of a thought experiment a new utopia, an alternative to the classical ideal of the national spectacle. He imagines circumstances that have brought together the component members of a provincial family unit, and hypothesizes an annual commemorative ritual whereby these members play themselves in a drama scripted by one of their number. For the purposes of this exercise in authenticity, only one role is played by an actor, that of the patriarch who has recently died, and there is only one spectator, Diderot himself, hiding in a corner but by his presence validating the event as a piece of theatre. Diderot goes on to analyse the minimum changes needed in order to transpose this play to the professional theatre, while retaining passages of silent action, broken speech rhythms, backs turned to the audience and other forms of verisimilitude.

The crucial hypothesis is that of the solitary spectator, the individual who has cast off his citizenship to function as a mere human being, watching a play that is not about social bonds but family bonds, which are conceived to be more 'natural'. In an earlier thought experiment, attacking the pretensions of classicism, Diderot tells of an African who, having

---

[103] *Réponse à la lettre de Madame Riccoboni* [1758]: Diderot (1936) 216; cf. p. 219 on Diderot's youth.
[104] *Entretiens sur 'Le Fils Naturel'*: Diderot (1980) 118.

never seen or heard of theatre, learns that he is to spy on a jealous king raging in his seraglio. The African is led into a theatre and through the grill fronting a private box watches a scene that might be Theseus raging in *Phèdre*. Instantly he knows that he is being fooled and that he is witnessing a false expression of feeling.[105] Again the experiment rests on the premise of isolated spectatorship, and it is clear that Diderot found it no easier than his friend Rousseau to participate in the collective emotions of a Parisian audience. 'I am often carried away', he records, 'when others do not think of being moved.'[106] A corollary of the isolated spectator is the isolated actor. When Diderot composes *A Natural Son*, he thinks of the pit as a window in the fourth wall of his study.[107] And in letters to the young actress Marie Madeleine Jodin, he advised: 'If, when you are on stage, you do not think yourself to be alone, all is lost. Mademoiselle, there is no good in the world save what is true; so be true on stage, true off stage.' And again, 'Let the stage have no front or back for you, but keep it scrupulously as a place where and from where no-one sees you. You must have the courage sometimes to turn your back to the spectator, and never must you think of him. Any actress who addresses him deserves to hear a voice rising from the pit and telling her: "Mademoiselle, I'm not there!"'[108]

It is no coincidence that this actress, taught to be true to herself and instructed in the moral integrity of the performer, became the author of a feminist manifesto at the start of the Revolution. She sought to establish a tribunal of female citizens that would be charged with supervising women's affairs, notably divorce, prostitution and the conduct of actresses. Diderot had taught her that the actress needs to resemble the true lover not the courtesan, and it followed that an actress, as the most prominent woman in the public sphere, had to differentiate herself from the prostitute.[109] The Revolution did nothing for women's rights and Olympe de Gouges, who in the wake of the libertarian revolution attempted to achieve parity for the citizeness as playwright, famously fell to the guillotine.[110]

In his later *Paradox upon the Actor*, Diderot was more sympathetic to the public theatre, happy that aristocrats had by now been driven from

[105] *Les bijoux indiscrets* [1748]: Diderot (1936) 225–6.
[106] *Réponse à la lettre de Madame Riccoboni*: Diderot (1936) 221. On the solitary spectator, see Roach (1985) 118–19 and Frantz (1998) 253.
[107] *Réponse à la lettre de Madame Riccoboni*: Diderot (1936) 215.
[108] Letters of 1765–7: Diderot (1936) 245–6.
[109] See Gordon and Furbank (2001) 65, 180–1, 188. Pp. 176–204 provide a translation of *Vues législatives pour les femmes* [1790].
[110] On De Gouges, see Landes (1988), Ozouf (1988) 101, Brown (2002) esp. 339ff. On the citizeness, see Sewell (1988).

their stools on stage to allow the development of pictorial staging, and he analysed the essential difference between performing on the stage of the Comédie Française and performing in a salon or small private theatre.[111] He rejects the Rousseauesque cult of lachrymose sensibility in favour of sense, and argues that the actor must never surrender to uncontrolled emotion. Rather than let citizen spectators descend to the moral condition of actors, he wants rational actors to be recognized as citizens, and hopes that civic respect will attract more principled persons into the profession.[112] Diderot's pictorial aesthetic is ultimately a political ethic, as is clear in his account of a chaotic street accident, an everyday scene that would appear to offer rich material to the artist.

In a performance, as in a well-ordered society, each sacrifices his rights for the good of the ensemble and of the whole. Who will appreciate best the measure of this sacrifice? Someone inspired? The fanatic? Indeed not. In society it will be the just man, on stage it will be the actor who keeps a cool head. Your street scene is to a dramatic scene as a horde of savages is to a civilized assembly.[113]

Cool-headed actors can be arranged in artistic tableaus on the pictorial stage, in what Brecht would later term the epic style, but missing from Diderot's reflections is any verdict on the proper sources of authority. Who is entitled to order society? And who orders actors into artistic groupings?[114]

As a theorist of citizenship in the *Encyclopaedia*, Diderot was essentially concerned with rights, and his running battle against censorship gave him reason to be passionate about tempering royal authority. He concedes to the pessimistic Hobbes that the moral category of the 'citizen' can be reconciled with the physical category of royal 'subject'.[115] Later, when philosopher-in-residence to Catherine the Great, who was a prolific dramatist and a supposedly enlightened despot, an increasingly uneasy Diderot would claim that the only true sovereign is the nation,[116] but he was never able to formulate a satisfactory theory of active citizenship because there was no foundation in his thinking for a communitarian view of the world. His own concept of the 'general will', which inspired Rousseau's bounded communitarian concept, relates to the benevolent mindset of the human

---

[111] On the shift in Diderot's aesthetics, see Roach (1985) 122.
[112] *Paradoxe sur le comédien* [written 1773]: Diderot (1951) 1068–9.
[113] *Paradoxe sur le comédien*: Diderot (1951) 1046. Cf. 'The street scene' in Brecht (1964) 121–8.
[114] In his *Encyclopaedia* article on *autorité politique*, he develops a contractual and relativist account: Diderot (1992) 6–12.
[115] Articles on *citoyen* and *Hobbisme*: Diderot (1992). See further Jaume (1987).
[116] *Observations sur le Nakaz* [written 1774–5]: Diderot (1992) 81.

race as a whole.[117] He rejected ethnic conceptions of nationhood, arguing that the moral characteristics of nations are a function of political systems, and it is universal human nature to love the place you come from.[118] And in the last pages of *On Dramatic Poetry* he describes how every human individual is physiologically and morally unique, moulded by its environment and in flux, so that any conception of the human ideal is but a convention. Given this understanding of the world, the 'citizen', in the thick value-laden sense of the word rather than the thin legal sense, must be seen as a thinking-feeling moral individual, a bearer of human rights, but not as an Aristotelian *zōon politikon*.

Diderot's vision of theatre anticipated late nineteenth-century naturalism, and was compatible both with modernist aesthetic tastes and with the philosophical assumptions of liberal individualism, though he remains a man of the eighteenth century in his moralism and his faith in the ability of audiences to be educated. He identifies but offers no solution to the fundamental problem which Rousseau tackled in his *Letter to d'Alembert*:

> The citizen who turns up at the doorway of the Comédie leaves his vices there, to collect them only as he leaves. Now he is just, impartial, a good father, good friend, friend to virtue – and I have often seen beside me wicked men become highly indignant at deeds they would unfailingly have perpetrated, if placed in the same circumstances as those in which the poet put the character whom they find abhorrent.[119]

It remains an article of faith that spectators learn, but it is unclear how Diderot's atomized spectator transposes lessons learned in the theatre to the world outside.

Diderot's tragicomic *genre sérieux* epitomizes 'bourgeois' theatre through its middle-class subject matter, but more importantly through its assumption that the normative spectator is the autonomous *bourgeois* who lives outside the old aristocratic web of privileges. When we contrast Diderot's bourgeois theatre with Chénier's classicism, it seems paradoxical that Diderot should demand restraint in the actor, Chénier an emotional surrender to nature. While Diderot idealized Clairon, famed for the classical control of her craft when performing Voltaire, Talma condemned Diderot as a cold spectator of human nature with no passion in his heart and championed Clairon's great rival Dumesnil, who was famed for untrammelled emotion.[120] The paradox of sense and sensibility is resolved when

[117] Article on *droit naturel*: Diderot (1992) 19–21.
[118] *Observations sur le Nakaz*: Diderot (1992) 85, 143.   [119] Diderot (1951) 1069.
[120] Diderot (1951) 1037–8, 1051; Talma (2002) 31. See also Paquet (1989), Roach (1985) 109–10, 135 and Howarth (1997) 545–51.

we see how the naturalistic idiom of Diderot requires the actor to take responsibility for intonation, speech rhythm and silent action, so that the actor becomes a surrogate writer shaping dramatic material, whereas the time-honoured form of the alexandrine and the protocols of neoclassical decorum created a framework within which the actor could give expression to an uninhibited sensibility. When Chénier was called to draw up a list of 300 aged artists and savants deserving of a state pension, *Citoyenne* Dumesnil was the only woman deemed to merit a pension by virtue of her achievements, and it is symptomatic of revolutionary attitudes to gender that the woman of pure sensibility should be seen as the quintessential female public servant.[121] As on stage, so in the auditorium, the dramatic idiom of Diderot demanded the respectful and disciplined attention of an audience which pretended it did not exist, while the closed formal rules of neoclassicism made it easy for the pit to break in and behave spontaneously, knowing the dramatic structure was secure enough to survive interruption.

The neoclassical genre is hard to appreciate today because we lack any equivalent to the public sphere presupposed by the form. The reference point is a classical utopia which lost its resonance when the ancient world ceased to be the focus of education. And there is, moreover, a cultural issue for the Anglophone world, since French neoclassical drama has never translated easily or found a regular place on the English-speaking stage. Inspired by seeing *Julius Caesar* in London, Voltaire typifies a French cultural viewpoint when he laments that play's barbaric deformities: 'The one surprising thing is that there are not more of them, in a work composed in a century of ignorance by a man who did not even know Latin and had no teacher save his genius.'[122] The aesthetic gulf between a mongrel Shakespearean form, slipping easily between genres, registers, timeframes and locations, and a disciplined French neoclassical form, replicates the difference between two traditions of citizenship. England since 1688 has been broadly content with a mongrel constitution which combines royal, aristocratic and representative parliamentary powers, and leaves the common population quite unclear whether they are citizens or subjects. In France under the *ancien régime*, absolute royal power permitted the emergence of its antithesis, a planned and centralized republic. As Gary Taylor points out, in the eighteenth century a French belief 'that a society could be rationally

---

[121] *Rapport sur des secours à accorder aux savans et aux artistes* [January 1795]: Chénier (1824–6) v.177–91. Two other women were named by virtue of kinship.
[122] *Discours sur la tragédie* prefatory to *Brutus* [1730]: Voltaire (1877–85) ii.316–17. The young Chénier echoed him: Chénier (1824–6) vi.191–2.

planned, that a blueprint could be intellectually conceived and then imposed upon recalcitrant human materials, was contrasted with the English belief that a society naturally evolved, organically, by gradations and consolidations... This political contrast has, obviously, its aesthetic corollary: French plays were constructed by rule, English drama grew organically.'[123]

The contrast of cultures remains as pertinent as ever. The United Kingdom seems content with the diversity and creative chaos of devolution, multiculturalism and private schooling, while France holds to an assimilative, universal and rigorously secular educational system. The point struck me forcibly when in 2008 I visited the Musée Victor Hugo in Paris. Two teachers were leading through the museum, formerly Hugo's house, their classes of multi-ethnic primary school children, and they expounded their knowledge of Hugo with passion and erudition, fielding questions from children of all colours who clearly were imaginatively engaged. In London it is inconceivable that teachers would think of introducing such classes to a figurehead of English or British culture in this manner, for such an act of assimilation would run counter to British respect for diversity. The second point that struck me in the Musée Victor Hugo, as I observed the induction of children into a cultural tradition, was the complete erasure of Hugo the dramatist by Hugo the novelist, and the only evocations of theatre in the museum concerned adaptations of *Les Misérables*. No knowledge was transmitted of the dramatist whose *Hernani* provoked a riot on the eve of the 1830 'July revolution', which threw out for the second time an absolutist monarchy.[124] Rewriting the rules of the neoclassical genre was still, in the Paris of 1829 as in 1798, a political act. Today the historic functioning of theatre as part of a public sphere with its citizen-actors and citizen-spectators has become so incomprehensible, or so undesired, that its story is no longer told. The timeless suffering of the poor in 'Les Mis' is something with which, as children and as adults, we are encouraged to empathize, but the possibility of alternative cultural-political systems is not on the educational agenda.

---

[123] Taylor (1991) 148–9.   [124] See Juin (1980) 1.583–605, Hovasse (2001) 1.412–38.

CHAPTER 7

The people, the folk and the modern public sphere

COLLECTIVISM IN PRE-WAR GERMANY

The French revolutionaries found no way of reconciling citizenship as a set of rights or negative freedoms with citizenship as a road to equality. The 1789 *Declaration of the Rights of Man and of the Citizen* never successfully elided the two terms 'Man' and 'Citizen', leaving human rights, supposedly rooted in nature, at odds with civic rights rooted in human artifice. When Robespierre turned from the negative ideals enshrined in the 1789 *Declaration* to the utopian dreams of the hungry proletariat of Paris, he relied increasingly on the emotive call of 'nation' to create communal fellow-feeling. 'France' as an entity barely featured in the 1789 *Declaration*, but the *patrie*, the fatherland, was invoked more and more to support the Terror.[1] In the famous words of the *Marseillaise*, a call to children of the fatherland – '*Allons enfants de la patrie*' – moves rapidly to the militaristic cry: '*Aux armes, citoyens!*' The armies of Napoleon were perhaps an inevitable outcome of the republican project, citizen solidarity realizing itself in the will to assail the outsider. The Athenian invasion of Sicily, Rome's conquest of Italy, Florence's siege of Pisa and Cromwell's oppression of Ireland are analogous outcomes of the project to build the internal unity of a republic.

Following the collapse of the French Revolution, and the eclipse of the republican figure called the 'Citizen', the human impulse to bond and transcend individuation took two major forms in Europe: communism and nationalism. The USA meanwhile performed its own painful journey from federation to union, and the eighteenth-century ideal of citizenship was pushed to one side by the intractable problem of race. Jürgen Habermas maintains that: 'The nation state and democracy are twins born of the French Revolution. From a cultural point of view both have been growing

---

[1] Hunt (2007) 16, Hampson (1988) 133.

under the shadow of *nationalism.*' And he emphasizes the crucial distinction that, since it implies membership of a state rather than a nation, citizenship 'was never conceptually tied to national identity'.[2] Rogers Brubaker likewise declares that: 'Modern national citizenship was an invention of the French revolution',[3] and he goes on to analyse the difference between a French nationalism defined by the idea of the *patrie* as a place and a Germanic nationalism defined by the idea of the *Volk* (the people, the 'folk') as a temporal category.[4] France had a long history of cultural and political centralization, and the revolutionaries pushed forward the Enlightenment ideal of linguistic homogenization, so the terms 'nation' and 'state' seemed more or less synonymous, while in Germany and Austria, with no such tradition of the monarchical nation-state, ethnicity and culture were far more important in creating a sense of the budding nation. Rousseau's *Observations on the Government of Poland* was a prophetic work, mapping out a cultural policy designed to build the sense of nationhood in an aspirational nation-state.[5] Whilst the rights of the citizen as member of a nation-state remained on the nineteenth-century agenda, the rights of man, celebrated by Jefferson as 'self-evident', were less easy to reconcile with the drive towards nationhood.

Nationalism can be interpreted as the glue holding society together in an industrial age when religious, craft and agrarian solidarities had all weakened, and the monarch was no longer the pinnacle of a god-given hierarchy.[6] Industrialization, however, threw up another basis of solidarity in the form of class, a solidarity which found its creed in the writings of Marx. Marx reflected back on the paradox of the French Revolution in his early essay *On the Jewish Question*, where the tension between religion and citizenship prompted broader reflections. He commented on the extraordinary phenomenon of the French *Declaration of the Rights of Man and of the Citizen*. Here was a nation which sought to 'tear down all the barriers between different sections of the people and to establish a political community', yet it formulated the rights of man as 'the rights of the egoistic

---

[2] Habermas (1994) 342, 344.   [3] Brubaker (1992) 35.

[4] Brubaker (1992) is fundamental on the distinction between an assimilative French *jus soli*, and a Germanic *jus sanguinis* tied to the idea of a *Volksgemeinschaft*. Anderson (1991) is a classic study of nationalism first published in 1983; cf. Hobsbawm on the distinction between old and invented national traditions in Hobsbawm and Ranger (1983) 10–14. Smith (1999) considers the limits of Anderson's social constructionism. Miller (2000) offers a philosophical defence of national citizenship as an ideal.

[5] Bell (2001) analyses the cultic forms taken by European nationalism. On Rousseau, see p. 142 above.

[6] Cf. Smith (1999) 100 and Bell (2001) 7.

man, separated from his fellow men and from the community'. For Marx, the crucial right of egoistic man, beyond practising his chosen religion, was to dispose of his private property.

The matter becomes still more incomprehensible when we observe that the political liberators reduce citizenship, the *political community*, to a mere *means* for preserving these so-called rights of man; and consequently, that the citizen is declared to be the servant of egoistic 'man', that the sphere in which man functions as a species-being is degraded to a level below the sphere where he functions as a partial being, and finally that it is man as a bourgeois and not man as a citizen who is considered the *true* and *authentic* man.[7]

To be sure, Marx adds, the practice of the French revolutionaries flatly contradicted the *Declaration*. The man/citizen dichotomy remained unresolved, with 'man in his sensuous, individual and *immediate* existence' inhabiting the non-political domain of civil society never reconciled with the artificial, moral and abstract person of the citizen formed in relation to the idea of the state. Marx's resolution to the problem lay in his quasi-biological conception that the human being finds wholeness as a 'species-being'. 'Human emancipation will only be complete when the real, individual man has absorbed into himself the abstract citizen; when as an individual man, in his everyday life, in his work, and in his relationships, he has become a *species-being*.'[8]

Marxism and nationalism were parallel reactions to the conundrum of the French Revolution. I shall examine in the first part of this chapter the case of Germany in the earlier twentieth century, where both strands converged as part of a widespread desire for some kind of species-being that would transcend bourgeois individualism. Arguments from biology, which once allowed thinkers of the Enlightenment to assume the superiority of men over women within a framework of 'natural' human rights, now legitimated assumptions about the superiority of one ethnically defined 'nation' over another. In an official commentary on the anti-semitic Reich citizenship law passed at the Nuremberg rally of 1935, Wilhelm Stuckart and his aide Hans Globke contrasted German with 'Romance' thought, alluding to the traditions of the French Enlightenment that lay behind the Weimar constitution. Romance thought had made the 'abstract personality' of the state central, its primary element being 'the free and independent individual'. In France, they complained,

---

[7] Marx (1963) 26.   [8] Marx (1963) 31.

with painstaking concern for the individual and his rights, the content of citizen-ship was discussed and precisely determined. Obviously, this concern referred essentially to the rights of the citizen, to his influence on the state and his independence from that state... There was no *völkisch* condition for citizen-ship. The question of the *völkisch* relationship of the individual citizen was never raised... The repudiation of the abstract state personality... does not prevent the Reich – as the political-*völkisch* organization of the *Volk* – from being the vehicle of rights and duties... Reich citizenship [*Reichsbürgerschaft*], the totality of all Reich citizens, is the *Volk* in its political configuration.[9]

The authors in this passage are concerned to distinguish *Staatsangehörigkeit* (membership of the state) from *Reichsbürgerrecht* (political rights within the Third Reich), and both terms are collapsed by the inadequate English translation 'citizenship'. Only those who combine German or kindred blood with the will to serve can aspire to the second category, implicitly distinct from the abstract and un-*völkisch* citizenship that characterized the Weimar republic.

Stuckart and Globke quote Hitler to the effect that 'the nation is to the state as content is to form'.[10] National Socialism and communism shared the same critique of the French Enlightenment and its tradition of citizenship, but where National Socialism gave primacy to the ideal of 'nation', communism was content with the abstraction of the 'state'. Nationalism and communism alike subordinate an ideal of the 'citizen' to an ideal of the 'people'. In its Latinate forms, we can trace the term 'people' (*popolo, peuple*, etc.) back to the *populus Romanus*, a term which in Rome did not connote ethnicity, and in a crucial semantic ambiguity may or may not allude to a lower-class majority.[11] The Germanic equivalent *Volk* (related to the English 'folk') has connotations of culture and ethnicity, and before the Fascist era it was always a positive term in opposition to the Latinate *Pöbel* which implies a rabble. The word remains contested. East Germans in 1989 transformed the slogan 'We are the *Volk*!', i.e. the masses oppressed by Soviet domination, into 'We are one *Volk*!', i.e. a single cultural/ethnic people that should be reunited politically.[12] Twentieth-century ideals of a 'popular' theatre have been ensnared by these semantic uncertainties, and Germany offers a crucial case study.

A feature of the nineteenth-century German quest for national unifica-tion was a Rousseauesque use of the festival to harness a 'general will'. The French revolutionary festival in honour of Voltaire inspired the 1851 festival

---

[9] Stuckart and Globke (1936) 19–25; translation in Mosse (2003) 327–31, slightly modified.
[10] Citation from *Mein Kampf*: Mosse (2003) 329.   [11] Cf. Millar (1998) 211.
[12] I am grateful to Margret Convery for this observation.

in honour of Schiller's centenary, which commandeered Germany's greatest dramatist to define a cultural conception of nationhood. Choirs, gymnastic groups and gun clubs were forms of choral behaviour that expressed a desire to transcend ego and become part of a supra-individual *völkisch* entity.[13] Nietzsche's essay on *The Birth of Tragedy out of the Spirit of Music* (1871) owed much to this festive culture, and lent philosophical support to the idea that a collective, embodied and intuitive chorus is more authentic, progressive and life-enhancing than the rational, language-bound and individuated actor. In the early twentieth century, theatre-makers of both left and right found inspiration in Nietzsche to support their hostility to bourgeois individualism.[14]

One of the most important cultural movements of the period was the Volksbühne ('People's stage'), which by 1930 had acquired half a million members nationwide.[15] Through either individual or group subscription, these members had the right to attend a certain number of performances, with lotteries ensuring a fair distribution of tickets. The movement was set up in 1890 under Social-democrat auspices to bring theatre to the workers, and it came to a point of crisis in 1927 with the 'Piscator affair'. The overtly communist productions of Erwin Piscator brought him into collision with those who believed variously in political neutrality or political pluralism, in high art or in entertainment. A journalist in the wake of Piscator's resignation maintained: 'The Volksbühne has not the tradition, intention or possibility of equating the word *Volk* in its name with "radical-socialist working-class"', for 'the membership of the Volksbühne in Berlin does not consist exclusively of proletarians'.[16] When Piscator left to found his own theatre, the competing arguments were set out at a conference in Magdeburg. The liberal Julius Bab distinguished the externality of politics from an inner world that is closer to the source of life and is the proper sphere of art. Kurt Baake took a middle position, distinguishing a *Zeitdrama* – drama that is not eternal but of the moment in its concerns – from *Zeitungstheater* – newspaper-theatre Piscator-style.[17] On behalf of Piscator, the playwright Ernst Toller argued that the *Volk* did not yet exist, but would only do so when class division had ended. Moreover, 'Theatre cannot create community: community is the precondition of theatre.' It followed that the artist needed to build upon the tentative forms of community already established by the socialist movement, and to follow the *Zeitgeist* like all

[13] Mosse (1975) 73–4, 87–9.
[14] See Aschheim (1992), esp. 168ff. for Nietzsche's influence on left-wing politics.
[15] Davies (2000) 181. [16] Georg Springer, cited in Davies (2000) 116. [17] Davies (2000) 172.

great artists of the past.[18] At the end of the debate the conference settled
for the broadly Kantian position that the Volksbühne existed in order to
bring together a free sovereign art and a free sovereign *Volk*, so theatre was
not to be used for social engineering. By failing to interrogate the notion
of a free, sovereign *Volk*, the movement eased the path to an eventual Nazi
takeover, when the Volksbühne was absorbed by the 'Deutsche Bühne'.[19]
Reflecting back on the controversy in 1929, Piscator put his case thus:

> When theatre flourished, it was always something deeply bound up with the
> popular community, but today, when the broad masses of the *Volk* have been
> awoken to political life, and justly demand that the form of the state should bear
> the imprint of their ideas, it is the destiny of theatre, unless it is to be a refined
> preserve of the upper echelon, to link itself in good times and bad to the needs,
> demands and sufferings of these masses. Its ultimate end is merely the job of
> bringing to the consciousness of human beings what as yet slumbers more or less
> opaque and confused in their subconscious.[20]

In Piscator's vocabulary, a notion of the *Volksgemeinschaft*, the popular
community,[21] slides into that of the 'masses', defined as a new kind of ego
(*Ich*).[22] Like a Freudian analyst, Piscator does not address the reasoning
mind but with his theatre draws out ideas and feelings that are already
latent. He was influenced by Béla Balázs' ideal of a mass-soul and a theatre
which 'in its Dionysian enthusiasm really achieves a unified consciousness', using techniques which dissolve the actor-audience boundary.[23] On
the one hand Piscator aspired to an educational theatre on the Enlightenment model, but on the other to a Dionysiac theatre of the Nietzschean
kind.[24] Theatre could not create a socialist community, but it could realize
something that was already latent.

    In the field of dance, Rudolf Laban developed the Platonist principle
that the rhythms of dance provide the fundamental tool for building community. 'The two great poles of human life are work and leisure', he wrote
in 1926. 'Work and leisure have their order, they have their rhythm, their
rule, and must be structured by the shape of this rhythm. Human beings
cry out for a rhythmic wave of strength, which from its repressed form

---

[18] Davies (2000) 283, 286.   [19] Davies (2000) 182.   [20] Piscator (1963) 93–4.
[21] Cf. Tönnies' classic sociological distinction between *Gemeinschaft*, a face-to-face community, and
    Gesellschaft, a rationally constituted society: Tönnies (1957) esp. 223–31. On *Volksgemeinschaft*, see
    Pois (1995).
[22] Piscator (1963) 131.
[23] 'Theatre for the People' (1919) cited in Innes (1972) 140; and in Piscator (1963) 96. Innes 145–51
    describes the integrative 'total theatre' planned by Piscator and Gropius. Cf. Shafer (1995) 105 on
    Piscator's performances at the Grosses Schauspielhaus.
[24] For the paradox, cf. Mosse (1975) 179.

in festival and work-life should be newly awoken and revived.'[25] To create such waves of strength he welded large groups of amateur dancers into disciplined 'movement choruses'.[26] His largest venture into community dance took place in Vienna in 1929, in partnership with Max Reinhardt. Here he sought to recreate a sense of the medieval citizen or *Bürger*, finding the work rhythms that belonged to each trade or craft, and he persuaded some 10,000 representatives of these trades and crafts to dance their way in a grand procession around the city, in the process revealing and releasing tensions and identity crises amongst the burghers of Vienna.[27] A month earlier, his more politically minded colleague Martin Gleisner had attempted a similar *Volkfest* ('People's festival') at the conference of the Social Democrats in Magdeburg. Some thousand amateurs again based their dance in the rhythms of the workplace, and sought to create participation by merging themselves with the audience of around 30,000 that had been watching from the other side of a lake. The socialist potential of Laban's work was clarified by Gleisner, though many activists protested that a political movement should not be grounded in such an abnegation of rationality.

Laban insisted that his project of bonding mind to body, person to person, and people to the cosmos, had no connection with politics, but ultimately found himself embroiled in the machinery of Fascism. By 1936 he had become the champion of *Volktanz* (people's dance) under the Nazis, and he was commissioned to produce a dance-drama in a new Greek-style theatre to celebrate the opening of the Berlin Olympics. The programme declared that this *Gemeinschaftstanz* (community dance) was designed 'to give the modern German people a harmonious unity of body, mind and intellect' with participants coming from all social classes.[28] The ceremony was to be replicated across the country, involving some thousand young amateur participants, subsidized by the state under the aegis of the Reich League for Community Dance.[29] Entitled *Of the Thawing Wind and the New Joy*, this dance-drama was framed by a text from Nietzsche. It began with the trauma of the First World War, and a gradual reawakening of the German national community, followed by representations of work which consolidated the new state, and ended with the circling of a sun-wheel, presented as a 'symbol of our ancestors and our *Volksgemeinschaft*' that aimed at 'rapturous unity' with the encircling audience.[30] Rehearsal

[25] Laban (1926) 35.   [26] See Maletic (1987) 8–14.
[27] Laban (1975) 142–51, with contextual information in Preston-Dunlop (1998) 145–8.
[28] Festival brochure in the John Hodgson Archive, University of Leeds (box 18/folder 10/file 2).
[29] Karina and Kant (2003) 119.   [30] Kew (1999) 80–1.

photos in the programme illustrate the transition from war to the sun-wheel, and show how the seating encircled the stage (Plates 7a/b). Hitler and Goebbels were amongst the 20,000 who watched the dress-rehearsal and disliked the performance, which was abruptly cancelled, a first step in Laban's fall from favour. Like Stalin, Hitler could not abide the intellectualism of a modernist aesthetic, and failure to celebrate the Führer's leadership clearly contributed to bringing an abrupt end to Laban's *völkisch* communitarianism.[31]

The huge Olympic theatre used for *Of the Thawing Wind* was originally conceived as a '*Thingplatz*', and a historical '*Thing*-play' written by E. W. Möller was another event staged to herald the Games and present Germany to the world.[32] The *Thingplatz* melded an architectural ideal from democratic Athens with the Germanic concept of the *Thing* or popular political assembly, and aspired to be a space where 'the spectator rises towards a feeling of total communion with the play and full participation'.[33] The *Thing*-play movement drew on the same festive and mystical traditions as Laban, but joined movement to choral speech within a dramatic narrative. The form evolved from a broad range of festive practices that had developed amongst workers' organizations, choral societies and the Catholic *Bühnenvolksbund*, to create outdoor dramas given by massed amateur casts, with the summer solstice a date specially favoured for performance. *Thing*-plays attacked the decadence of Weimar life, praised the work ethic and conjured up a mood of spiritual redemption. The Nazis did not create this movement, but Goebbels sought to harness it, identifying its potential for transforming a class-free *Volk* into a racially configured *Volk*. He related the *Thing*-play to his ideal of creating *Volksgemeinschaft* through 'festivals in which government and people become one unity',[34] and tried to lure Piscator back to Germany to direct such work.[35] Goebbels withdrew support for the movement at the same time as he abandoned Laban's community dance, for its aspiration to realize a General Will was incompatible with celebration of the Führer, the individual possessed of a unique vision and charisma. He experienced the same difficulty as Piscator in finding new scripts written by an author of genius and supportive of a predetermined ideology. To unleash an organic collectivism seemed in the end too risky.

---

[31] Kew (1999) 82, 87. Karina and Kant (2003) 120–1 emphasizes Hitler's taste.
[32] On the space, see Gadberry (1980) 106. On the form, see Eichberg (1977), Niven (2000), Fischer-Lichte (2005) 122–58.
[33] L. Moshammer in *Die Bauweld* [1935]: Fischer-Lichte (2005) 129.
[34] 'Der Sinn unsere grossen Feiern' [1933]: Fischer–Lichte (2005) 131–2.
[35] Fischer-Lichte (2005) 136.

Plate 7a. War.

Plate 7b. The sun-wheel.

Within the Nazi hierarchy, Rosenberg as head of the 'National Socialist Cultural Community' favoured a traditionalist approach, seeking out conventional drama that enshrined the desired ideology, while Hitler himself favoured light entertainment, having little interest in either high art or *völkisch* spiritualism.[36] The *Thing*-play withered, and political rallies took over the task of indoctrination with no claim to artistic roots in indigenous cultural traditions. Theatre was not in the end the chosen tool to create the mentality of the *Reichsbürger*, the citizen of Nazi Germany. The polarities of education and festival allowed of no satisfactory middle point, and the future under Fascism lay in bourgeois rather than collectivist modes of theatrical expression.

THE INDIAN PEOPLE'S THEATRE ASSOCIATION

The ideal of the citizen was in a sense reborn in 1948 when the United Nations *Universal Declaration of Human Rights* was passed, as its preamble declares, in response to 'barbarous acts which have outraged the conscience of mankind'.[37] The UN Declaration was modelled on the French *Declaration of the Rights of Man and of the Citizen* of 1789, and the transformation of 'Man' into 'Human' emphasized that gender equality had become a fundamental premise. The romantic Nietzschean dream of transcending ego to find authenticity in collective experience was dead, and the UN Declaration, like its French predecessor, construed the world as a world of autonomous individuals. National identity was secondary to personal identity, and indeed according to Article 15 individuals should not be denied the right to change their nationality. Under Article 27, human rights extend to 'the right freely to participate in the cultural life of the community' and 'to enjoy the arts', a statement which formally demarcates the sphere of culture and the arts from political life. Amidst the battery of negative liberties to be enjoyed by the individual, a number of positives stand out. The rights to social security, work, education and an 'adequate' standard of living (Articles 22, 23, 25, 26) have redistributive implications, and Article 29 proclaims that 'Everyone has duties to the community in which alone the free and full development of his personality is possible.'[38] Some ideal of localized citizenship flickers in these Articles, but the overall drive of the UN Declaration is to construct a notion of *Weltbürgerschaft*, world

---

[36] See Niven (2000) 88–90; on Rosenberg, see Kamenetsky (1972), Gadberry (1995) 134.
[37] Text in Brownlie and Goodwin-Gill (2002) 18–23. The USSR and seven other states declined to sign.
[38] On theories of freedom, see e.g. Skinner (1991), Skinner (2003).

citizenship, whereby all people are equal, free and individual members of as it were a single global republic.

In the established nations of Europe, nationalism lost much of its affective hold, and the surrender of many aspects of citizenship to the European Union was made possible by the feeling that personal identity and nationhood can be placed in separate boxes. Whilst Europe was deconstructing national boundaries, many other parts of the world were engaged in processes of nation-building, often constructing nation-states on the basis of arbitrary territorial lines drawn by colonial administrators, and in this context the notion of 'citizenship' takes on a very different complexion. The case of India exemplifies the issues, and I shall focus on the particular case study of the Indian People's Theatre Association (IPTA), active between 1942 and the mid 1950s, where the three problematic terms 'India', 'People' and 'Theatre' had to be negotiated against the claims of nationalism and communism. Whilst Indians were formally constituted as citizens by the Constitution of 1947, 'citizenship' as a moral ideal played little part in discourses of the time, for the term was contaminated not by its Frenchness but by its Englishness. Take for example complaints by a colonial judge in 1909 about the way education bred politicization: 'Surveying the educated classes as a whole, I doubt whether any one who really knows them would confidently say that their utility as citizens, or their morality as men, has been increased or heightened by a fraction of a fraction.' For this representative of British authority the 'citizen' was but a *useful* subject of the crown, India had no basis to be a 'nation' and there could be no grounds for Indians claiming equal rights of free citizenship on abstract ethical principles. They could not claim to have been enslaved by the British, who had merely brought law and order to these 'children of inexorable inequality'.[39]

The case of India raises a question of first principle: are democracy and citizenship inherently western concepts? And with that question goes its rider: what of theatre? Are citizenship and theatre not twin parts of a suspect postcolonial legacy derived from classical antiquity? Is the spread of bourgeois representational theatre not in fact simply part of a hegemonic process, fostering the individualism which is a necessary counterpart of modernity and global capitalism? To deal with the first of these questions, let me start with the influential contemporary voice of Amartya Sen, who argues that we misunderstand democracy if we see it as a set of formal

[39] Mr Justice Beaman 'The Situation in India' *Empire Review* (February 1909), cited in Alston (1910) 202, 174, 194. On the political legacy of colonialism, see Kaviraj (2003). Niraja Jayal examined colonial definitions of citizenship in the first of her Radhakrishnan lectures in Oxford in 2009, related to a forthcoming book on the Indian idea of citizenship.

institutional structures. Like Habermas, Sen prefers a 'deliberative' concept, whereby true democratic government rests on widespread formal and informal processes of discussion. In his book *The Argumentative Indian*, Sen explores a tradition of democratic discussion at the local level in India, and describes the tolerant imperial regimes of the Buddhist Ashoka and the Moslem Akbar which once fostered heterodoxy and debate, finding their cultural counterpart in the great ethical debate between Krishna and Arjuna in the *Bhagavad Gita*.[40] It follows from Sen's perspective that, although Greece and Rome have no special status as point of origin, their legacy should not be discarded. Sen sets up his rationalism in opposition both to Hindutva, the communitarian movement which defines India's uniqueness in terms of its Hindu religion, and to the liberalism of John Rawls who fails to account for the continuing negotiations needed to create consensus about what is fair and just.[41] A model of the participatory citizen emerges very clearly from Sen's account.

For Sen in the twenty-first century, the nation-state is a *de facto* reality which has to be accommodated, but at the end of the colonial period the world offered a more open prospect to the three giant figures of that era: Mahatma Gandhi, Rabindranath Tagore and Jawaharlal Nehru. Gandhi had much in common with Rousseau in his taste for spiritualism and the simple peasant life. He conceived of freedom and citizenship in terms of *swaraj* or 'self-rule', arguing that 'swaraj comes only from performance by individuals of their duty as citizens. In it no one thinks of his rights.'[42] The search for an authentic mode of living left no space in Gandhi's philosophy for the mimetic mode of theatre, and there is a ring of Plato in his account of viewing the Indian night sky:

> Both children and grown-ups love dramas and the spectacular scenes which they present. But no drama composed or acted by human beings can even equal the great spectacle which Nature has arranged for us on the stage of the sky. Moreover in a theatre we may harm our eyes, breathe unclean air and also run a great risk of our moral sense being weakened. On the other hand this drama arranged by Nature can do us nothing but good.[43]

A close associate of Gandhi, Tagore was a more cosmopolitan figure, and as a playwright himself he had a very different attitude to theatre. He

---

[40] Sen (2005), esp. 3–33, the title essay. Sen (2009) develops the argument into a systematic political philosophy. Drèze and Sen (2002) presents the fieldwork from which these theoretical views emerge.
[41] Sen (2009).   [42] 'Appeal to people of Rajkot' [1939]: Gandhi (1958–91) LXXV.179.
[43] 'Watching the heavens' [1932]: Gandhi (1958–91) LV.226.

condemned the professional theatre of Calcutta as an example of European materialism, and argued that a play should be served up unadorned just as 'at a banquet we eat off plantain leaves'. Playing Aristotle to Gandhi's Plato, as it were, he argued for a theatre stripped of its visual excrescences and reduced to the poetic text.[44] The argument placed him, in the end, in the same camp as many a European modernist aggrieved by bourgeois society. Tagore was fiercely opposed to the whole European concept of the nation-state, and maintained that: 'In the West the national machinery of commerce and politics turns out neatly compressed bales of humanity which have their use and high market value; but they are bound in iron hoops.'[45] Like Gandhi he preferred to think in terms of civilizations rather than nations, a mode of thinking somewhat discredited in recent years by the neo-conservative thesis of Samuel Huntington.[46] The problem of colonialism for Tagore was not so much rule by the British as government through the principle of the Nation.

Nehru had no option but to accept the principle of the nation-state in order to win freedom from the British, and the consequences of compromise were tragic, with partition from Pakistan entailing bloodshed and decades of political turmoil. European assumptions about the convergence of nation and state could not in the end be reconciled with a land that saw itself as comprising a multiplicity of nations. Prior to the challenge of nation-building, Nehru formulated his thoughts in his great work written in prison, *The Discovery of India*, and attempted to break down a series of important dichotomies. Alongside the religious and racial diversity of India, he portrayed cultural unity. Against the 3,000-year continuity of Indian civilization he set the obvious need to modernize. Comparing a nationalist concern for tradition with communism's contempt for the past, he noted how much Stalin had done to reinstate nationalism. Setting out an approach to the organization of society, Nehru contrasted the excessive individualism of the west with a Hindu conception of the group that resulted in the excesses of caste, and against individual rights he set universalist obligations enshrined in the Hindu concept of *dharma*.[47] Mapping out this model of India, Nehru gave a key place to Sanskrit theatre, emblematic of an ancient cultural unity and allegedly drawing on a shared language. The fundamental unity of India could still be discerned, he argued, in the taste of the illiterate masses for the *Mahabarata*

---

[44] 'The theatre' [1903]: Tagore (2001) 95–9.
[45] 'Nationalism in the west' [1917]: Tagore (1996) 419–35, at 420.
[46] Huntington (1996).   [47] Nehru (1946) 444, 62, 202–3.

and other epic poems.[48] Nehru tried not to essentialize the dichotomy of east and west, and dismissed as bogus the claims of Europe and America to some organic connection with ancient Greek civilization, believing that Greece had more in common with polytheistic India, a land that loved philosophical debate, while Europe and America yearned for Greece as a symbolic oasis in the desert of their modern existence. He positioned Greek tragedy and Sanskrit theatre as historically parallel forms, and if Sanskrit theatre did not ask such searching moral questions, that it is because it belonged to a more stable civilization.[49] Though Nehru did not address the relative merits of a traditionalist and a modernist theatre in a future independent India, his taste was clearly for tradition.

IPTA sprang up in very loose association with the Communist Party at a time when Nehru and other Congress leaders were in prison. The Communists were free to operate because, out of a desire to support the Soviet Union, they supported the war against Fascism, which they saw as a necessary prelude to the ending of British imperialism. Countless theatre artists and intellectuals centred on Bombay (Mumbai) and Calcutta were drawn into the movement, driven on by the same idealism that had sent British intellectuals to fight Franco a few years earlier, and by the war-time closure of mainstream theatres which left many in search of a creative outlet. Members of the Association, subdivided into different squads, took a medley of simply staged musical sketches, agit-prop playlets, plays, dance-dramas and the occasional film to workers and peasants across India. An important spur was the Bengal famine, in which millions died unheeded by the British government during the last three years of the war, and IPTA performances served both to raise funds and to reveal the political roots of the famine. There has been no book-length study of IPTA because of the exceptional historiographic problems posed by the Association.[50] Plays were improvised or based on ephemeral typescripts, and performed in multiple languages often far from centres of cultural authority and transmission. The forms and methods were diverse. There were no newspaper reviews and no subsequent research funds to support oral historians. The subsequent challenge which IPTA presents to the theatre historian is bound up with the historic significance of the movement as an attempt to build citizenship.

---

[48] Nehru (1946) 125–6, 45, 79.   [49] Nehru (1946) 117–28.

[50] The best short studies are Bhatia (2004) 76–94, Chatterjee (2004) 206–44 and Bhattacharya (2009). I have not seen forthcoming work by Bishnupriya Dutt.

Manifestos provide our most substantive source. The annual report for the Bombay conference of 1946, for example, looked back at what had been achieved:

Those who grouped together in our movement were inspired by a deep and abiding faith that our ancient culture cannot be allowed to die, that it must be used to serve and save our people; that art can and should flourish not as a weapon of luxury but as a means of portraying life and reality of our people, of reviving their faith in themselves and in their past, and of rousing them to the will to live and the will to be free . . . In the present situation we aim to make our cultural activities a strong unifying movement among our people – to interpret the thought and feelings of every section of our people to the other, to foster understanding and appreciation of what is just and good.

As an organisation we belong to no party, we belong to the people of our country . . . I.P.T.A. aims at being a truly people's theatre starring the people, an organisation that will cover the whole of India, which will serve as a medium for all local writers and artists.[51]

The key aspirations are all here. First is the ideal of Tagore and Nehru, that cultural continuity must be maintained. The idea that a people can be saved by its culture is foreign to classic Marxist thought, but the success of IPTA lay in its ability to use popular traditional forms in order to reach audiences that had hitherto had no contact with intellectuals or metropolitan theatre professionals. The folk ideal is balanced by realism, and a determination to put the truth of human suffering before superficial concerns of aesthetic form, though of course art can never exist without form and modernist agit-prop experiments like the Russian *Proletkult* did much to shape IPTA's work. Within a broad educational agenda, the emphasis is less upon reason than on shaping the will. In the new post-war situation, with Moslem-Hindu tensions building, the report argues that the focus of the organization must now be upon Indian unity, using theatre to create inter-communal understanding. In contrast to the actor-manager system and the old cult of the individual star, the theatre experience must be a participatory one, and the long-term aim is not to carry art to the people but to galvanize local activity.

The Punjabi playwright Balwant Gargi provides one of the few available eyewitness accounts of an early IPTA production. He describes a packed, evidently middle-class audience in a hall in Lahore (in modern Pakistan). The actors are not professionally trained, but are young communist activists who have come across India by train from Calcutta, centre of the famine.

---

[51] Report by N. M. Joshi, President, and Ahmed Abbas, Secretary: Pradhan (1979) 237–8.

They emerge from the audience and at first it is not clear that they are actors. Without props and against a black backdrop they perform a version of the play *Nabanna* ('New Harvest'), which in short scenes punctuated by songs told of a peasant family who move from the starving countryside to Calcutta in vain hopes of help.

All the suffering of famine and poverty was expressed in their voices and strained faces. Their movements, gestures, expressions and speech had no theatricality; it was as real as the street scenes we experience daily. These faces were familiar to us in the poor quarters of Lahore. In a larger sense they mirrored Indian life, the poverty and suffering under the heel of a foreign power.

Significantly, Gargi does not mention what language was used, but he remarks on how the drive to communicate resulted in artistic forms that seemed new whilst reviving much that had been discarded. The fund-raising performance in middle-class Lahore, he explains, was not the predominant IPTA mode:

The theatre came out of the closed halls to perform under open skies, on street corners, on sandy beaches, on mounds in villages, in city courtyards – anywhere, in fact. The same pulse beat in the players as in the people who came to see them. People and players, the two halves of theatre, kept apart for so long, joined and became one whole.[52]

The aspiration to a restored wholeness recalls the theatrical ideal which we have observed in Germany, but this Indian *Volksgemeinschaft* pictured in Lahore conjoins Punjabis and Bengalis who are separated by language, ethnicity and a huge geographical distance.

Another very successful production was *Zubeida* (1944), written by one of the authors of the 1946 report. The heroine is a young Moslem woman who abandons her purdah in order to help the victims of a cholera epidemic. She herself dies because there is a shortage of vaccine, a tragedy for which the British administration is plainly to blame. As Nandi Bhatia points out, there are two ways of reading this story in terms of gender: on the one hand a woman becomes an activist, but on the other she is confined to the feminized role of nurturer.[53] By the same token, a Moslem becomes the embodiment of Indian heroism, but at the same time a condition of this heroism is shedding a symbol of Islam. The success of the play owed much to the ideological issues which it opened up, and it must have had

[52] Gargi (1962) 188–9. On the play *Nabanna* and Gargi's identification of it, see Bhatia (2004) 82, 86. On the play and its author, see Bharucha (1983) 44–9.
[53] Bhatia (2004) 94.

fundamentally different meanings in different performance contexts, when it was transposed into different languages and modified for different audiences. Debates regularly accompanied performances, and many spectators would have known that the play was based on a real-life story, albeit transposed from southern to northern India. The play staged a *baithak* or gathering of the village elders, and this traditional event provided a paradigm for the performance event.[54]

In the experience of performance, the activism of the semi-fictional Zubeida would have merged with the real activism of the actress, a woman who contrary to social custom ventured with men into remote places, playing female roles which in traditional theatre would have been taken by men. Manikuntala Sen, a communist activist who briefly took on a role in *Nabanna*, comments: 'It is a matter of pride that most of those female artists who had stepped onto the stage for the first time and those who became famous were activists of the women's movement. They themselves had witnessed the tragedy [of the famine], which is probably why they were able to depict it so movingly.'[55] She also notes the enlightened attitude of P. C. Joshi, secretary of the Communist Party, who wanted women to be pioneers in the class struggle.[56] All-female audiences were common, and for many women who were watching a play for the first time Zubeida's emergence from purdah was a metaphor for the act of theatre-going.[57] When Sen took to the stage, she played a decrepit old woman who becomes an activist not from the threat of starvation but from the threat to her honour as a woman,[58] in a scene that reflects how many women had no choice but to change traditional patterns of behaviour. Tension between public and private worlds has characterized western theatre ever since an Aeschylean stage wall separated the private space of the *oikos* from the public space occupied by the chorus,[59] and the imaginary fourth wall of the twentieth-century box set does the same work, separating a fictional domestic interior from the public world of the auditorium. An oral history of Bombay mill-workers comments on the erosion of public and private, when men lived separated from family in crowded sleeping quarters and all personal privacy vanished.[60] Zubeida's transgressive journey into public space echoed the experience of many impoverished spectators for whom privacy now scarcely existed.

---

[54] I rely on the account of the play in Bharucha (1983) 41–2.
[55] Sen (2001) 115. On women in IPTA, cf. Dalmia (2009) 262.   [56] Sen (2001) 95.
[57] Bharucha (1983) 42.   [58] Sen (2001) 115.
[59] Cf. Wiles (1997) 166–7.   [60] Chandavarkar (2009) 136.

Tension between the moral claim of gender equality and the moral claim of respect for minorities has today become all too familiar.[61] The issue of religion is intractable, and brings us back to the dilemma explored by Marx: how can the orthodox Jew also be, in the French republican sense, a 'citizen'? Marx offered the solvent of class identity, but in India where personal and religious identities were so often intertwined, the classic Marxist answer too often seemed inadequate. Manikuntala Sen, for example, describes her own youthful resistance to the idea that in order to be a communist one has also to be an atheist.[62] When Nehru invoked the *Mahabarata* as a symbol of Indian unity, an 'encyclopaedia of tradition and legend',[63] many would have preferred to see the poem in more explicitly religious terms. The Bombay oral history documentation provides glimpses of a rich substructure of dramatic activity, invisible to conventional theatre research, into which IPTA inserted its activities. A maker of clay idols, for example, describes how plays were regularly performed as part of a great religious festival when the statue of Ganesh is immersed in the sea. The folk plays brought to such festivals helped maintain links between mill-workers and their home villages, but membership of these village troupes was a specific function of caste membership, and the Ganesh festival was a product of early twentieth-century Hindu revivalism.[64] When exploiting the emotional resonances of folk theatre, IPTA were obliged to eviscerate the form of its cultural content. For Bharucha, IPTA's idealization of 'folk' culture was symptomatic of urban thinking, and he discerns 'an unspoken assumption that it was the "folk" who performed for the "people", not the other way around'. Although it was beneficial to substitute the positive image of a 'folk' for a negative image of the 'peasant', folk culture became too easily an empty vessel waiting to be filled with political content.[65] Given the religious basis of so much traditional culture, it is hard to see what alternative there was for a movement inspired by communism.

There are three obvious reasons why IPTA disintegrated. Theatre artists, finding it hard to reconcile art with politics, returned to the city and the world they had known before the war. Joshi lost his sway and the Communist Party machine was Stalinized. And the Nehru government

---

[61] For the Indian context, cf. Jayal (2001) 209, Alam (2004) 84.

[62] Sen (2001) 40.   [63] Nehru (1946) 78.

[64] Adarkar and Menon (2004) 115–18; cf. 142 on caste, 138–9 on IPTA. On caste and performance, see also Srampickal (1994) 68–71. N. P. Ashley informed me about the revivalism of Balagangadhara Tilak in 1903.

[65] Bharucha (1990) 198–9. It is also to be noted that IPTA in Bengal, with its large Moslem population, drew rather less upon the folk tradition than the Bombay branch: see Srampickal (1994) 79.

suppressed IPTA's activities.[66] Nehru had been sympathetic to IPTA insofar as it postulated and revitalized a lost Indian dramatic tradition, and one of IPTA's most successful productions was a balletic interpretation of Nehru's *Discovery of India*, but giving a voice to the masses was incompatible with Nehru's project of centralization and nation-building.[67] A seminar of 1957 under the aegis of the Sangeet Natak Akademi, a government-funded academy of the arts in Delhi, proved a crucial moment in the making of a new cultural policy. When scholars and practitioners weighed the competing claims of a resuscitated folk theatre against an all-Indian brand of modernist theatre, it was taken for granted that the impetus for the development of Indian theatre should come from Delhi.[68] Bharucha explains how this debate turned upon a reified concept of the 'folk', and argues that state-sponsored festivals which reduce 'our people' to 'folk material' can be no substitute for the genuine attempts made by IPTA to bridge the gap between urban and rural cultures.[69] Though pre-war German attempts to foster a *Volksgemeinschaft* have something in common with Indian attempts to recover a folk culture in order to manufacture a sense of the national community, we should not simply dismiss out of hand the emotive and memorializing notion of the *Volk* or 'folk' in favour of an abstract republican concept of the citizen. Arguably this abstraction, like the Marxist concept of an overarching class identity, is the product of a specifically western modernity.[70]

Whilst IPTA was merely a hiatus in the history of mainstream urban Indian theatre, it was the significant ancestor of what became known as 'Theatre for Development'.[71] It is worth pondering, therefore, how the notion of culture impacts on the twin apostles of the international Theatre for Development movement, the Brazilian educationalist Paulo Freire and his theatrical interpreter Augusto Boal. Freire developed a powerful dialogic theory of education involving the consciousness-raising of the 'people', and he critiques a neo-colonial process of 'cultural invasion', without offering in his eclectic methodology any definition of quite what he understands by the words 'people' and 'culture'.[72] Boal developed his ideal

---

[66] Cf. Bhatia (2004) 90–2, Dalmia (2006) 167–8, Bhattacharya (2009) 173–4. Thapar (1991) 66 provides a glimpse of Stalinization in action.

[67] Bhattacharya (2009) 175–8. On the context of nation-building, see Sheth (2005).

[68] Bharucha (1990) 197, Dalmia (2006) 169ff., Mee (2008) 179–87, Dharwadker (2009) 61–4.

[69] Bharucha (1990) 23; cf. 192–210, an essay entitled 'Notes on the invention of tradition'. The argument is developed in Chatterjee (2004) esp. 231–3, and Dalmia (2006) esp. 154–8, 211.

[70] On competing modernities, see e.g. Taylor (1999), Eisenstadt (2000).

[71] On the legacy of IPTA, see Bharucha (1983) 54, Mee (2008) 89, Yarrow (2001) 176–82. From a very different perspective, Dharwadker (2005) 36 conceives IPTA as an 'interregnum'.

[72] Freire [1970] (2003) esp. 152–4, 160–1.

of the participant spectator in relation to a classical model of theatre, a point underlined in the second edition of *Theatre of the Oppressed* where he develops a foundation myth for theatre around the figure of Thespis the Athenian rebel. He is happy to cite Machiavelli's *Mandragola* as an instance of popular theatre telling the truth about bourgeois hypocrisy, and he consistently uses the language of enlightenment, appealing to the spectator's reason in order to create a capacity for action, while his term 'Forum Theatre' evokes ancient Rome.[73] Transferred from monoglot urban Brazil to the Indian countryside, Boal's classical rationalism becomes problematic. Jacob Srampickal, for example, describes how street-theatre groups and 'Social Action Groups' which draw upon the ideas of Freire and Boal repeatedly find that they cannot discard the notion of the 'folk',[74] and he cites the rationale of one director for integrating social education with the annual *yatra* festival: 'The traditional concept of *yatra*, the feelings and emotions it evokes have deep roots in the psyche of the masses . . . Even the social consciousness assumes the form of religio-cultural representations.'[75] Srampickal endorses the IPTA argument that although the themes of folk theatre may be retrograde, adoption of such forms is inherently radical because they foster local community identity, all the more important in an age of mediatization.[76] We are pushed back in this debate to unresolved questions about human identity.

The Indian Constitution of 1947 provides a useful lens through which to consider Indian citizenship. The preamble to the Constitution salutes the values of the French Enlightenment, declaring that the people of India have resolved to create a republic which will secure justice, liberty and equality for its citizens and will promote fraternity. The promotion of fraternity and equality means in practice that certain freedoms have to be qualified, and so, for example, no citizen according to Article 15 may suffer discrimination, but the state reserves the right to discriminate 'for the advancement of any socially and educationally backward classes of citizens or for the Scheduled Castes and the Scheduled Tribes'. According to Articles 29–30, any 'section of the citizens residing in the territory of India or any part thereof having a distinct language, script or culture of its own shall have the right to conserve the same', and this right includes administering an education system. Such provisions construe Indian citizens not simply as atomized individuals but

---

[73] Boal (2000). The book was first published in Argentina in 1973. On Boal and 'Theatre for Development', see Prentki (1998), Amkpa (2006). Boal (1998) extends the notion of Forum Theatre in order to conceive the citizen as a surrogate legislator.
[74] Srampickal (1994) 54–98, 182–6.   [75] Ajit Murickan cited in Srampickal (1994) 183.
[76] Srampickal (1994) 235.

also as members of distinct communities.[77] When Indira Gandhi like a latterday Robespierre suspended the negative freedoms enshrined in the Constitution under a much-resented 'State of Emergency', she sought justification by adding a set of fundamental positive duties. Every citizen, for example, was now expected 'to value and preserve the rich heritage of our composite culture'.[78] The 'Emergency' was short-lived, but the inherent contradictions within a rights-based conception of citizenship did not vanish as quickly.

Around the start of the 1990s, as elsewhere in the world, 'citizenship' emerged in India as a progressive aspiration because of the way it mingled a notion of rights with a notion of moral duty, and suggested an ideal of community that was not contaminated by religion or ethnicity, while inviting local as much as national modes of public engagement.[79] The masculinist associations of citizenship in the earlier republican tradition vanished once the citizen was no longer equated with the warrior, and women as a category were plainly greater beneficiaries of a rights-based discourse than the poor as a category.[80] I will cite two examples that come to hand. In a 1991 programme note to a classic play by Tagore about nationhood and modernity, the director summed up the problematic raised by her feminist production: 'how we construct the meaning of the word citizen in today's India is a vexed question'.[81] And in Rohinton Mistry's 2002 novel *Family Matters*, a young teacher in Bombay looks to the future: '"If you are good citizens of my classroom," said Miss Alvarez, "you will be good citizens of India." She believed this was the way to fight the backwardness and rot and corruption in the country: classroom by classroom.'[82] In the event her style of classroom management merely breeds more corruption, but her intentions seem admirable in the Bombay that Mistry describes, torn by religious tensions yet enriched by religious traditions.

The IPTA project was triangulated upon three once convergent ideals: modernism linked to the ideal of artistic free expression, rationalism linked to the goal of education and traditionalism with its celebration of the folk. We might think of modern citizenship as triangulated

---

[77] See Jayal (2001) 205–6, Alam (2004) 77ff., Xaxa (2008) 42–7. Jayal's forthcoming study will analyse 'group-differentiated citizenship' in India.

[78] *Article* 51A (f) added in 1976. See Kashyap (1997) 257–8, Oommen (2004) 351. Kashyap's commentary on the constitution was published under the auspices of the Citizenship Development Society.

[79] Cf. Frevert (2005) 59.

[80] There are no ambiguities about gender equality in the national constitution. At the local Panchayat level a quota of seats is reserved for women: Jayal (2001) 31.

[81] Anuradha Kapur cited in Dalmia (2009) 276. Cf. Kapur's contribution to the same volume.

[82] Mistry (2002) 210.

in a similar fashion: on the libertarian ideal of the individual vested with rights, on the moral ideal of duty to others and on the communitarian ideal whereby citizenship is a mode of belonging. A prerequisite of both theatre and citizenship is the existence of a public sphere where people come together and make contact with each other. The nature and presence of the public sphere seemed self-evident in the salons, coffee-houses and theatres of eighteenth-century Paris where all of 'society' converged, but in India Delhi seems an imposed rather than a natural centre, and the urban intelligentsia form all too obviously an elite within a vast country that ascribes formal democratic rights to all. Whether the proper denizens of the Indian public sphere are individuals or communities is a burning issue, since it is only by functioning within groups that individuals can achieve meaningful forms of social citizenship commensurate with their civic rights.[83] Threading the country on its network of railways, the activists of IPTA, despite whatever limitations of hasty art and doctrinaire politics, did more than anyone since to create an inclusive public sphere where the masses, both as individuals and as communities, had a voice as well as a vote.

IN SEARCH OF THE PUBLIC SPHERE

It is in the public sphere that theatre and citizenship converge. In the age of 'spin' and of 'Fox News', public opinion seems ever more open to manipulation, so it becomes increasingly irrelevant to talk of democracy in the absence of a functional 'public sphere'. Theatre, as I have shown in this book, was for centuries a place of public encounter where opinion was shaped and relations of power were negotiated. Today we must ask ourselves whether that space of interaction has devolved to the internet, or whether the face-to-face encounter of theatre is indeed still of relevance in the making of an active citizenship. Since it lies outside my brief as a historian to look into the future, I shall confine myself to conceptualizing the public sphere, and examining theatre's place within it in the post-war period.

The reference point for all discussions of the public sphere is Jürgen Habermas' *Structural Transformation of the Public Sphere: An Inquiry into a Category of Bourgeois Society*, published in German in 1962, and translated into English in 1989, around the time when 'citizenship' regained its place in political discourse. The English phrase 'public sphere' spatializes the

---

[83] See Alam (2005) 357.

more abstract German *Öffentlichkeit*, which implies the act of opening up.[84] Habermas describes a *bürgerlich Gesellschaft*, a phrase which implies both the phenomenon of 'civil society' and a particular bourgeois epoch.[85] Habermas' account of the 'bourgeois public sphere' rests on a Marxist historiography which pertains to theatre even though theatre is not his major concern, and I shall sketch out the bones of that historical narrative.

Antiquity, when citizens were free to participate directly in political life thanks to slavery, was replaced by a medieval world characterized by the need for public representations of status.[86] Habermas mentions street theatre in this connection,[87] and we saw in Chapter 4 how the Coventry Weavers' pageant was just such a means of winning status within a milieu that left no room for a separate sphere of private life. A retreat into royal absolutism characterized by court theatre was followed by the French Enlightenment, and Habermas describes how the frustrated hero of Goethe's novel goes on stage to play Hamlet because he felt that, as a bourgeois in an aristocratic world, he had no other means of achieving public visibility. However, 'Wilhelm Meister's theatrical mission had to fail. It was out of step, as it were, with the bourgeois public sphere whose platform the theatre had meanwhile become. Beaumarchais' Figaro had already entered the stage and along with him, according to Napoleon, the revolution.'[88] The theatre for Habermas was one component of an eighteenth-century world of letters that facilitated free public discussion, and it gained a true *Publikum* when the cultured bourgeoisie took control of the pit. He dismisses earlier forms of theatre like the Elizabethan Globe as spaces of representation where the aristocracy paraded and the people had to applaud them.[89] In fourth-wall domestic drama, which demanded the same empathetic responses as the novel,[90] privatized experiences furnished material for public debate, yielding a sense of what it was to be universally human. The flaw in this bourgeois public sphere lay in the simple equation: *homme* = *citoyen* = owner of property.[91] The notion of human rights was bound up with the right to property, and people without property were excluded from the public sphere. Despite this major reservation, Habermas has no truck with Rousseau's revolutionary counter-argument, that the creation of a public space permits the emergence of a collective public

---

[84] Cf. Warner (2002) 47.
[85] Habermas 1989. Habermas (1992) explains in response to criticism that he did not want the bourgeois *Öffentlichkeit* to be seen as the only operative public sphere.
[86] Habermas (1989) 3–10.   [87] Habermas (1989) 10.   [88] Habermas (1989) 14.
[89] Habermas (1989) 38–9. Pincus (2007) critiques Habermas' periodization in relation to English theatre.
[90] Habermas (1989) 43, 50.   [91] Habermas (1989) 55–6, 87.

voice. As Habermas later put it, in preference to Rousseau's consensus of hearts he wanted a consensus of arguments, for it is the public exercise of reason and debate that generate valid forms of public opinion.[92]

Habermas concludes with a story of decline, the private sphere being reduced to the 'intimate sphere' of the nuclear family, and the public sphere transformed into a world of leisure, in a conception of the present (effectively, the 1950s) that was heavily influenced by Adorno and the Frankfurt School. Culture has become a product to be consumed, and the practice of public reasoning has been delegated to professionals like theatre critics or television hosts, while a group of intellectuals has split off from the educated bourgeoisie, and the avant-garde has been institutionalized. The split between mass media and connoisseurs of modernist art left no space for a novel like Richardson's *Pamela* to be debated by an entire reading public,[93] and Habermas might have added, to underline his point about a universal culture, that a Franco-Italian stage adaptation of this English novel became a cause célèbre during the French Revolution.[94] Habermas laments the loss of what is now most needed, 'literary and critical debate' and 'the communicative interconnectedness of a *public*'.[95] In his later work, as he moves away from Marxism to become the apostle of modern social-democratic liberalism, Habermas becomes more optimistic about the present, seeing the eighteenth century less as an ideal than as the beginnings of an unfinished modernist project.[96] He propounds a theory of 'communicative action', involving the development of mutually acceptable validity claims, as the basis for a republican society whose citizens are patriots but not nationalists,[97] and his continuing attention to rational discourse very obviously marks a profound reaction to the irrationalism of mass movements in pre-war Germany.

From the Habermasian point of view, modern theatre should in principle be a place where citizens engage in communicative action, positioned not at the fringe or creases of society,[98] but in the centre of a public sphere. Arguing that 'by the mid 1990s the public square was nearly barren of healthy discourse', the playwright and performer Anne Deavere Smith set up an Institute on the Arts and Civic Dialogue based at Harvard University, seeking to overcome the localism of community arts.[99] The project was entirely in the spirit of Habermas, but the idea of building a bridge between an elite east-coast university and the entire US body politic was utopian. In

---

[92] Habermas (1989) 98–9, Habermas (1992) 445.   [93] Habermas (1989) 174–5.
[94] See Carlson (1966) 159–60.   [95] Habermas (1989) 163, 249.   [96] Habermas (1996).
[97] Finlayson (2005) 40–1.   [98] On crease phenomena, see Schechner (1988) 164.
[99] Citation from Institute's website. See further Cohen-Cruz (2001) 104–5.

the UK, David Hare seems a more pragmatic exponent of the same ideal. He has to date written some fourteen plays for the National Theatre addressing the state of the nation, but at the same time, often in collaboration with Max Stafford-Clark, he has been at pains to extend the public sphere by reaching out to non-standard audiences. He aspires with his work to shape public opinion in accordance with the ethos of the National Theatre which, with its platform discussions and social foyer space, aims to be a place where citizens interact and discuss. In an essay of 2005 Hare sought to reposition himself as an artist rather than spokesman for a left-wing movement, but he claimed nevertheless that 'my views as a citizen are stronger than ever, my politics more resilient'.[100] As Chris Megson and Dan Rebellato have demonstrated, there is an unresolved tension in Hare's work between art and journalism. His carefully researched plays are driven by content more than form, and seek to show how life *really* is, a reality supposedly ignored by politicians bent on power. Megson and Rebellato are unimpressed by the metaphysics of his claim that in live performance the play exists 'in the air' between stage and audience, and they argue 'that the condition to which Hare strives in the theatre is that of the lecture'.[101] When Hare refers in a 2008 interview to 'a whole lot of unspoken stuff that's going on in the air', it becomes hard to reconcile mysteries of art with the Habermasian ideal of rational discourse.[102]

Hare's work confronts us with a number of unanswered questions. Despite the best efforts of the National Theatre management, partly driven by pressures of public funding, to reach a broad audience by means of cheap 'Travelex' seats, creative programming, Discovery and New Connections programmes, performances relayed to cinemas, outdoor performances and so forth, it is arguable that the core audience for David Hare's plays still equates with the exclusive audience of property owners who once constituted the Enlightenment public sphere. Nicholas Hytner, Director of the NT, maintains that his theatre has demonstrably reached 'a large public that craves engagement with the kind of art that asks difficult questions and provides the kind of insight that can only come with sustained concentration, a public that seeks to understand more, to explore more and to expand its intellectual and imaginative horizons',[103] but what Hytner cannot demonstrate in this public is *public* reasoning and communicative interconnectedness involving the mutual recognition of truth claims. We also have to ask whether Hare is the creator of theatrical art, or merely

---

[100] Hare (2005) 27.   [101] Megson and Rebellato (2007) esp. 240, 246.
[102] Hammond and Steward (2008) 59.   [103] Cited from the 2009 Annual Report.

journalism by another means. What Habermas admired in the eighteenth
century was a civil society where private life was made public in order to
debate foundational values, and the Parisian controversy about *Pamela*, for
example, concerned the heroine's parentage, raising questions of principle about identity and class. By going directly to issues of public policy,
Hare arguably creates through his reportage the instant and illusory thrill
of an engaged citizenship, while not actually identifying the fundamental
issues upon which social consensus must rest prior to effective political
action. In 2004 Hare described his play about the British railway system
as 'a rallying point, for better or worse, even if it confirms people in their
own feelings, just makes people feel less lonely about what they feel'.[104]
This remark points us to a final question, a recurrent one in this book.
Is theatre more potent as a medium for articulating debates, or for building communities? In the German idiom, is it a tool for *Gesellschaft* or
Gemeinschaft?

Hannah Arendt like Habermas combines a horror of totalitarian government with dismay at the consumerist mass culture of so-called democracies.
Like Habermas she regrets the loss of a public sphere, though her preferred
term is 'public realm' with its connotations of popular sovereignty, and
she finds little to celebrate in the rise of a modern intimate sphere once
the individual in the nineteenth century had as it were 'got the better of
the citizen'.[105] Where Habermas sites the citizen in a civil society that lies
between the domestic and political worlds, Arendt is interested in the citizen's capacity to act within political society, and is concerned with material
speech acts rather than abstract discourses, persuasion being the crux of
political action. While Habermas wants to push the boundaries of the
nation-state in the direction of world citizenship, Arendt is committed to
smaller communities on the model of the Athenian polis, or the Jeffersonian
township, seeing the nation-state as the manifestation of a new and reduc-
tive 'social realm' which blurs private and public.[106] She respects the Greek
polis and Roman Republic because they were once a 'guarantee against the
futility of individual life', providing a public space where actions enjoyed a
certain permanence,[107] and she argues that 'wherever the man-made world
does not become the scene for action and speech – as in despotically ruled
communities which banish their subjects into the narrowness of the home

[104] Platform conversation with Richard Boon: Cottesloe Theatre, 27 January 2004.
[105] Arendt (1963) 137.
[106] Arendt's most important discussion of 'the public and the private realm' forms chapter 11 of *The Human Condition*: Arendt (1958). On the Jeffersonian ideal, see Arendt (1963) 236–42.
[107] Arendt (1958) 55–6.

and thus prevent the rise of a public realm – freedom has no worldly reality'. She adds that freedom 'may still dwell in men's hearts . . . but the human heart, as we all know, is a very dark place'.[108] It is only through emerging from this private darkness into a community that humans can act politically and thus be free. Arendt's work connects to a modern politics of identity when she claims that answering the question 'who are you?' is the primordial human act.[109] Satisfactory answers to this question can be generated only through repeated speech-acts in the public realm.

In a 2007 editorial in *Research in Drama Education*, Joe Winston flags the importance of Arendt for underpinning work with young and marginalized people in the field of 'applied drama'. Arendt's belief that the citizen needs to act before an audience in the public sphere, and that 'the form of drama creates a public space that mirrors the public sphere of politics', offer inspiration to 'applied' practitioners.[110] Helen Nicholson argues in a similar vein that 'applied drama' should constitute a 'practice of citizenship', taking as her preferred theorist of democratic citizenship Chantal Mouffe, whose conception of democracy has much in common with Arendt's 'agonistic politics of performativity', though Mouffe has less faith in ultimate consensus.[111]

Arendt is not a straightforward figurehead for 'applied' drama practitioners because, heeding Kant and the Frankfurt School, she refuses to relinquish notions of beauty, and believes that artists should mistrust politics even though their artworks belong in the public realm. Her major work, *The Human Condition*, maps a threefold segmentation of human existence into labour, work and action. Arendt has no truck with the notion of artistic 'self-expression', arguing that the artist as *homo faber*, the craftsman or fabricator, creates a 'work', and creating a work involves thinking instrumentally, while self-disclosure is only possible in the transient political sphere of 'action'.[112] Her distinction between work and action implies a privileged place for drama amongst the arts because drama is the imitation of action, and although a text may be fixed as a 'work', performances in the public realm can never be replicated because audiences are never constant. Theatre, she argues, 'is the political art par excellence; only there is the political sphere of human life transposed into art'.[113] She ends her book

---

[108] Arendt (1961) 148–9.   [109] Arendt (1958) 178–9.   [110] Winston (2007).

[111] See Nicholson (2005) 19–37; cf. Mouffe (1993). This summation of Arendt is attributed to Bonnie Honig in Warner (2002) 58.

[112] Arendt (1958) 156, 322. Arendt's notion that personal qualities can only be revealed through action owes something to Aristotle's *Poetics*.

[113] Arendt (1958) 188, Arendt (1978) I.96.

On Revolution with a citation from Sophocles on the nature of the polis because the artist is one 'whose business it is to find and make the words we live by'.

Arendt identifies a 'conflict between art and politics' which 'cannot and must not be solved'. Though both belong to the public world, the artist in order to fabricate objects of beauty needs to remain isolated from the public.[114] Since a domain of the aesthetic implies detached spectatorship rather than active participation, Arendt develops a paradox of the spectator. As spectator but not participant one can 'see the whole play', like the ancient philosopher who was a contemplative spectator of life, or like Kant whose enthusiastic spectatorship of and 'wishful participation' in the French Revolution stand in contrast to his political passivity, a physical inertia shared by 'every intellectual circle in Europe'. To resolve this difficulty she adopts Kant's distinction between thinking and judging. Theatre does not fundamentally concern *thought*, for 'the spectator's viewpoint is not determined by the categorical imperatives of practical reason, that is, reason's answer to the question What ought I to do? That answer is moral and concerns the individual qua individual.' Rather, theatre is a matter of *judgement*, including the judgement of beauty, and spectators are neither solitary nor self-sufficient, for 'you can never speak of the spectator: spectators exist only in the plural'. Spectators cannot form judgements independent of the views of others, but only through what Kant calls an 'enlarged mentality'.[115] It follows that art, and theatre par excellence, help to create 'the We, the true plural of action' and the 'citizen' as distinct from 'man in general'.[116] Put another way, 'Judging is one, if not the most, important activity in which this sharing-the-world-with-others comes to pass.' Because it 'depends on the presence of others... the capacity to judge is a specifically political ability in exactly the sense denoted by Kant, namely, the ability to see things not only from one's own point of view but in the perspective of all those who happen to be present'.[117] Aristotle's concept of *synaisthēsis* captures precisely this notion of collective viewing characteristic of the human as a political animal.[118]

Arendt articulates an ideal of political theatre that sits at a far remove from the tradition exemplified by Brecht which harnesses emotion to reason in order to lay before the spectator questions of individual moral choice, but accords perfectly with Rousseau, who understood the principle that art creates taste and sent Emile to the theatre to study taste not morals.[119]

[114] 'The crisis in culture' in Arendt (1961) 217–18.   [115] Arendt (1978) I.93–7, II.262.
[116] Arendt (1978) II.200.   [117] Arendt (1961) 221.
[118] See p. 15 above.   [119] Rousseau (1969) 677.

Arendt's emphasis on 'judgement' steers her clear of the Dionysiac collectivism that culminated in German Fascism without surrendering the principle that theatre generates communities, and it allows her to address the faultline between art and activism that we have seen in the Volksbühne, in IPTA and in Hare. Though Arendt's acceptance of an aesthetic domain sets her at odds with prevailing twentieth-century academic criticism of theatre, which has tended to collapse aesthetic concerns into ethical concerns, it chimes with current thinking by applied theatre practitioners in the UK, troubled by a gut feeling that they are creating art and frustrated by the pressure to articulate their work only in terms of social instrumentality. Joe Winston has reflected upon the instinctive pleasure taken by children in the classroom when they create beautiful things,[120] and, partly inspired by Winston, James Thompson has recently explored the moral value of beauty and the capacity of emotion to generate action, seeking to reconcile Kantian ideals of beauty and feeling with radical social intervention.[121] Winston and Thompson have initiated a debate that has clearly only just begun.

Richard Sennett, once a pupil of Arendt, shares her perception that the eighteenth-century balance of public and private has been sacrificed to the tyrannies of individualism and corporate capitalism. Reflecting a contemporary sense of the personal as political in *The Fall of Public Man* (1976), Sennett portrays a citizen who is neither the quiet deliberator of Habermas, nor Arendt's assertive public speaker, but someone who is fully embodied and emotionally expressive. His focus is less upon 'citizenship' than 'civility', the ability of strangers to meet in the city and interact, and in the modern urban context he dismisses Arendt's call for localized community as 'retribalization'.[122] The theatre sits at the centre of his analysis as the exemplary site of social encounter, where beneath the mask of civility eighteenth-century spectators were free to be emotionally expressive. Cosmetics, clothing and manners all contributed to this liberating social mask.[123] The story Sennett tells of the nineteenth century is of a newly disciplined and silent audience, relieved in the privacy of a darkened auditorium to escape the oppression of respectable domestic life and the terror of revealing an authentic interior selfhood. This silent and passive spectatorship generates, as in the exemplary case of Wagner's Bayreuth, theatre as 'Art'.[124]

---

[120] Winston (2006); see also Winston (2008), Jackson (2007) 23–38.   [121] Thompson (2009).
[122] Sennett (1977) 339. Sennett (1994) 370–6 argues the case for 'civic bodies' in a multicultural society.
[123] Sennett (1977) 264 etc.   [124] Sennett (1977) 208–9.

Diderot's conception of a gap between the person of the eighteenth-century actor and the representation of emotion epitomizes all that Sennett admires about the social actors of the auditorium, unconstrained by the modern tyranny of truthful self-expression.[125] In Sennett's model, the individual spectator did not identify with Figaro in order to feel the human equality of the servant, for what mattered was the shared witnessing of a public enactment, a story told by Beaumarchais.[126] Rousseau is the prophet of an unwelcome modernity, celebrating intimacy and the expression of authentic feeling, while recoiling in horror from the falsity of metropolitan life, and in Rousseau's cult of the natural man Sennett sees the negation of civility.[127] When one compares Sennett, who wrote in the wake of the Paris *Événements* of 1968, to Arendt and Habermas, one finds less faith in the possibility of political change, and particularly in effecting change through the power of language. For Sennett, the essence of citizenship lies in the convergence of strangers within whom there is no distinction of mind from body, or reason from emotion. It is enough for his spectator to be 'active' as a social performer, without activity in any political arena.

Sennett's argument of 1976 has in one respect been accepted as public policy across much of Europe, with the conversion of old industrial buildings or flamboyant modern architectural designs yielding theatres that reanimate city centres, reconnecting the idea of the citizen to the idea of the city.[128] Yet Sennett's ideal of the citizen is more elusive. The comfortable nooks and foyers of London's National Theatre are a perfect setting for the Habermasian citizen to deliberate the work of the playwright, but are less efficacious as a space of display for Sennett's social actor. The public spaces of the Royal Opera House in Covent Garden, opened in 1999, provide more panoramas and fewer private retreats, reflecting not only a less demotic audience, one traditionally more willing to dress up, but also perhaps some move towards the social actor. From Sennett's perspective, David Hare's desire to reveal the private human being behind the public figure panders to individualism, and is complicit with a political system which invites citizens to judge politicians on the basis of personality.

When he looked back at the twentieth century, Sennett deployed the theatre spectator as a metaphor, standing for the assimilation of the politically constituted citizen by the passive consumer.[129] Sennett's condemnation of

[125] Sennett (1977) 110–15.	[126] Sennett (1977) 79–80.	[127] Sennett (1977) 115–22.
[128] See for example Khan (2002), reporting on an international seminar of arts managers.
[129] Sennett (2006) 161–2.

consumerism results in a certain nostalgia for the medieval ideal of the citizen-as-craftsman, an ideal which lives on in Diderot's *Encyclopédie*.[130] On this basis he criticizes Arendt's conception that *homo faber*, the artist as artisan, comes second to those who partake in political action. For Sennett, understanding how things work is an essential part of democracy, and politics is essentially 'statecraft'.[131] Since the embodied knowledge of the craftsman is as valuable as intellectual knowledge, Sennett celebrates fifth-century Athenian spectators who carried the skills of choral dancing in their bodies over against later Aristotelian spectators who separated understanding from doing and saw 'with the mind's eye'.[132] Sennett's celebration of the craftsman's 'workshop' may remind theatre scholars of the way Brecht foregrounded the skills of the actor and the machinery of the stage, or of historical landmarks like Littlewood's Theatre Workshop and Schechner's Performing Garage. Albeit superficially, the modern infrastructure of pre-play talks, post-play discussions and schools workshops respond to Sennett's ideal, demonstrating that the play is an object made with skill and love, and not a product of consumer capitalism. It is arguable, of course, that these are but marketing ploys and provide the illusion of authenticity repeatedly sought by modernist art.

Zygmunt Bauman is an influential interpreter of postmodernity who will help to draw the strands of my discussion towards the present. In *Liquid Modernity* (2000) he describes a transition from a 'solid' to a 'fluid' modernity, whereby power has passed from those who once controlled space to those nomadic figures whose velocity allows them control of time. He prepares the ground for this thesis in *In Search of Politics* (1999), borrowing his account of the public sphere from Sennett's description of Athens, and defining the *agora* as the vital intermediate space which sits between the *ecclesia* (the political assembly) and the *oikos* (domestic space). In the wake of Fascism, Habermas saw the threat to the *agora* coming from the *ecclesia*, but today the *ecclesia* has been evacuated of its old inhabitants and the major threat comes from the *oikos*, reducing public life to the trivialities of personality.[133] Bauman describes the breakdown of a long-standing love-hate union between 'republic' and 'nation' once sealed by the 'nation-state'. Whilst 'nation' assumes that the national community is a given, and offers escape from the uncomfortable freedoms proposed by liberalism and globalization, the republican idea insists that communities

---

[130] Sennett (2006) 169–171, Sennett (2008) 90–1.
[131] Sennett (2008) 6–7, 290.   [132] Sennett (2008) 124–5.
[133] Bauman (1999) 3–4, 86–98; cf. Bauman (2000) 69–70, Sennett (1994) 52–67.

need to be made, and in this idea Bauman sees the only hope for the future in the world of liquid modernity, despite inevitable tensions within the republican concept between the individual's liberty from interference and the citizen's right to interfere. Though he endorses an ideal of community which we do not find in Habermas, there is a ring of Habermas in Bauman's statement that the republican idea 'puts critical enquiry in the heart of community membership'.[134]

A striking theatrical metaphor provides the climax of *Liquid Modernity*. Bauman takes the theatre audience to stand for the 'explosive', short-term and essentially spurious sense of community exemplified, at the point when he wrote the book, by Serbian nationalism, and he dubs this audience a 'cloakroom community'.

> During the performance all eyes are on the stage; so is everybody's attention. Mirth and sadness, laughter and silence, rounds of applause, shouts of approval and gasps of surprise are synchronized – as if carefully scripted and directed. After the last fall of the curtain, however, the spectators collect their belongings from the cloakroom and when putting their street clothes on once more return to their ordinary mundane and different roles, a few moments later dissolving in the variegated crowd filling the city streets from which they emerged a few hours earlier.

The trope of theatre as deception is a familiar one, but has lost none of its force. Bauman's audience, like the prisoners in Plato's cave, are aware not of each other but only of the spectacle. The delusions of the theatre are dangerous because they

> ward off the condensation of 'genuine' (that is, comprehensive and lasting) communities which they mime and (misleadingly) promise to replicate or generate from scratch. They scatter instead of condense the untapped energy of sociality impulses and so contribute to the perpetuation of the solitude desperately yet vainly seeking redress in the rare and far-between concerted and harmonious collective undertakings.[135]

Bauman is sympathetic to Arendt's yearning for genuine communities, though he is wary of the consequences.

The image of the cloakroom recalls Bauman's Polish compatriot Tadeusz Kantor, who once placed the audience in a cloakroom, seeking thus to escape from 'artistic activity' into '"r e a l i t y" and truth'. A cloakroom, Kantor wrote

---

[134] Bauman (1999) 166.   [135] Bauman (2000) 200–1. On Plato, see Wiles (2003) 209–11.

is shameless
in its invasion of one's privacy:
we are forced to leave there
an intimate part of us.
It is a terrorist act.
We could push this metaphor even further and say that
during a production
parts of us are hanging there mixed together
with people we do not know.[136]

Kantor's cloakroom experiment of 1973 belonged to an age when the ideal of an 'alternative' or 'underground' theatre was premised on the existence of marginal places where authentic intimate encounters between strangers were possible. It is Bauman's thesis that no salvation can be found in such heterotopias, or alternative spaces, because in the age of liquid modernity power is vested in time not place.[137] He endorses Sennett's ideal of 'civility', lamenting the emergence of paradoxically 'public but not civil' places where people insulate themselves against any risk of interaction.[138] In a multicultural society Bauman's priority is to reclaim control of the *agora*. There should be no more escaping from the republican category of the citizen into the modernist category of the authentic human individual.

The final and most recent theorist of the public sphere whom I wish to discuss is Jacques Rancière, who approaches the same issues from a philosophical rather than sociological standpoint. Clinging to a progressive dialectical model of history, Rancière is unwilling to concede either ancient Athens or the eighteenth-century Enlightenment as an era when the public sphere was healthier than today. He sees today's democratic public sphere as the product of a historic break with 'natural' titles to govern, so that it has become the 'sphere of encounters and conflicts between the two opposed logics of . . . the natural government of social competences and the government of anyone and everyone. The spontaneous practices of any government tend to shrink this public sphere, making it into its own private affair'. Democracy, for Rancière, is 'a process of struggle against this privatization', and enlarging the public sphere 'entails struggling against the distribution of the public and the private' which ultimately shores up oligarchy.[139] The duality of man and citizen, so prominent a feature of French revolutionary debate, illustrates how power always lies in the

---

[136] 'A Cloakroom' in Kantor and Kobialka (1993) 103–5, and cf. 301–4.
[137] On 'heterotopias', cf. Wiles (2003) 8–9.
[138] Bauman (2000) 104–5.   [139] Rancière (2006) 55.

'distribution' of terms and places, and political action in this case must involve 'playing man against citizen and citizen against man'.[140] Since there is no democratic order in nature, Rancière condemns Platonist and French republican visions of a harmonious order within which citizens must be educated to play their proper parts. Republican efforts to erase the boundary between state and society have repeatedly furnished a cover for oligarchy.[141]

When he turns to theatre, Rancière identifies a 'paradox of the spectator' which catches the central dilemma that I have explored in this book. According to this paradox, there can be no theatre without a spectator, yet mere spectatorship is by definition a bad thing.

First, viewing is the opposite of knowing: the spectator is held before an appearance in a state of ignorance about the process of production of this appearance and about the reality it conceals. Second, it is the opposite of acting: the spectator remains immobile in her seat, passive. To be a spectator is to be separated from both the capacity to know and the power to act.[142]

Rancière traces these objections to theatrical illusion from Plato and Rousseau to Debord's *The Society of the Spectacle*, a situationist manifesto which inspired many Parisian radicals in 1968. The critique of passivity relates to an ideal of active citizenship. The active citizen for Plato and Rousseau is someone who joins the communal dance, rather than watch a performance.

Rancière picks apart two competing principles that have positioned theatre as a force for good in the public sphere. On the one hand there is the educational ideal. Questioning the Brechtian alienation effect, Rancière sees no reason why 'the clash of heterogeneous elements should bring about an understanding of the state of the world; and no reason either why understanding the state of the world should prompt a decision to change it'. Molière and Voltaire claimed that their plays taught spectators about the perils of religious hypocrisy or fanaticism, but Rousseau in his *Letter to d'Alembert* exposed the fallacy of this argument: theatre depends on the gap between the act and what is enacted, so there can be no stable correspondence between theatre and life outside the theatre.[143] Rancière holds up the ideal of the 'ignorant schoolmaster' who, somewhat in the tradition of Socrates, Rousseau and Freire, without dispensing knowledge allows the pupil to create knowledge. Theatre-makers, by the

[140] Rancière (2006) 59. The French term *partition* implies both distribution and division.
[141] Rancière (2006) 63–70   [142] Rancière (2009) 2.   [143] Rancière (2009) 74–5, 60.

same token, are doomed to fail if they set out to dispense their superior wisdom.[144]

Against this educational ideal Rancière sets the Artaudian ideal of total theatre involving communion with the audience. Rousseau's communitarian dance in Geneva anticipates, for example, the way Appia and Dalcroze worked on Wagnerian choruses with movement choirs incorporating the children of German industrial workers.[145] Laban's choreography likewise 'developed in a context favouring the liberation of bodies and became the model for the large Nazi demonstrations before regaining, in the anti-establishment context of performance art, a new subversive virginity', and with Plato always in mind Rancière perceives 'a long-standing connection between the unanimous consensus of the citizenry and exaltation of the free movement of bodies'.[146]

Rancière sets out the paradox of the spectator very clearly, but does little to clarify how theatre might assist in a contemporary struggle for the public sphere. His broad thesis is that power operates through sensory partition or distribution, and thus binary oppositions like viewing/knowing, appearance/reality and activity/passivity are 'embodied allegories of inequality', unstable oppositions that need to be challenged. When he finally considers where that challenge might come from, Rancière reveals an underlying assumption about the nature of theatre.

[W]hat exactly occurs among theatre spectators that cannot happen elsewhere? What is more interactive, more communitarian, about these spectators than a mass of individuals watching the same television show at the same hour?
This something, I believe, is simply the presupposition that theatre is in and of itself communitarian. This presupposition continues to precede theatrical performances and anticipate its effects. But in a theatre, in front of a performance, just as in a museum, school or street, there are only ever individuals plotting their own paths in the forest of things, acts and signs that confront or surround them.[147]

A sense of distance from the stage and from fellow spectators leads him, like Arendt, back to Kant and the notion of aesthetic distance: any artist must accept the gap between *poiesis* and *aisthesis*, making and perceiving, in order to allow for the creativity of the spectator.[148]

Rancière emerges here, from behind the smokescreen of his epigrammatic prose, as the Cartesian intellectual. His equation of the theatre audience with the television audience may be broadly reasonable in respect

---

[144] Rancière (2009) 8–11.   [145] Rancière (2009) 63.   [146] Rancière (2004) 18.
[147] Rancière (2009) 16. This passage was not included in the first English version of 'The emancipated spectator' published in *ArtForum* in March 2007.
[148] Rancière (2009) 10, 64.

of his world in 2009, but it does not respond to the historical otherness of performances as they were experienced in the Athens of Plato or the Paris of Rousseau, the factories of Piscator or the villages of Bengal. At the end of 'The emancipated spectator' Rancière argues for 'spectators who play the role of individual interpreters, who develop their own translation in order to appropriate the "story" and make it their own story. An emancipated community is a community of narrators and translators.'[149] Amongst the binary 'distributions' which he seems disinclined to collapse are those of body/mind, movement/speech and emotion/reason. I have argued in this book that people are more than individuals, and therefore it is insufficient to conceive liberated citizens as forming a community of individuals, however creative those individuals may be. Rancière's paradox of the spectator defines the problem that we need to resolve, but despite his best efforts he operates within a 'distribution of the sensible' that separates the insights of the philosopher, dedicated to the contemplative life, from those of theatre studies, with its collectivist and participant traditions of pedagogy, in yet another 'allegory of inequality'.

Rancière is a representative cultural commentator of 2009, looking back to the securities of Marxism without a clear vision of the future. The philosophical challenge in a post-Marxist world is to reconcile the liberalism of a Voltaire or a Habermas, based upon faith in individual reason, with the communitarian tradition that includes Rousseau and Arendt and insists that the human being is in the first instance a *zōon politikon*, a collective or political being. I have organized this book around a series of pairings, including Aristotle and Plato, Terence and Machiavelli, Milton and Shakespeare, Diderot and Chénier, which relate in different ways to this central dilemma, at the core of which is a question about self and singularity. Jean-Luc Nancy attempts a philosophical answer to this conundrum when he argues that a '"we", even one that is not articulated, is the condition for the possibility of each "I"'. Rousseau's ideal society, which exists without spectacle once the 'I' has disappeared, rests on a fallacy because society is but the spectacle of itself. Nancy urges us to relinquish the paradigm of Athenian theatre with its promise of uniting *logos* to mimesis because the world is neither logical nor representable, and invites us to settle for the ideal of together 'co-appearing'.[150] This is a useful formulation, but it does not offer a clear programme for action. There are practical questions to be answered. How far should we value private against public living? In terms of ethics, how should we weigh individual rights against mutual obligations?

---

[149] Rancière (2009) 22.   [150] Nancy (2000) 65–73.

In terms of social policy, should we value diversity or seek assimilation? As makers of theatre, should we try to teach spectators, or embrace them as a community? The 'citizen' provides a focus and intersection point for these questions.

Within the concept of citizenship, the individual as holder of human rights collides with the collectivity that gives human life its purpose. And between these two principles, the historian can perceive the swing of a pendulum. I have examined in this chapter a swing towards collectivity in pre-war Germany that was countered by a swing back towards the individual. The power of capital and the loneliness of the consumer are functions of modern individualism and the pendulum will need to swing back again if the planet is to survive. Citizenship is a valuable concept in helping people to negotiate these macro processes, and to separate positive from destructive forms of collectivity.

Although it has lost some of its former cultural eminence, theatre remains a uniquely valuable testing ground for citizenship both because it brings citizens face to face in an interactive space, and because of its history. Today's problems are modifications of yesterday's problems. Theatre practitioners characteristically have a strong awareness of theatrical tradition, and if they understood more clearly how art and politics have always been locked into each other, they would perhaps find new creative resources to address present political situations.

Epilogue: Washington's monuments to citizenship

This book germinated from a lecture given in Washington at a conference dedicated to the 'Citizen Artist'.[1] The organizers perceived in their nation's historic ideal of good 'citizenship' the stuff of international relevance. Seeking an education in US history, I set off during the conference rest day on a walk around the tidal basin to visit the famous republican monuments which fix in stone a sequence of contradictory ideas about citizenship. I was accompanied in my search for cultural enlightenment by an authority on Hindu dance-poetry, who had chastised me after my lecture for the western nature of my preoccupations.

Walking clockwise we came first to the Jefferson Memorial, a romantic classical rotunda built on a promontory. While Greek and Roman buildings are rooted in the earth, the Jefferson reaches skywards from a series of terraces. Freedom of the spirit is the main burden of the inscriptions, in accordance with the ideals of the earliest European settlers. The author of the Declaration of Independence stands proudly upright to attest the legend that 'Almighty God hath created the mind free.' The statement on the northeast wall that 'Commerce between master and slave is despotism' compelled us to observe how all the visitors were white, while the maintenance staff scrubbing the floors at Jefferson's feet were black. Freedom of the mind and social equality are competing ideals, and as a man of the Enlightenment Jefferson was more interested in the first. The Jeffersonian citizen had equal rights to freedom of thought and expression, but not to food and medicine. As in the Grecian world evoked by the architecture, slavery was an inconvenient complication. The romantic lakeside setting suggests that the 'Almighty God' evoked in this pagan architectural form could be a synonym for Nature, and helps the visitor to sense that the human being is by nature free, and is enchained by society.

[1] Conference of the IFTR/FIRT at the University of Maryland, 2005.

Next in our circuit, the Franklin D. Roosevelt Memorial spoke to a different idea, a social ideal familiar to me as a European,[2] but one that I had not expected to find in a country so resistant to the healthcare provisions normal in Europe. The presidential wheelchair and the welfare claimants in bronze relief illustrate the message that, under the 'new deal', citizenship involves rights and entitlements. While the Jefferson pushes upwards, the FDR is organized on a horizontal plane, for its message is about social levelling, and the waterfall proclaims the naturalness of this human equality.

Though the Lincoln Memorial was allegedly inspired by the temple of Zeus at Olympia, its proportions are more Roman than Greek, and the fasces carved in relief on the arms of the throne recall the neo-Roman architecture of Mussolini. Everything in this monument speaks to the power of the state, celebrating Lincoln's triumph in saving the Union. When Lincoln-as-Jupiter gazes across at the Capitol, an architectural allusion to a Rome that shaped the Constitution, his sightline runs past Washington's obelisk and crosses a neoclassical arrangement of space that recalls royal Versailles. We ponder the complex relationship between democracy and neo-imperialism. In Europe, such a temple would be an unabashed monument to nationhood, fixing the idea that citizenship equals membership of the nation-state, but here in America citizens have traditionally aspired to being patriots without being nationalists, reluctant to surrender the importance of locality within the US federation.[3] As we gaze up at Lincoln in appropriate awe, the triumphal architecture offers little grounds sustaining any separation of nation from state.

We retrace to the Korean War memorial where nineteen multi-ethnic servicemen advance towards the US flag. The protagonists of this drama are individualized, yet also form a collective like a Greek chorus. Whereas the Lincoln invited a passive and submissive gaze, the Korean requires a more active mode of viewing, each chosen angle of viewing creating different configurations and reflections in water and stone. This monument celebrates diversity within unity, a perfect balance called into question by the trio of female soldiers positioned nearby beside the Vietnam memorial. Inclusiveness is an ideal doomed to recede the moment it has been achieved.

The Vietnam Memorial rejects the vertical dimension even more emphatically than the Korean and FDR. The folk piety of the bereaved was expressed by little envelopes and badges placed against the individual

---

[2] On T. H. Marshall's classic analysis, see Turner (1993) 6ff., Fraser and Gordon (1994).
[3] On American nationalism, see Lieven (2005).

names of the dead. In this monument to the humbling of the State, we are shown how society comprises nothing but a multiplicity of unique human beings, death being a more powerful leveller than any state intervention. The citizen is merely a cover for the human individual, mourned in this public arena by family members. The Vietnam Memorial offers us, in Arthur Miller's phrase, the tragedy of the common man,[4] and we file past this record of human suffering as atomized individuals.

Each of these architectural representations of citizenship correlates with an idea about theatre. The Jeffersonian citizen will seek a play that defies censorship and is a vehicle for new ideas. The FDR brand of citizen demands state subsidy for a theatre that brings culture to the people. Lincoln's citizen wants a national theatre that other nations might envy, creating political unity through fixing shared memories. The Korean ideal reflects the choral energies of the fifties musical and stresses the participatory nature of theatre experience, while the Vietnam ideal turns upon the emotional power of intimacy. The theatrical force of these installations in the Washington landscape is not easily matched today by live human bodies, because they are of their time, and theatre is transient.

On this tour of the monuments I encountered a discourse about citizenship hitherto unfamiliar to me, being accustomed to an English landscape littered with monuments to aristocracy not republicanism. I was grateful for my acquaintance with the classics, recalling the famous text of Thomas Hobbes about reading the political and historical works of ancient authors: 'From the reading, I say, of such books, men have undertaken to kill their kings, because the Greek and Latin writers, in their books, and discourses of policy, make it lawful, and laudable, for any man so to do; provided, before he do it, he call him tyrant . . . From the same books, they that live under a monarch conceive an opinion, that the subjects in a popular commonwealth enjoy liberty; but that in a monarchy they are all slaves.'[5] Hobbes likens the infection produced by Plutarch *et al.* to an attack of rabies. Our tour pinpointed a historical threshold, the Jefferson being dedicated in 1943. Hitherto antiquity had provided Europeans and North Americans with a collective means of conceptualizing citizenship; after that time, classics ceased to be the basis of western education. Arendt and Rancière perhaps belong to the last generation reared in that virtual world. Without the classical frame of reference it became harder to place ideas about citizenship in a historical perspective, weigh them, and imagine other political possibilities.

---

[4] Clark (1965) 537–9.   [5] Hobbes *Leviathan* II.29.

Born in the aftermath of the French Revolution, Alexis de Tocqueville had mixed feelings about the classical tradition, which can provide a 'wholesome medicine for the mind' but can equally create 'a very dangerous set of citizens' who may 'perturb the state, in the name of the Greeks and Romans, instead of enriching it by their productive industry'.[6] His account of American theatre continues to resonate. He saw European theatre as the recurrent site of a power struggle between people and aristocracy, with the pit often making laws for the boxes, and in the USA his sense of cultural impoverishment is mingled with relief when he sees how American democrats 'care but little for what occurred at Rome and Athens; they want to hear something that concerns themselves ... The drama becomes more striking, more vulgar, and more true.' In democratic theatre generally, De Tocqueville observes, the spectators 'do not go there to seek the pleasures of the mind but the keen emotions of the heart', and provided the 'characters excite curiosity and awaken sympathy, the audience are satisfied'. There can be 'no dramatic subjects in a country which has witnessed no great political catastrophes and in which love invariably leads by a straight and easy road to matrimony', and the American puritan tradition imposes an unexpected level of censorship.[7] Whilst nineteenth-century French theatre remained a political space, a site of confrontation, theatre was of marginal cultural importance in democratic America. Today the American condition described by De Tocqueville has become the European condition, and to a large extent the global condition. The American founding fathers clearly once fell into De Tocqueville's category of 'dangerous citizens', and this book has been a quest for other dangerous citizens who once sought through the making of theatre to change their worlds.

---

[6] Tocqueville (1954) ii.66.   [7] Tocqueville (1954) ii.85–8.

References

Adarkar, Neera, and Meena Menon. 2004. *One hundred years, one hundred voices: the millworkers of Girangaon: an oral history.* Calcutta: Seagull.

Alam, Javeed. 2004. *Who wants democracy?* New Delhi: Orient Longman.

2005. 'Civil society, democracy and public sphere in India'. In *Civil society, public sphere and citizenship: dialogues and perceptions,* ed. Rajeev Bhargava and Helmut Reifeld, 348–64. New Delhi and London: Sage.

Alston, David. 1993. 'David et le théâtre'. In *David contre David: actes du colloque organisé au Musée du Louvre par le service culturel du 6 au 10 décembre 1989,* ed. Régis Michel. Vol. 1, 165–98. Paris: Documentation Française.

Alston, Leonard. 1910. *Education and citizenship in India.* London: Longmans, Green, and Co.

Amkpa, Awam. 2006. 'Theatre, activism and citizenship in neocolonial contexts'. In *A Boal companion: dialogues on theatre and cultural politics,* ed. Jan Cohen-Cruz and Mady Schutzman, 161–72. New York: Routledge.

Anderson, Benedict. 1991. *Imagined communities: reflections on the origin and spread of nationalism.* Rev. edn. London and New York: Verso.

Anon. 1842. *Du théâtre de Genève.* Geneva: P.-A. Bonnant.

Appiah, Kwame Anthony. 1998. 'Cosmopolitan patriots'. In *Cosmopolitics: thinking and feeling beyond the nation,* ed. Pheng Cheah and Bruce Robbins, 91–114. Minneapolis: University of Minnesota Press.

Archer, Ian W. 1991. *The pursuit of stability: social relations in Elizabethan London.* Cambridge: Cambridge University Press.

Arendt, Hannah. 1958. *The human condition.* Chicago: University of Chicago Press.

1961. *Between past and future: six exercises in political thought.* New York: Viking.

1963. *On revolution.* London: Faber and Faber.

1967. *The origins of totalitarianism.* 3rd edn. London: Allen & Unwin.

1978. *The life of the mind.* London: Secker & Warburg.

Arnold, Oliver. 2007. *The third citizen: Shakespeare's theater and the early modern house of commons.* Baltimore, Md.: Johns Hopkins University Press.

Artaud, Antonin. 1970. *The theatre and its double.* London: Calder & Boyars.

Arts Council of England. 1996. *The policy for drama of the English arts funding system.* London: Arts Council of England.

228

1998. *Cultural diversity action plan for the Arts Council of England*. London: Arts Council of England.

Aschheim, Steven E. 1992. *The Nietzsche legacy in Germany, 1890–1990*. Berkeley: University of California Press.

Aslan, Odette. 1989. *Voies de la création théâtrale*. Vol. xvi: *Strehler*. Paris: Centre National de la Recherche Scientifique.

Atkinson, James B., and David Sices, eds. 1996. *Machiavelli and his friends: their personal correspondence*. DeKalb: Northern Illinois University Press.

Aulard, François Victor Alphonse. 1892. *Le culte de la raison et le culte de l'être suprême, 1793–1794*. Paris: Alcan.

Avagnina, Maria Elisa. 2005. *The Teatro Olimpico*. Venice: Marsilio.

Ayckbourn, Alan. 1979. *Joking Apart; Ten Times Table; Just Between Ourselves*. London: Chatto & Windus.

Baker, Keith Michael. 1987. *The French Revolution and the creation of modern political culture*. Oxford: Pergamon.

Bakhtin, Mikhail. 1968. *Rabelais and his world*. Trans. Hélène Iswolsky. Cambridge, Mass.: MIT Press.

Balibar, Etienne. 1991. 'Citizen subject'. In *Who comes after the subject?*, ed. Eduardo Cadava, Peter Connor and Jean-Luc Nancy, 33–57. New York and London: Routledge.

Banu, Georges. 1989. *Le rouge et or: une poétique du théâtre à l'italienne*. Paris: Flammarion.

Barker, Derek W. M. 2009. *Tragedy and citizenship: conflict, reconciliation, and democracy from Haemon to Hegel*. Albany: State University of New York Press.

Barron, Caroline. 2000. 'London 1300–1540'. In *The Cambridge urban history of Britain*. Vol. i: *600–1540*, ed. D. M. Palliser, Peter Clark and M. J. Daunton, 395–440. Cambridge: Cambridge University Press.

2004. *London in the later Middle Ages: government and people, 1200–1500*. Oxford: Oxford University Press.

Bauman, Zygmunt. 1999. *In search of politics*. Cambridge: Polity.

2000. *Liquid modernity*. Cambridge: Polity.

Bayley, C. C. 1961. *War and society in renaissance Florence: the 'De Militia' of Leonardo Bruni*. Toronto: University of Toronto Press.

Beckwith, Sarah. 1994. 'Making the world in York and the York cycle'. In *Framing medieval bodies*, ed. Sarah Kay, Miri Rubin, 254–76. Manchester: Manchester University Press.

Bell, David Avrom. 2001. *The cult of the nation in France: inventing nationalism, 1680–1800*. Cambridge, Mass.: Harvard University Press.

Bellah, Robert Neelly, *et al.* 1996. *Habits of the heart: individualism and commitment in American life*. Updated edn. Berkeley: University of California Press.

Belsey, Catherine. 2007. 'Historicizing New Historicism'. In *Presentist Shakespeares*, ed. Hugh Grady and Terence Hawkes, 27–45. London: Routledge.

Bennett, Susan. 1990. *Theatre audiences: a theory of production and reception.* London: Routledge.

1997. *Theatre audiences: a theory of production and reception.* 2nd edn. London: Routledge.

Bentley, Eric. 1964. *The genius of the Italian theater.* New York: New American Library.

Berghaus, Günter. 1996. *Fascism and theatre: comparative studies on the aesthetics and politics of performance in Europe, 1925–1945.* Providence: Berghahn Books.

Beringer, Mrs Oscar. 1900. 'Women dramatists' – extracted in "Dramatic Notes". *Womanhood* 3(17): 367–9.

Berlin, Michael. 1986. 'Civic ceremony in early modern London'. *Urban History* 13: 15–27.

Bharucha, Rustom. 1983. *Rehearsals of revolution: the political theater of Bengal.* Honolulu: University of Hawaii Press.

1990. *Theatre and the world: essays on performance and politics of culture.* New Delhi: Manohar.

Bhatia, Nandi. 2004. *Acts of authority, acts of resistance: theater and politics in colonial and postcolonial India.* New Delhi and Oxford: Oxford University Press.

Bhattacharya, Malini. 2009. 'The Indian People's Theatre Association: a preliminary sketch of the movement and the organization 1942–47'. In *Modern Indian theatre: a reader*, ed. Nandi Bhatia, 158–81. New Delhi and Oxford: Oxford University Press.

Biet, Christian. 1994. *Oedipe en monarchie: tragédie et théorie juridique à l'âge classique.* Paris: Klincksieck.

Bingham, Alfred Jepson. 1939. *Marie-Joseph Chénier: early political life and ideas (1789–1794).* New York: Privately printed.

1963. 'Napoléon et Marie-Joseph Chénier'. *Studi francesi* 7: 438–49.

Black, Antony. 2003. *Guild & state: European political thought from the twelfth century to the present.* New Brunswick and London: Transaction Publishers.

Black, Robert. 1990. 'Machiavelli, servant of the Florentine republic'. In *Machiavelli and republicanism*, ed. Gisela Bock, Quentin Skinner and Maurizio Viroli, 71–99. Cambridge: Cambridge University Press.

Boal, Augusto. 1998. *Legislative theatre: using performance to make theatre.* London: Routledge.

2000. *Theater of the oppressed.* New edn. Trans. Charles A. Leal-McBride and Maria-Odilia Leal-McBride. London: Pluto Press.

Boës, Anne. 1982. *La lanterne magique de l'histoire: essai sur le théâtre historique en France de 1750 à 1789.* Studies on Voltaire and the eighteenth century 213. Oxford: Voltaire Foundation.

Bolton, Diane K. 1969a. 'The city of Coventry: social history to 1700'. In *The Victoria history of the counties of England: a history of the county of Warwick.* Volume VIII: *The city of Coventry and borough of Warwick*, ed. W. B. Stephens, 208–21. London: Oxford University Press.

1969b. 'The city of Coventry: the legend of Lady Godiva'. In *The Victoria history of the counties of England: a history of the county of Warwick*. Volume VIII: *The city of Coventry and borough of Warwick*, ed. W. B. Stephens, 242–7. London: Oxford University Press.

Brannan, Tessa, Peter John, and Gerry Stoker. 2007. *Re-energizing citizenship: strategies for civil renewal*. Basingstoke: Palgrave.

Brecht, Bertolt. 1964. *Brecht on theatre: the development of an aesthetic*, ed. John Willett. London: Eyre Methuen.

Brigden, Susan. 1989. *London and the Reformation*. Oxford: Clarendon.

1997. 'Youth and the English Reformation'. In *The impact of the English Reformation, 1500–1640*, ed. Peter Marshall, 55–85. London: Arnold.

Brooks, Douglas A. 2008. *Milton and the Jews*. Cambridge: Cambridge University Press.

Brown, Gregory S. 2002. *A field of honor: writers, court culture, and public theater in French literary life from Racine to the Revolution*. New York: Columbia University Press.

Brownlie, Ian, and Guy S. Goodwin-Gill. 2002. *Basic documents on human rights*. 4th edn. Oxford: Oxford University Press.

Brubaker, Rogers. 1992. *Citizenship and nationhood in France and Germany*. Cambridge, Mass.: Harvard University Press.

Bryce, Judith. 1995. 'The oral world of the early Accademia Fiorentina'. *Renaissance Studies* 9(1): 77–103.

Burbery, Timothy J. 2007. *Milton the dramatist*. Pittsburgh: Duquesne University Press.

Cahn, Steven M. 1997. *Classics of modern political theory: Machiavelli to Mill*. Oxford: Oxford University Press.

Camino, Mercedes Maroto. 1995. *The stage am I?: raping Lucrece in early modern England*. Lewiston, N.Y.: Edwin Mellen.

Canetti, Elias. 1962. *Crowds and power*. Trans. Carol Stewart. London: Gollancz.

Carey, Christopher. 1994. 'Comic ridicule and democracy'. In *Ritual, finance, politics: Athenian democratic accounts presented to David Lewis*, ed. Robin Osborne and Simon Hornblower, 69–83. Oxford: Clarendon.

Carlson, Marvin A. 1966. *The theatre of the French Revolution*. Ithaca, N.Y.: Cornell University Press.

1998. *Voltaire and the theatre of the eighteenth century*. Westport, Conn.: Greenwood Press.

Castiglione, Baldassare. 1976. *The courtier*. Trans. George Bull. Harmondsworth: Penguin.

Chambers, E. K. 1923. *The Elizabethan stage*. Oxford: Clarendon.

Chandavarkar, Rajnarayan. 2009. *History, culture and the Indian city: essays*. Cambridge: Cambridge University Press.

Chaponnière, Paul. 1936. *Voltaire chez les calvinistes*. Paris: Perrin.

Chatterjee, Minoti. 2004. *Theatre beyond the threshold: colonialism, nationalism and the Bengali stage, 1905–1947*. New Delhi: Indialog Publications.

Chénier, Marie-Joseph. 1824–6. *Œuvres de M. J. Chénier*. Paris: Guillaume.

2002. *Théâtre*, ed. Gauthier Ambrus and François Jacob. Paris: Flammarion.

Chevalley, Sylvie Bostsarron. 1961. *La Comédie-Française*. Paris: Comédie-Française.

Clark, Arthur Melville. 1931. *Thomas Heywood: playwright and miscellanist*. Oxford: Blackwell.

Clark, Barrett H. 1965. *European theories of the drama: an anthology of dramatic theory and criticism from Aristotle to the present day*. New York: Crown.

Cohen-Cruz, Jan. 2001. 'Motion of the ocean: the shifting face of U.S. theatre for social change since the 1960s'. *Theater* 31(3): 95–107.

Collins, Herbert Frederick. 1964. *Talma, a biography of an actor*. London: Faber and Faber.

Collinson, Patrick. 1988. *The birthpangs of Protestant England: religious and cultural change in the sixteenth and seventeenth centuries*. Basingstoke: Macmillan.

1996. 'Elizabethan and Jacobean puritanism as forms of popular religious culture'. In *The culture of English puritanism, 1560–1700*, ed. Christopher Durston and Jacqueline Eales, 32–57. Basingstoke: Macmillan.

Cook, Ann Jennalie. 1981. *The privileged playgoers of Shakespeare's London 1576–1642*. Princeton: Princeton University Press.

Corfield, P. J. 2007. *Time and the shape of history*. New Haven, Conn.: Yale University Press.

Cox Jensen, Freyja. 2009. *The ending of the Roman republic: its interpretation and representation in early modern England, c. 1570–1640*. DPhil., University of Oxford.

Cradock, Joseph. 1828. *Literary and miscellaneous memoirs*, ed. John Bowyer Nichols. 4 vols. London: J. B. Nichols.

Craig, Hardin. 1957. *Two Coventry Corpus Christi plays*. 2nd edn. Early English Text Society 87. London: Oxford University Press.

Cranston, Maurice William. 1983. *Jean-Jacques: the early life and work of Jean-Jacques Rousseau, 1712–1754*. London: Allen Lane.

1991. *The noble savage: Jean-Jacques Rousseau, 1754–1762*. London: Allen Lane.

1997. *The solitary self: Jean-Jacques Rousseau in exile and adversity*. London: Allen Lane.

Cropp, Martin, K. H. Lee, and David Sansone. 2000. *Euripides and tragic theatre in the late fifth century*. Illinois Classical Studies 24/25. Champaign: Stipes.

Crow, Thomas E. 1985. *Painters and public life in eighteenth-century Paris*. New Haven: Yale University Press.

Csapo, Eric. 2004. 'The politics of the new music'. In *Music and the Muses: the culture of 'mousike' in the classical Athenian city*, ed. P. Murray and P. J. Wilson, 207–48. Oxford: Oxford University Press.

2007. 'The men who built the theatres: *theatropolai, theatronai* and *arkhitektones*'. In *The Greek theatre and festivals: documentary studies*, ed. Peter Wilson, 87–115. Oxford: Oxford University Press.

Cummings, Anthony M. 2004. *The Maecenas and the madrigalist: patrons, patronage, and the origins of the Italian madrigal*. Philadelphia: American Philosophical Society.

Dalmia, Vasudha. 2006. *Poetics, plays and performances: the politics of modern Indian theatre*. New Delhi and Oxford: Oxford University Press.

    2009. '"I am a Hindu": assertions and queries'. In *Modern Indian theatre: a reader*, ed. Nandi Bhatia, 261–91. New Delhi and Oxford: Oxford University Press.

Daniell, David, ed. 1998. *Julius Caesar*. The Arden Shakespeare, 3rd series. Walton-on-Thames: Nelson.

Darnton, Robert. 1987. 'The facts of literary life in eighteenth-century France'. In *The French Revolution and the creation of modern political culture*, ed. Keith Michael Baker, 261–91. Oxford: Pergamon.

Davidson, Clifford. 2007. *Festivals and plays in late medieval Britain*. Aldershot: Ashgate.

Davies, Cecil W. 2000. *The Volksbühne movement: a history*. Amsterdam: Harwood Academic.

Davies, J. K. 1977–8. 'Athenian citizenship: the descent group and the alternatives'. *Classical Journal* 73: 105–21.

    1992. 'Society and economy'. In *The Cambridge ancient history*. Vol. v: *The fifth century B.C.*, ed. D. M. Lewis, John Boardman, J. K. Davies, and M. Ostwald, 2nd edn, 287–305. Cambridge: Cambridge University Press.

Dawson, Anthony B., and Paul Edward Yachnin. 2001. *The culture of playgoing in Shakespeare's England: a collaborative debate*. Cambridge: Cambridge University Press.

Debord, Guy. 1970. *Society of the spectacle*. Detroit: Black & Red.

Deeney, John F. 2007. 'National causes / moral clauses? The National Theatre, young people and citizenship'. *Research in Drama Education* 12(1): 331–4.

Dennett, Daniel Clement. 1992. *Consciousness explained*. London: Allen Lane.

Depew, David. 2007. 'From hymn to tragedy: Aristotle's genealogy of poetic kinds'. In *The origins of theater in ancient Greece and beyond: from ritual to drama*, ed. Eric Csapo and Margaret C. Miller, 126–49. Cambridge: Cambridge University Press.

Derrida, Jacques. 1997. *Of grammatology*. Baltimore, Md.: Johns Hopkins University Press.

Desnoiresterres, Gustave. 1875. *Voltaire et la société au XVIII siècle*. 2nd edn. Paris: Librairie Académique.

Dharwadker, Aparna Bhargava. 2005. *Theatres of independence: drama, theory, and urban performance in India since 1947*. Iowa City: University of Iowa Press.

    2009. 'The critique of western modernity in post-independence India'. In *Modern Indian theatre: a reader*, ed. Nandi Bhatia, 56–74. New Delhi and Oxford: Oxford University Press.

Diderot, Denis. 1936. *Diderot's writings on the theatre*, ed. F. C. Green. Cambridge: Cambridge University Press.

    1951. *Œuvres*. Bibliothèque de la Pléiade, ed. André Billy. Paris: Gallimard.

    1980. *Œuvres complètes*. Vol. x, ed. J. Chouillet and A.-M. Chouillet. Paris: Hermann.

1992. *Political writings*, ed. Robert Wokler and John Hope Mason. Cambridge: Cambridge University Press.

2005. *Theatres of independence: drama, theory, and urban performance in India since 1947*. Iowa City: University of Iowa Press.

Dillon, Matthew, and Lynda Garland. 2005. *Ancient Rome: from the early republic to the assassination of Julius Caesar*. London and New York: Routledge.

Dionisotti, Carlo. 1993. 'Machiavelli man of letters'. In *Machiavelli and the discourse of literature*, ed. Albert Russell Ascoli and Victoria Ann Kahn, 17–51. Ithaca, N. Y.: Cornell University Press.

Dover, Kenneth James. 1993. *Aristophanes: 'Frogs'*. Oxford: Clarendon.

Dowd, David Lloyd. 1948. *Pageant-master of the republic, Jacques-Louis David and the French Revolution*. Lincoln: University of Nebraska Press.

1960. 'Art and the theater during the French Revolution: the role of Louis David'. *Art Quarterly* 23: 3–22.

Drèze, Jean, and Amartya Sen. 2002. *India: development and participation*. 2nd edn. Oxford: Oxford University Press.

Dryzek, John S. 2002. *Deliberative democracy and beyond*. Oxford: Oxford University Press.

Duffy, Eamon. 2005. *The stripping of the altars: traditional religion in England c.1400–c.1580*. 2nd edn. New Haven, Conn.: Yale University Press.

Edmonds, David, and John Eidinow. 2006. *Rousseau's dog: two great thinkers at war in the age of enlightenment*. London: Faber and Faber.

Eichberg, Henning. 1977. 'The Nazi Thingspiel: theater for the masses in Fascism and proletarian culture', trans. Robert A. Jones. *New German Critique* 11: 133–50.

Eisenstadt, S. N. 2000. 'Multiple modernities'. *Daedalus* 129(1): 1–29.

Emery, Nathan, Nicola Clayton, and Christopher D. Frith. 2008. *Social intelligence: from brain to culture*. Oxford: Oxford University Press.

English, Mary. 2005. 'Aristophanes' *Frogs*: Brek-kek-kek-kek! on Broadway'. *American Journal of Philology* 126(1): 127–33.

Epstein, Steven. 1991. *Wage labor & guilds in medieval Europe*. Chapel Hill: University of North Carolina Press.

Estrée, Paul d'. 1913. *Le théâtre sous la terreur: 1793–1794. D'après des publications récentes et d'après les documents révolutionnaires du temps, imprimés ou inédits*. Paris: Émile-Paul.

Everitt, Anthony. 2001. 'Culture and citizenship'. In *Citizens: towards a citizenship culture*, ed. Bernard Crick, 64–73. Oxford: Blackwell.

Faulks, Keith. 2000. *Citizenship*. London: Routledge.

Feagin, Susan L., and Patrick Maynard. 1997. *Aesthetics*. Oxford: Oxford University Press.

Finlayson, James Gordon. 2005. *Habermas: a very short introduction*. Oxford: Oxford University Press.

Fischer-Lichte, Erika. 2005. *Theatre, sacrifice, ritual: exploring forms of political theatre*. London: Routledge.

Fletcher, Stella, and Christine Shaw. 2000. *The world of Savonarola: Italian élites and perceptions of crisis: papers from the conference held at the University of Warwick, 29–31 May 1998, to mark the fifth centenary of the death of Fra Girolamo Savonarola.* Aldershot: Ashgate.

Foley, Helene. 2000. 'The comic body in Greek art and drama'. In *Not the classical ideal: Athens and the construction of the other in Greek art*, ed. Beth Cohen, 275–311. Leiden: Brill.

Fontes-Baratto, Anna. 1974. 'Les fêtes à Urbin en 1513 et la "Calandria" de Bernardo Dovizi da Bibbiena'. In *Les écrivains et le pouvoir en Italie à l'époque de la renaissance*, ed. André Rochon. Vol. III, 45–79. Paris: Centre Interuniversitaire de Recherche sur la Renaissance Italienne.

Forsyth, Neil. 2008. *John Milton: a biography.* Oxford: Lion.

Frantz, Pierre. 1998. *L'esthétique du tableau dans le théâtre du XVIIIe siècle.* Paris: Presses Universitaires de France.

Fraser, Nancy, and Linda Gordon. 1994. 'Civil citizenship against social citizenship?' In *The condition of citizenship*, ed. Bart van Steenbergen, 90–107. London: Sage.

Freire, Paulo. 2003. *Pedagogy of the oppressed.* Trans. Myra Bergman Ramos. New York: Continuum.

Freud, Sigmund. 1985. *Civilization, society and religion: group psychology, civilization and its discontents and other works.* Trans. Albert Dickson. Pelican Freud library 12. Harmondsworth: Penguin.

Frevert, Ute. 2005. 'Civil society and citizenship in western democracies: historical developments and challenges'. In *Civil society, public sphere and citizenship: dialogues and perceptions*, ed. Rajeev Bhargava and Helmut Reifeld, 59–83. New Delhi and London: Sage.

Frézouls, E. 1983. 'La construction du *theatrum lapideum* et son contexte politique'. In *Théâtre et spectacles dans l antiquité, actes du colloque de Strasbourg (novembre 1981)*, 193–214. Strasbourg: Travaux du Centre de Recherche sur le Proche-Orient et la Grèce Antiques.

Friedland, Paul. 2002. *Political actors: representative bodies and theatricality in the age of the French revolution.* Ithaca, N. Y.: Cornell University Press.

Furet, François. 1981. *Interpreting the French Revolution.* Cambridge; Paris: Cambridge University Press; Éditions de la Maison des Sciences de l'Homme.

Gabarel, Jean Pierre. 1856. *Voltaire et les genevois.* Geneva: J. Cherbuliez.

Gadberry, Glen W. 1980. 'The Thingspiel and *das Frankenberger Wurfelspiel*'. *Drama Review* 24(1) (German theatre issue): 103–14.

1995. 'The first National Socialist theatre festival – Dresden 1934'. In *Theatre in the Third Reich, the prewar years: essays on theatre in Nazi Germany*, ed. Glen W. Gadberry, 121–39. Westport, Conn.: Greenwood Press.

Gandhi, Mohandas K. 1958–91. *The collected works of Mahatma Gandhi.* 100 vols. New Delhi: Publications Division, Government of India.

Gardiner, Harold C. 1946. *Mysteries' end: an investigation of the last days of the medieval religious stage.* New Haven: Yale University Press.

Gardner, Jane F. 1993. *Being a Roman citizen*. London: Routledge.

Gareffi, Andrea. 1991. *La scrittura e la festa: teatro, festa e letteratura nella Firenze del rinascimento*. Bologna: Mulino.

Gargett, Graham. 1994. *Jacob Vernet, Geneva, and the philosophes*. Studies on Voltaire and the eighteenth century 321. Oxford: Voltaire Foundation.

Gargi, Balwant. 1962. *Theatre in India*. New York: Theatre Arts Books.

Gay, Peter. 1959. *Voltaire's politics: the poet as realist*. Princeton: Princeton University Press.

Gellinek, Christian. 1983. *Hugo Grotius*. Boston, Mass.: Twayne.

Gilbert, Felix. 1949. 'Bernardo Rucellai and the Orti Oricellari: a study on the origin of modern political thought'. *Journal of the Warburg and Courtauld Institutes* 12: 101–31.

Godman, Peter. 1998. *From Poliziano to Machiavelli: Florentine humanism in the high renaissance*. Princeton, N. J.: Princeton University Press.

Goethe, Johann Wolfgang von. 1994. *Italian journey*. Trans. Robert R. Heitner. Princeton: Princeton University Press.

Goffman, Erving. 1959. *The presentation of self in everyday life*. Garden City, N. Y.: Doubleday.

Goldberg, Sander M. 1986. *Understanding Terence*. Princeton, N. J.: Princeton University Press.

Goldhill, Simon. 1991. *The poet's voice: essays on poetics and Greek literature*. Cambridge: Cambridge University Press.

    1997. 'The audience of Athenian tragedy'. In *The Cambridge companion to Greek tragedy*, ed. P. E. Easterling, 54–68. Cambridge: Cambridge University Press.

Gordon, Felicia, and Philip Nicholas Furbank. 2001. *Marie-Madeleine Jodin, 1741–1790: actress, philosophe and feminist*. Aldershot: Ashgate.

Goulbourne, Russell. 2000. 'The eighteenth-century "querelle des vers" and Jean Du Castre d'Auvigny's *La Tragédie en prose*'. *Studies on Voltaire and the Eighteenth Century* 5: 371–410.

Grange, Henri. 1977. 'La Revelliere-Lepeaux: théoricien de la fête nationale (1797)'. In *Les fêtes de la révolution: colloque de Clermont-Ferrand, juin 1974*, ed. Jean Ehrard and Paul Viallaneix, 493–502. Paris: Société des Études Robespierristes.

Gray, Chris Hables. 2001. *Cyborg citizen: politics in the posthuman age*. New York and London: Routledge.

Green, John. 1615. *A refutation of the Apology for Actors by J. G*. London: W. White.

Greenblatt, Stephen. 1980. *Renaissance self-fashioning: from More to Shakespeare*. Chicago: University of Chicago Press.

    1981. 'Invisible bullets: Renaissance authority and its subversion'. *Glyph: textual studies* 8: 40–61.

Grosby, Steven Elliott. 2005. *Nationalism: a very short introduction*. Oxford: Oxford University Press.

Grotius, Hugo. 1640. *Christs passion: a tragedie*. Trans. George Sandys. London: John Legatt.

1652. *Hugo Grotius his Sophompaneas, or Joseph: a tragedy.* Trans. Francis Gold-smith. London: W. H.

Gruen, Erich S. 1992. *Culture and national identity in republican Rome.* Ithaca, N.Y.: Cornell University Press.

Guibert, Noëlle. 1986. 'Talma et la création dramatique'. In *Dramaturgies, langages dramatiques: mélanges pour Jacques Scherer*, ed. Jacqueline Jomaron, 441–50. Paris: A.-G. Nizet.

Guibert, Noëlle, and Jacqueline Razgonnikoff. 1989. *Le journal de la Comédie-Française: 1787–1799, la comédie aux trois couleurs.* Paris: Sides.

Guichonnet, Paul. 1974. *Histoire de Genève.* Toulouse; Lausanne: Privately published; Payot.

Gurr, Andrew. 1991. *The Shakespearian stage 1574–1642.* Cambridge: Cambridge University Press.

1996a. *Playgoing in Shakespeare's London.* 2nd edn. Cambridge: Cambridge University Press.

1996b. *The Shakespearian playing companies.* Oxford: Clarendon.

2004. *The Shakespeare company, 1594–1642.* Cambridge: Cambridge University Press.

Habermas, Jürgen. 1989. *The structural transformation of the public sphere: an inquiry into a category of bourgeois society.* Cambridge: Polity.

1992. 'Further reflections on the public sphere'. In *Habermas and the public sphere*, ed. Craig Calhoun, 421–61. Cambridge, Mass.: MIT Press.

1994. 'Citizenship and national identity: some reflections on the future of Europe'. In *Citizenship: critical concepts*, ed. Bryan S. Turner and Peter Hamilton, 341–58. London: Routledge.

1996. 'Modernity: an unfinished project'. In *Habermas and the unfinished project of modernity: critical essays on the philosophical discourse of modernity*, ed. Maurizio Passerin d'Entrèves and Seyla Benhabib, 38–55. Cambridge: Polity.

Hadfield, Andrew. 2005. *Shakespeare and republicanism.* Cambridge: Cambridge University Press.

Hale, John K. 1991. 'Milton's Euripides marginalia: their significance for Milton studies'. *Milton Studies* 27: 23–35.

Hamiche, Daniel. 1973. *Le théâtre et la révolution: la lutte de classes au théâtre en 1789 et en 1793.* Paris: Union Générale d'Éditions.

Hammond, William, and Dan Steward. 2008. *Verbatim verbatim: contemporary documentary theatre.* London: Oberon.

Hampson, Norman. 1978. *Danton.* London: Duckworth.

1988. 'La Patrie'. In *The French Revolution and the creation of modern political culture*, ed. Colin Lucas, 125–37. Oxford: Pergamon.

Hansen, Mogens Herman. 1991. *The Athenian democracy in the age of Demosthenes: structure, principles and ideology.* Trans. J. A. Crook. Oxford: Blackwell.

Hare, David. 2005. *Obedience, struggle & revolt: lectures on theatre*. London: Faber and Faber.

Harris, Mary Dormer. 1911. *The story of Coventry*. London: Dent.

Hattaway, Michael, ed. 1969. *Francis Beaumont: the Knight of the Burning Pestle*. New Mermaids. London: Benn.

Haywood, Eric, ed. 2002. *Mandragola*. Dublin: UCD Foundation for Italian Studies.

Heater, Derek Benjamin, 1999. *What is citizenship?*. Cambridge: Polity.

2004. *Citizenship: the civic ideal in world history, politics and education*. 3rd edn. Manchester: Manchester University Press.

Hemmings, F. W. J. 1994. *Theatre and state in France, 1760–1905*. Cambridge: Cambridge University Press.

Henderson, J. J. 1998. 'Attic old comedy, frank speech, and democracy'. In *Democracy, empire, and the arts in fifth-century Athens*, ed. Deborah Dickmann Boedeker and Kurt A. Raaflaub, 255–73. Cambridge, Mass.: Harvard University Press.

Henke, Robert. 2007. 'Virtuosity and mimesis in the commedia dell'arte and *Hamlet*'. In *Italian culture in the drama of Shakespeare & his contemporaries: rewriting, remaking, refashioning*, ed. Michele Marrapodi, 69–82. Aldershot: Ashgate.

Herbert, Robert L. 1973. *David, Voltaire, 'Brutus' and the French Revolution: an essay in art and politics*. New York: Viking Press.

Heywood, Thomas. 1612. *An apology for actors*. London: N. Okes.

Hill, Aaron. 1736. *The tragedy of Zara*. London: John Watts.

Hill, Christopher. 1964. *Society and Puritanism in pre-revolutionary England*. London: Secker & Warburg.

1968. 'The Norman yoke'. In *Puritanism and revolution: studies in interpretation of the English revolution of the 17th century*, 58–125. London: Panther.

Hill, Tracey. 2004. *Anthony Munday and civic culture: theatre, history, and power in early modern London: 1580–1633*. Manchester: Manchester University Press.

Hobsbawm, E. J., and T. O. Ranger. 1983. *The invention of tradition*. Cambridge: Cambridge University Press.

Hoggett, Paul. 1997. *Contested communities: experiences, struggles, policies*. Bristol: Policy Press.

Holaday, Allan, ed. 1950. *Thomas Heywood: The Rape of Lucrece*. Illinois Studies in Language and Literature 34(3). Urbana: University of Illinois Press.

Honigmann, E. A. J., and Susan Brock. 1993. *Playhouse wills, 1558–1642: an edition of wills by Shakespeare and his contemporaries in the London theatre*. Manchester: Manchester University Press.

Hovasse, Jean-Marc. 2001. *Victor Hugo*. 4 vols. Paris: Fayard.

Howarth, W. D. 1997. *French theatre in the neo-classical era, 1550–1789*. Cambridge: Cambridge University Press.

Hulliung, Mark. 1983. *Citizen Machiavelli*. Princeton: Princeton University Press.

Hulton, Mary H. M. 1987. *'Company and fellowship': the medieval weavers of Coventry*. Oxford: Dugdale Society.

Hunt, Lynn Avery. 1986. *Politics, culture, and class in the French Revolution.* London: Methuen.

  2007. *Inventing human rights: a history.* New York: Norton.

Hunt, Peter. 1998. *Slaves, warfare and ideology in the Greek historians.* Cambridge: Cambridge University Press.

Huntington, Samuel P. 1996. *The clash of civilizations and the remaking of world order.* New York: Simon & Schuster.

Hutton, Ronald. 1996. *The stations of the sun: a history of the ritual year in Britain.* Oxford: Oxford University Press.

Ingram, R. W. 1979. '"Pleyng geire accustumed belongyng & necessarie": guild records and pageant production at Coventry'. In *Proceedings of the first colloquium at Erindale College, University of Toronto, 31 August–3 September 1978,* ed. Joanna Dutka, 60–100. Toronto: Records of Early English Drama.

  1981. *Records of Early English Drama. Coventry.* Manchester: Manchester University Press.

Innes, C. D. 1972. *Erwin Piscator's political theatre: the development of modern German drama.* Cambridge: Cambridge University Press.

Jackson, Tony. 2007. *Theatre, education and the making of meanings: art or instrument?.* Manchester: Manchester University Press.

James, Mervyn. 1983. 'Ritual, drama and social body in the late medieval town'. *Past and Present* 98: 3–29.

Jameson, Frederic. 2002. *A singular modernity: essay on the ontology of the present.* London: Verso.

Jaume, Lucien. 1987. 'Citoyenneté et souveraineté: le poids de l'absolutisme'. In *The French Revolution and the creation of modern political culture,* ed. Keith Michael Baker, 515–34. Oxford: Pergamon.

  2003. 'Citizen and state under the French Revolution'. In *States and citizens: history, theory, prospects,* ed. Quentin Skinner and Bo Stråth, 131–44. Cambridge: Cambridge University Press.

Jayal, Niraja Gopal. 2001. *Democracy in India.* New Delhi and Oxford: Oxford University Press.

Jelgerhuis, J. 1984. *Classicistic acting: two centuries of a performance tradition at the Amsterdam Schouwburg,* ed. Alfred Siemon Golding. Lanham, Md.: University Press of America.

Johnson, James H. 1992. 'Revolutionary audiences and the impossible imperatives of fraternity'. In *Re-creating authority in revolutionary France,* ed. Bryant T. Ragan and Elizabeth A. Williams, 57–78. New Brunswick, N. J.: Rutgers University Press.

  1995. *Listening in Paris: a cultural history.* Berkeley: University of California Press.

Jomaron, Jacqueline, ed. 1986. *Dramaturgies, langages dramatiques: mélanges pour Jacques Scherer.* Paris: A.-G. Nizet.

Jones, Colin. 2002. *The great nation: France from Louis XV to Napoleon 1715–99.* London: Allen Lane.

Jones, Nicholas F. 2004. *Rural Athens under the democracy.* Philadelphia: University of Pennsylvania Press.

Jones, Rosemary Devonshire. 1972. *Francesco Vettori, Florentine citizen and Medici servant.* University of London Historical Studies 34. London: Athlone.

Jose, Nicholas. 1984. *Ideas of the Restoration in English literature, 1660–71.* London: Macmillan.

Joseph, Stephen. 1967. *Theatre in the round.* London: Barrie & Rockcliff.

Juin, Hubert. 1980–6. *Victor Hugo.* 3 vols. Paris: Flammarion.

Kagan, Donald. 1987. *The fall of the Athenian empire.* Ithaca, N. Y.: Cornell University Press.

2003. *The Peloponnesian War.* New York: Viking Press.

Kamenetsky, Christa. 1972. 'Folklore as a political tool in Nazi Germany'. *Journal of American Folklore* 85: 221–35.

Kantor, Tadeusz, and Michal Kobialka. 1993. *A journey through other spaces: essays and manifestos.* Berkeley: University of California Press.

Karina, Lilian, and Marion Kant. 2003. *Hitler's dancers: German modern dance and the Third Reich.* New York and Oxford: Berghahn Books.

Kashyap, Subhash C. 1997. *Citizens and the constitution: citizenship values under the constitution.* 2nd edn. New Delhi: Publications Division, Government of India.

Kathman, David. 2004. 'Grocers, goldsmiths, and drapers: freemen and apprentices in the Elizabethan theater'. *Shakespeare Quarterly* 55(1): 1–49.

Kaviraj, Sudipta. 2003. 'A state of contradictions: the post-colonial state in India'. In *States and citizens: history, theory, prospects*, ed. Quentin Skinner and Bo Stråth, 145–63. Cambridge: Cambridge University Press.

Kew, Carole. 1999. 'From Weimar movement choir to Nazi community dance: the rise and fall of Rudolf Laban's "Festkultur"'. *Dance Research* 17(2): 73–96.

Kewes, Paulina. 2002. 'Roman history and the early Stuart drama: Thomas Heywood's *The Rape of Lucrece*'. *English Literary Renaissance* 32: 239–67.

Khan, Naseem. 2002. *The shared space: cultural diversity and the public domain: report from a working seminar held by the Arts Council of England and the Council of Europe, February 2002.* London: Arts Council of England.

King, Pamela M., and Clifford Davidson. 2000. *The Coventry Corpus Christi plays.* Kalamazoo: Medieval Institute Publications, Western Michigan University.

Kirchmeyer, Thomas. 1570. *The Popish Kingdome, or reigne of Antichrist, written in Latine verse by Thomas Naogeorgus.* Trans. Barnabe Googe. London: Henry Denham, for Richard Watkins.

Kirk, Linda. 1998. '"Going soft": Genevan decadence in the eighteenth century'. In *The identity of Geneva: the Christian commonwealth, 1564–1864*, ed. John B. Roney and Martin I. Klauber, 143–54. Westport, Conn.: Greenwood Press.

Kirkconnell, Watson. 1952. *The celestial cycle; the theme of Paradise Lost in world literature, with translations of the major analogues.* Toronto: University of Toronto Press.

Klein, Robert, and Henri Zerner. 1964. 'Vitruve et le théâtre de la renaissance italienne'. In *Le lieu théâtral à la renaissance: Royaumont, 22–27 mars, 1963*, ed. Jean Jacquot, Elie Konigson and Marcel Oddon, 49–60. Paris: Centre National de la Recherche Scientifique.

Knee, Philip. 2005. 'Sincérité et théâtralité'. *Annales de la Société Jean-Jacques Rousseau* 46: 137–54.

Knutson, Roslyn Lander. 2001. *Playing companies and commerce in Shakespeare's time*. Cambridge: Cambridge University Press.

Konstan, David. 1995. *Greek comedy and ideology*. Oxford: Oxford University Press.

Kowalzig, Barbara. 2004. 'Changing choral worlds: song-dance and society in Athens and beyond'. In *Music and the muses: the culture of 'mousikē' in the classical Athenian city*, ed. Penelope Murray and Peter Wilson, 39–65. Oxford: Oxford University Press.

2007a. *Singing for the gods: performances of myth and ritual in archaic and classical Greece*. Oxford: Oxford University Press.

2007b. '"And now all the world shall dance!" (Eur. *Bacch.* 114): Dionysus' *choroi* between drama and ritual'. In *The origins of theater in ancient Greece and beyond: from ritual to drama*, ed. Eric Csapo and Margaret C. Miller, 221–51. Cambridge: Cambridge University Press.

Kunz-Aubert, Ulysse. 1963. *Le théâtre à Genève: l'art lyrique et dramatique à Genève depuis le moyen-âge*. Geneva: Perret-Gentil.

Kymlicka, Will. 2001. *Politics in the vernacular: nationalism, multiculturalism and citizenship*. Oxford: Oxford University Press.

2002. *Contemporary political philosophy: an introduction*. 2nd edn. Oxford: Oxford University Press.

La Harpe, Jean François de. 1790. *Discours sur la liberté du théâtre*. Paris: Société des amis de la constitution.

Laban, Rudolf von. 1926. *Gymnastik und Tanz*. Oldenburg: G. Stalling.

1975. *A life for dance: reminiscences*. London: Macdonald & Evans.

Lada-Richards, Ismene. 1999. *Initiating Dionysus: ritual and theatre in Aristophanes' 'Frogs'*. Oxford: Clarendon.

Lancashire, Anne Begor. 2002. *London civic theatre: city drama and pageantry from Roman times to 1558*. Cambridge: Cambridge University Press.

Landes, Joan B. 1988. *Women and the public sphere in the age of the French Revolution*. Ithaca, N.Y.: Cornell University Press.

Lape, Susan. 2004. *Reproducing Athens: Menander's comedy, democratic culture, and the Hellenistic city*. Princeton: Princeton University Press.

Launay, Michel. 1989. *Jean-Jacques Rousseau, écrivain politique (1712–1762)*. 2nd edn. Geneva: Slatkine.

Le Bon, Gustave. 1977. *The crowd: a study of the popular mind*. New York: Viking.

Le Pors, Anicet. 1999. *La citoyenneté*. Paris: Presses Universitaires de France.

Lee, Simon. 1999. *David*. London: Phaidon.

Lefebvre, Georges. 1964. *The French Revolution: from 1793–1799*. Trans. John Hall Stewart and James Friguglietti. London: Routledge and Kegan Paul.

Leigh, Matthew. 2004. *Comedy and the rise of Rome*. Oxford: Oxford University Press.

Leoni, Sylviane. 1998. *Le poison et le remède: théâtre, morale et rhétorique en France et en Italie, 1694–1758*. Studies on Voltaire and the eighteenth century 360. Oxford: Voltaire Foundation.

Lever, Maurice. 2001. *Théâtre et lumières: les spectacles de Paris au XVIIIe siècle*. Paris: Fayard.

Lieby, Adolphe. 1901. *Étude sur le théâtre de Marie-Joseph Chénier*. Paris: Société Française d'Imprimerie et de Librairie.

Lieven, Anatol. 2005; 2004. *America right or wrong: an anatomy of American nationalism*. London: Harper Perennial.

Lintott, Andrew. 1999. *The constitution of the Roman republic*. Oxford: Clarendon.

Liu, Alan. 1989. 'The power of formalism: the new historicism'. *ELH* 56: 721–71.

Long des Clavières, Pauline. 1920. *La jeunesse de Grétry et ses débuts à Paris*. Besançon: Jacques et Demontrond.

Loraux, Nicole. 1986. *The invention of Athens: the funeral oration in the classical city*. Trans. Alan Sheridan. Cambridge, Mass.: Harvard University Press.

Lunari, Luigi, and Carlo Pedretti, eds. 1978. *Goldoni: Le Baruffe Chiozzotte*. Milan: Rizzoli.

Lupton, Julia Reinhard. 2005. *Citizen-saints: Shakespeare and political theology*. Chicago: University of Chicago Press.

Lüsebrink, Hans-Jürgen. 1992. 'Réécritures et formes de réception du *Brutus* de Voltaire au dix-huitième siècle'. In *Transactions of the eighth international congress on the Enlightenment*, 1871–4. Oxford: Voltaire Foundation.

Machiavelli, Niccolò. 1961. *The literary works of Machiavelli*, ed. and trans. J. R. Hale. London: Oxford University Press.

  1989. *The chief works and others*, ed. and trans. Allan H. Gilbert. 3 vols. Durham, N. C.: Duke University Press.

  2005. *Opere*, ed. Corrado Vivanti. 3 vols. Turin: Einaudi.

MacKendrick, Paul Lachlan, and Karen Lee Singh. 1989. *The philosophical books of Cicero*. London: Duckworth.

Magnette, Paul. 2005. *Citizenship: the history of an idea*. Trans. Katya Long. Colchester: ECPR.

Maletic, Vera. 1987. *Body, space, expression: the development of Rudolf Laban's movement and dance concepts*. Berlin: Mouton de Gruyter.

Manin, Bernard. 1997. *The principles of representative government*. Cambridge: Cambridge University Press.

Marcus, Leah S. 1986. *The politics of mirth: Jonson, Herrick, Milton, Marvell, and the defense of old holiday pastimes*. Chicago: University of Chicago Press.

Marmontel, Jean François. 1777. 'Parterre'. In *Supplément à l'Encyclopédie*. Vol. IV, 241–2. Amsterdam: Rey.

Martinez, Lauro. 2000. 'Literary crisis in the generation of 1494'. In *The world of Savonarola: Italian élites and perceptions of crisis: papers from the conference held at the University of Warwick, 29–31 May 1998*, ed. Stella Fletcher and Christine Shaw, 5–21. Aldershot: Ashgate.

Marx, Karl. 1963. *Early writings*. Trans. T. B. Bottomore. London: Watts.

Maslan, Susan. 2005. *Revolutionary acts: theater, democracy, and the French Revolution*. Baltimore, Md.: Johns Hopkins University Press.

Maynard, Michel Ulysse. 1867. *Voltaire, sa vie et ses oeuvres*. 2 vols. Paris: A. Bray.

McGlew, James F. 2002. *Citizens on stage: comedy and political culture in the Athenian democracy*. Ann Arbor: University of Michigan Press.

McGrath, John. 1996. *A good night out: popular theatre: audience, class, and form*. 2nd edn. London: Nick Hern.

McGuire, Maryann Cale. 1983. *Milton's puritan masque*. Athens: University of Georgia Press.

McPhail, Clark. 1991. *The myth of the madding crowd*. New York: Aldine de Gruyter.

Mee, Erin B. 2008. *Theatre of roots: redirecting the modern Indian stage*. London: Seagull.

Megson, Chris, and Dan Rebellato. 2007. '"Theatre and anti-theatre": David Hare and public speaking'. In *The Cambridge companion to David Hare*, ed. Richard Boon, 236–49. Cambridge: Cambridge University Press.

Melton, James Van Horn. 2001. *The rise of the public in Enlightenment Europe*. Cambridge: Cambridge University Press.

Mercier, Louis-Sébastien. 1773. *Du théâtre, ou, nouvel essai sur l'art dramatique*. Amsterdam: E. van Harrevelt.

Millar, Fergus. 1998. *The crowd in Rome in the late republic*. Ann Arbor: University of Michigan Press.

2002. *The Roman Republic in political thought*. Hanover: University Press of New England.

Miller, David. 2000. *Citizenship and national identity*. Cambridge: Polity.

Millin, A. L. 1790. *Sur la liberté du théâtre*. Paris: Lagrange.

Milton, John. 1931–8. *The works of John Milton*, ed. Frank Allen Patterson. 18 vols. New York: Columbia University Press.

1953–82. *Complete prose works of John Milton*, ed. Don Marion Wolfe. 8 vols. New Haven; London: Yale University Press; Oxford University Press.

Mistry, Rohinton. 2002. *Family matters*. London: Faber and Faber.

Mitchell, Thomas N. 1991. *Cicero, the senior statesman*. New Haven: Yale University Press.

Mohamed, Feisal G. 2005. 'Confronting religious violence: Milton's *Samson Agonistes*'. *PMLA* 120: 327–40.

Molinari, C. 1964. 'Les rapports entre la scène et les spectateurs dans le theatre italien du XVIe siècle'. In *Le lieu théâtral à la renaissance: Royaumont, 22–27 mars, 1963*, ed. Jean Jacquot, Elie Konigson and Marcel Oddon, 61–71. Paris: Centre National de la Recherche Scientifique.

Montrose, Louis A. 1995. 'A kingdom of shadows'. In *The theatrical city: culture, theatre, and politics in London, 1576–1649*, ed. David L. Smith, Richard Strier and David M. Bevington, 68–86. Cambridge: Cambridge University Press.

Moraw, Susanne, and Eckehart Nölle. 2002. *Die Geburt des Theaters in der griechischen Antike*. Mainz am Rhein: Philipp Von Zabern.

Moretti, Jean-Charles. 2000. 'The theater of the sanctuary of Dionysus Eleuthereus in late fifth-century Athens'. *Illinois Classical Studies* 24–5: 377–98.

Moscovici, Serge. 1985. *The age of the crowd: a historical treatise on mass psychology*. Cambridge; Paris: Cambridge University Press; Maison des Sciences de l'Homme.

Mosse, George L. 1975. *The nationalization of the masses: political symbolism and mass movements in Germany from the Napoleonic wars through the Third Reich.* New York: H. Fertig.

    2003. *Nazi culture: intellectual, cultural, and social life in the Third Reich.* Madison: University of Wisconsin Press.

Mouffe, Chantal. 1993. *The return of the political.* London: Verso.

Mozzati, Tommaso. 2008. *Giovanfrancesco Rustici: le compagnie del Paiuolo e della Cazzuola; arte, letteratura, festa nell'età della maniera.* Florence: L. S. Olschki.

Mullaney, Steve. 1988. *The place of the stage: license, play and power in renaissance England.* Chicago: University of Chicago Press.

Muraro, M. T. 1964. 'Le lieu des spectacles (publics ou privés) dans le théâtre italien du XVIe siècle'. In *Le lieu théâtral à la renaissance: Royaumont, 22–27 mars, 1963*, ed. Jean Jacquot, Elie Konigson and Marcel Oddon, 61–71. Paris: Éditions du Centre National de la Recherche Scientifique.

Nancy, Jean-Luc. 1991. *The inoperative community.* Minneapolis: University of Minnesota Press.

    2000. *Being singular plural.* Stanford, Calif.: Stanford University Press.

Nehru, Jawaharlal. 1946. *The discovery of India.* London: Meridian.

Newbigin, Nerida. 1996. *Feste d'Oltrarno: plays in churches in fifteenth-century Florence.* Florence: L. S. Olschki.

Nicholson, Helen. 2005. *Applied drama: the gift of theatre.* Basingstoke and New York: Palgrave Macmillan.

Nicolet, Claude. 1976. *Le métier de citoyen dans la Rome républicaine.* Paris: Gallimard.

Niven, William. 2000. 'The birth of Nazi drama? *Thing* plays'. In *Theatre under the Nazis*, ed. John London, 54–95. Manchester: Manchester University Press.

Oommen, T. K. 2004. 'Crisis of citizenship education in the Indian republic: contestation between cultural monists and pluralists'. In *Diversity and citizenship education: global perspectives*, ed. James A. Banks, 333–54. San Francisco: Jossey-Bass.

Orgel, Stephen. 1975. *The illusion of power: political theater in the English renaissance.* Berkeley: University of California Press.

Orrell, John. 1988. *The human stage: English theatre design, 1567–1640.* Cambridge: Cambridge University Press.

Ozouf, Mona. 1988. *Festivals and the French Revolution.* Trans. Alan Sheridan. Cambridge, Mass.: Harvard University Press.

    1992. 'Liberté, égalité, fraternité'. In *Les lieux de mémoire*, ed. Pierre Nora. Vol. III, 582–629. Paris: Gallimard.

Padoan, Giorgio. 1978. *Momenti del rinascimento veneto*. Padova: Antenore.

Paquet, Dominique. 1989. 'Le jeu de l'acteur'. In *Actes du colloque théâtre et révolution*, ed. Lucile Garbagnati and Marita Gilli, 69–82. Besançon; Paris: Université de Besançon; Les Belles Lettres.

Parker, Robert. 2005. *Polytheism and society at Athens*. Oxford: Oxford University Press.

Parker, William Riley, and Gordon Campbell. 1996. *Milton: a biography*. 2nd edn. Oxford: Clarendon.

Pearl, Valerie. 1961. *London and the outbreak of the puritan revolution: city government and national politics, 1625–43*. London: Oxford University Press.

Peltonen, Markku. 1995. *Classical humanism and republicanism in English political thought, 1570–1640*. Cambridge: Cambridge University Press.

Petrini, Armando. 1996. *La 'Signoria di madonna Finzione': teatro, attori e poetiche nel Rinascimento italiano*. Genova: Costa & Nolan.

Phythian-Adams, Charles. 1979. *Desolation of a city: Coventry and the urban crisis of the late middle ages*. Cambridge: Cambridge University Press.

Piccioli, Gianandrea. 1968. 'Gli Orti Oricellari'. In *Contributi dell'Istituto di Filologia Moderna: serie storia del teatro*. Vol. 1: 60–93. Milan: Istituto di Filologia Moderna.

Pickard-Cambridge, Arthur Wallace. 1988. *The dramatic festivals of Athens*, revised by John Gould and David M. Lewis. 2nd edn. Oxford: Clarendon.

Picot, Jean. 1811. *Histoire de Genève, depuis les tems les plus anciens, jusqu'à nos jours*. 3 vols. Genève: Manget & Cherbuliez.

Pincus, Steven C. A. 2007. 'The state and civil society in early modern England: capitalism, causation and Habermas' bourgeois public sphere'. In *The politics of the public sphere in early modern England*, ed. Peter Lake and Steven C. A. Pincus, 213–31. Manchester: Manchester University Press.

Piscator, Erwin. 1963. *Das politische Theater*, ed. Felix Gasbarra. Reinbek bei Hamburg: Rowohlt.

Pois, Robert A. 1995. 'National Socialist *Volksgemeinschaft* fantasy and the drama of national rebirth'. In *Theatre in the Third Reich, the prewar years: essays on theatre in Nazi Germany*, ed. Glen W. Gadberry, 17–31. Westport, Conn.: Greenwood Press.

Poli-Palladini, Letizia. 2001. 'Some reflections on Aeschylus' "Aetnae(ae)"'. *Rheinisches Museum* 144: 287–325.

Poliziano, Angelo. 1973. *La commedia antica e l'Andria di Terenzio*, ed. Rosetta Lattanzi Roselli. Florence: Sansoni.

Pomeau, René. 1955. *Voltaire par lui-même*. Paris: Seuil.
1994a. *'Écraser l'infâme': 1759–1770*. Voltaire en son temps 4. Oxford: Voltaire Foundation.
1994b. *On a voulu l'enterrer: 1770–1791*. Voltaire en son temps 5. Oxford: Voltaire Foundation.

Pomeau, René, and Christiane Mervaud. 1991. *De la cour au jardin: 1750–1759*. Voltaire en son temps 3. Oxford: Voltaire Foundation.

Porter, Roy. 1996. *London: a social history*. London: Penguin.

Pradhan, Sudhi. 1979. *Marxist cultural movements in India: chronicles and documents, 1936–1947*. Calcutta: Santi Pradhan.

Prentki, Tim. 1998. '"Must the show go on?" The case for Theatre for Development'. *Development in Practice* 8(4): 419–29.

Preston-Dunlop, Valerie Monthland. 1998. *Rudolf Laban: an extraordinary life*. London: Dance.

Raaflaub, Kurt A., Josiah Ober, and Robert W. Wallace. 2007. *Origins of democracy in ancient Greece*. Berkeley: University of California Press.

Rancière, Jacques. 2004. *The politics of aesthetics: the distribution of the sensible*. Trans. Gabriel Rockhill. London: Continuum.

  2006. *Hatred of democracy*. Trans. Steve Corcoran. London: Verso.

  2009. *The emancipated spectator*. Trans. Gregory Elliott. London: Verso.

Rappaport, Steve Lee. 1989. *Worlds within worlds: structures of life in sixteenth-century London*. Cambridge: Cambridge University Press.

Ravel, Jeffrey S. 1999. *The contested parterre: public theater and French political culture, 1680–1791*. Ithaca, N. Y.: Cornell University Press.

Ravenhill, Mark. 2008. *Plays: 2*. London: Methuen.

Rawson, Elizabeth. 1989. 'Roman tradition and the Greek world'. In *The Cambridge ancient history*. Vol. VIII: *Rome and the Mediterranean to 133 B.C.*, ed. A. E. Astin, 2nd edn, 422–76. Cambridge: Cambridge University Press.

Rebhorn, Wayne A. 1990. 'The crisis of the aristocracy in *Julius Caesar*'. *Renaissance Quarterly* 43: 75–111.

Regnault-Warin, J.-J. 1904. *Mémoires sur Talma*, ed. Henri d' Alméras. Paris: Société Parisienne d'Édition.

Reiter, William. 1988. *Aemilius Paullus: conqueror of Greece*. London: Croom Helm.

Renwick, John, ed. 1998. *Voltaire: Oeuvres 5, 1728–1730*. Oxford: Voltaire Foundation.

Revermann, Martin. 2001. 'Euripides, tragedy and Macedon: some conditions of reception'. *Illinois Classical Studies* 25: 451–68.

Rhodes, P. J. 2003. 'Nothing to do with democracy: Athenian drama and the polis'. *Journal of Hellenic Studies* 123: 104–19.

Ridolfi, Roberto. 1963. *The life of Niccolò Machiavelli*. Trans. Cecil Grayson. London: Routledge & Kegan Paul.

Riesenberg, Peter. 1992. *Citizenship in the western tradition: Plato to Rousseau*. Chapel Hill: University of North Carolina Press.

Ripley, John. 1980. *Julius Caesar on stage in England and America, 1599–1973*. Cambridge: Cambridge University Press.

Roach, Joseph R. 1985. *The player's passion: studies in the science of acting*. Newark; London: University of Delaware Press; Associated University Presses.

Roberts, Warren. 1989. *Jacques-Louis David, revolutionary artist: art, politics and the French Revolution*. Chapel Hill: University of North Carolina Press.

Robespierre, Maximilien. 1965. *Discours et rapports à la Convention*. Paris: Union Générale d'Éditions.

Rorty, Richard. 1998. 'Justice as a larger loyalty'. In *Cosmopolitics: thinking and feeling beyond the nation*, ed. Pheng Cheah and Bruce Robbins, 45–58. Minneapolis: University of Minnesota Press.

Rose, Mark. 1989. 'Conjuring Caesar: ceremony, history, and authority in 1599'. *English Literary Renaissance* 19: 291–304.

Rose, R. B. 1969. 'The city of Coventry: the common lands'. In *The Victoria history of the counties of England: a history of the county of Warwick*. Volume viii: *The city of Coventry and borough of Warwick*, ed. W. B. Stephens, 199–207. London: Oxford University Press.

Rosenberg, Pierre. 2002. *Jacques-Louis David, 1748–1825: catalogue raisonné des dessins*. Milan: Leonardo Arte.

Rosenblatt, Helena. 1997. *Rousseau and Geneva: from the First Discourse to the Social Contract, 1749–1762*. Cambridge: Cambridge University Press.

Rousseau, Jean-Jacques. 1959. *Les confessions; autres textes autobiographiques*, ed. Bernard Gagnebin and Marcel Raymond. Bibliothèque de la Pléiade 1. Paris: Gallimard.

    1961. *La nouvelle Héloïse: théâtre; poésies; essais littéraires*, ed. Bernard Gagnebin and Marcel Raymond. Bibliothèque de la Pléiade 2. Paris: Gallimard.

    1964. *Du contrat social: écrits politiques*, ed. Bernard Gagnebin and Marcel Raymond. Bibliothèque de la Pléiade 3. Paris: Gallimard.

    1965–98. *Correspondance complète de Jean Jacques Rousseau: édition critique*, ed. R. A. Leigh. Geneva: Institut et Musée Voltaire.

    1969. *Emile: éducation, morale, botanique*, ed. Bernard Gagnebin and Marcel Raymond. Bibliothèque de la Pléiade 4. Paris: Gallimard.

    1992. *Discours sur les sciences et les arts; Discours sur l'origine de l'inégalité*, ed. Jacques Roger. Paris: Flammarion.

    1995. *Écrits sur la musique, la langue et le théâtre*, ed. Bernard Gagnebin, Marcel Raymond and Samuel Baud-Bovy. Bibliothèque de la Pléiade 5. Paris: Gallimard.

    1997a. *The Discourses and other early political writings*. Trans. Victor Gourevitch. Cambridge: Cambridge University Press.

    1997b. *The Social Contract and other later political writings*. Trans. Victor Gourevitch. Cambridge: Cambridge University Press.

    2003. *Lettre à d'Alembert*, ed. Marc Buffat. Paris: Flammarion.

Royle, Nicholas. 2006. '*Julius Caesar* and the democracy to come'. In *Julius Caesar in western culture*, ed. Maria Wyke, 203–27. Oxford: Blackwell.

Rubin, Miri. 1991. *Corpus Christi: the Eucharist in late medieval culture*. Cambridge: Cambridge University Press.

Rubinstein, Nicolai. 1990. 'Machiavelli and Florentine republican experience'. In *Machiavelli and republicanism*, ed. Gisela Bock, Quentin Skinner and Maurizio Viroli, 3–16. Cambridge: Cambridge University Press.

Saïd, Suzanne. 1998. 'Tragedy and politics'. In *Democracy, empire, and the arts in fifth-century Athens*, ed. Deborah Dickmann Boedeker and Kurt A. Raaflaub, 275–96. Cambridge, Mass.: Harvard University Press.

Sandel, Michael J. 1998. *Liberalism and the limits of justice*. 2nd edn. Cambridge: Cambridge University Press.

Sarrazac, Jean-Pierre. 1992. 'Le drame selon les moralistes et les philosophes'. In *Le théâtre en France du moyen age à nos jours*, ed. Jacqueline Jomaron, 295–353. Paris: A. Colin.

Sauer, Elizabeth. 1998. 'The politics of performance in the inner theater: *Samson Agonistes* as closet drama'. In *Milton and heresy*, ed. Stephen B. Dobranski and John Peter Rumrich, 199–215. Cambridge: Cambridge University Press.

Schama, Simon. 1989. *Citizens: a chronicle of the French Revolution*. London: Penguin.

Schechner, Richard. 1988. *Performance theory*. 2nd edn. New York and London: Routledge.

Schoenbaum, S. 1993. *Shakespeare's lives*. Oxford: Oxford University Press.

Scurr, Ruth. 2006. *Fatal purity: Robespierre and the French Revolution*. London: Chatto & Windus.

Seaford, Richard. 1994. *Reciprocity and ritual: Homer and tragedy in the developing city-state*. Oxford: Clarendon.

Segal, Erich. 1968. *Roman laughter: the comedy of Plautus*. Cambridge, Mass.: Harvard University Press.

Sen, Amartya. 2005. *The argumentative Indian: writings on Indian history, culture and identity*. London: Allen Lane.

2009. *The idea of justice*. London: Allen Lane.

Sen, Manikuntala. 2001. *In search of freedom: an unfinished journey*. Calcutta: Stree.

Sennett, Richard. 1977. *The fall of public man*. Cambridge: Cambridge University Press.

1994. *Flesh and stone: the body and the city in western civilization*. London: Faber and Faber.

2006. *The culture of the new capitalism*. New Haven: Yale University Press.

2008. *The craftsman*. London: Allen Lane.

Sewell, William H. 1988. 'Le citoyen/la citoyenne: activity, passivity, and the revolutionary concept of citizenship'. In *The French Revolution and the creation of modern political culture*, ed. Colin Lucas, 105–23. Oxford: Pergamon.

Shafer, Yvonne. 1995. 'Nazi Berlin and the Grosses Schauspielhaus'. In *Theatre in the Third Reich, the prewar years: essays on theatre in Nazi Germany*, ed. Glen W. Gadberry, 103–19. Westport, Conn.: Greenwood Press.

Shapiro, James S. 2005. *1599: a year in the life of William Shakespeare*. London: Faber and Faber.

Sharp, Thomas. 1825. *A dissertation on the pageants or dramatic mysteries anciently performed at Coventry by the trading companies of that city . . . To which are added the pageant of the Shearmen & Taylors' company, and other municipal entertainments of a public nature*. Coventry: Merridew.

Shearman, John. 1962. 'Pontormo and Andrea del Sarto, 1513'. *Burlington Magazine* 104 (November): 478–50.

Shell, Susan Meld. 2000. 'Machiavelli's discourse on language'. In *The comedy and tragedy of Machiavelli: essays on the literary works*, ed. Vickie B. Sullivan, 78–101. New Haven: Yale University Press.

Sheth, D. L. 2005. 'Nation-building and the making of civil society'. In *Civil society, public sphere and citizenship: dialogues and perceptions*, ed. Rajeev Bhargava and Helmut Reifeld, 384–401. New Delhi and London: Sage Publications.

Sices, David, and James B. Atkinson, eds. 1985. *The comedies of Machiavelli*. Hanover: University Press of New England.

Skinner, Quentin. 1991. 'The paradoxes of political liberty'. In *Liberty*, ed. David Miller, 183–205. Oxford: Oxford University Press.

2000. *Machiavelli: a very short introduction*. Oxford: Oxford University Press.

2003. 'States and the freedom of citizens'. In *States and citizens: history, theory, prospects*, ed. Quentin Skinner and Bo Stråth, 11–27. Cambridge: Cambridge University Press.

Smith, Anthony D. 1999. *Myths and memories of the nation*. Oxford: Oxford University Press.

Smith, David L., Richard Strier, and David M. Bevington. 1995. *The theatrical city: culture, theatre, and politics in London, 1576–1649*. Cambridge: Cambridge University Press.

Société d'Histoire et d'Archéologie de Genève. 1951. *Histoire de Genève des origines à 1798*. Geneva: Société d'Histoire et d'Archéologie.

Sommerstein, Alan H. 1993. 'Kleophon and the restaging of *Frogs*'. In *Tragedy, comedy and the polis: papers from the Greek drama conference, Nottingham, 18–20 July 1990*, ed. Alan H. Sommerstein, 461–76. Bari: Levante.

Sommerstein, Alan H., ed. 1996. *Aristophanes: 'Frogs'*. Warminster: Aris & Phillips.

Sommerstein, Alan H., and David Barrett. 1978. *The knights; [and] Peace; [and] The birds; [and] The assemblywomen; [and] Wealth / [by] Aristophanes; translated [from the Greek] by David Barrett and Alan H. Sommerstein*. Harmondsworth and New York: Penguin.

Sorabji, Richard. 2006. *Self: ancient and modern insights about individuality, life, and death*. Oxford: Clarendon.

Spevack, Marvin, ed. 2003. *Julius Caesar*. The New Cambridge Shakespeare. 2nd edn. Cambridge: Cambridge University Press.

Srampickal, Jacob. 1994. *Voice to the voiceless: the power of people's theatre in India*. London: Hurst & Company.

Starobinski, Jean. 1979. *1789: les emblèmes de la raison*. Paris: Flammarion.

1987. *The invention of liberty, 1700–1789*. Trans. Bernard C. Swift. Geneva; New York: Skira; Rizzoli.

1988. *Jean-Jacques Rousseau: transparency and obstruction*. Trans. Arthur Gold-hammer. Chicago: University of Chicago Press.

1991. *Diderot dans l'espace des peintres; suivi de, Le sacrifice en rêve*. Paris: Réunion des Musées Nationaux.

Stäuble, Antonio, ed. 2004. *Mandragola*. Florence: F. Cesati.

Stoppelli, Pasquale. 2005. *La mandragola: storia e filologia: con l'edizione critica del testo secondo il laurenziano redi 129*. Roma: Bulzoni.

Stow, John. 1908. *A survey of London*, ed. Charles Lethbridge Kingsford. Oxford: Clarendon.

Strype, John. 1720. *A survey of the cities of London and Westminster*. London: Printed for A. Churchill, *et al.*

Stuckart, Wilhelm, and H. Globke. 1936. *Kommentare zur deutschen Rassengesetzgebung*. Munich and Berlin: Beck.

Swanson, Heather. 1988. 'The illusion of economic structure: craft guilds in late medieval English towns'. *Past and Present* 121: 29–48.

1989. *Medieval artisans: an urban class in late medieval England*. Oxford: Blackwell.

Symes, Carol. 2007. *A common stage: theater and public life in medieval Arras*. Ithaca, N. Y.: Cornell University Press.

Szondi, Peter. 1984. 'Denis Diderot: théorie et pratique dramatique'. In *Diderot: les grands dramaturges*, ed. Jacques Chouillet, 33–61. Paris: Comédie Française.

Tagore, Rabindranath. 1996. *The English writings of Rabindranath Tagore*, ed. Sisir Kumar Das. New Delhi: Sahitya Akademi.

2001. *Selected writings on literature and language*, ed. Sisir Kumar Das and Sukanta Chaudhuri. New Delhi: Oxford University Press.

Talma, François Joseph. 2002. *Réflexions sur Lekain et sur l'art théâtral*, ed. Pierre Frantz. Paris: Desjonquères.

Tarin, René. 1998. *Le théâtre de la constituante, ou, l'école du peuple*. Paris: H. Champion.

Taylor, Charles. 1985. *Philosophy and the human sciences*. Philosophical papers 2. Cambridge: Cambridge University Press.

1999. 'Two theories of modernity'. In *Alter/native modernities*, ed. Dilip Parameshwar Gaonkar, 153–74. Durham, N. C.: Duke University Press.

2004. 'No community, no democracy'. In *The communitarian reader: beyond the essentials*, ed. Amitai Etzioni, Drew Volmert and Elanit Rothschild, 27–43. Lanham, Md. and Oxford: Rowman & Littlefield.

Taylor, Gary. 1991. *Reinventing Shakespeare: a cultural history from the Restoration to the present*. London: Vintage.

Thapar, Raj. 1991. *All these years: a memoir*. New Delhi: Seminar Publications.

Thompson, J. M. 1968 (1935). *Robespierre*. New York: H. Fertig.

Thompson, James. 2009. *Performance affects: applied theatre and the end of effect*. Basingstoke: Palgrave Macmillan.

Tocqueville, Alexis de. 1954. *Democracy in America*, trans. Henry Reeve, rev. Francis Bowen, corrected and edited by Phillips Bradley. 2 vols. New York: Vintage.

1998. *The old regime and the revolution*, ed. François Furet, Françoise Mélonio and Alan S. Kahan. Vol. 1: *The complete text*. Chicago: University of Chicago Press.

Tönnies, Ferdinand. 1957. *Community & society*. East Lansing: Michigan State University Press.

Touchefeu, Yves. 1999. *L'antiquité et le christianisme dans la pensée de Jean-Jacques Rousseau*. Studies on Voltaire and the eighteenth century 372. Oxford: Voltaire Foundation.

Trachtenberg, Zev M. 1993. *Making citizens: Rousseau's political theory of culture.* London: Routledge.

Trexler, Richard C. 1980. *Public life in renaissance Florence.* New York and London: Academic Press.

Trexler, Richard C., and Mary E. Lewis. 1981. 'Two captains and three kings: new light on the Medici chapel'. *Studies in Medieval and Renaissance History* 4: 99–177.

Tulard, Jean. 1989. *La Révolution.* Paris: Association pour la Publication d'une Histoire de Paris.

Turner, Bryan S. 1993. *Citizenship and social theory.* London: Sage.

Unwin, George. 1908. *The gilds and companies of London.* London: Methuen.

Van Steen, Gonda. 2007. 'Aristophanes and politics: watchword "caution!"'. In *The Cambridge companion to Greek and Roman theatre*, ed. Marianne McDonald and J. Michael Walton, 108–23. Cambridge: Cambridge University Press.

Van Steenbergen, Bart. 1994. *The condition of citizenship.* London: Sage.

Vanderbroeck, Paul J. J. 1987. *Popular leadership and collective behavior in the late roman republic (ca. 80–50 B.C.).* Amsterdam: Gieben.

Vasari, Giorgio. 1996. *Lives of the painters, sculptors and architects*, trans. Gaston du C. De Vere. London: David Campbell.

Ventrone, Paola, ed. 1992. *Le temps revient: 'l tempo si rinuova: feste e spettacoli nella Firenze di Lorenzo il Magnifico.* Milan: Silvana Editoriale.

  1996. 'Lorenzo's *politica festiva*'. In *Lorenzo the Magnificent: culture and politics*, ed. Michael Edward Mallett and Nicholas Mann, 105–16. London: Warburg Institute.

Vernant, Jean Pierre, and Pierre Vidal-Naquet. 1988. *Myth and tragedy in ancient Greece.* Trans. Janet Lloyd. New York: Zone Books.

Voltaire. 1792. *Œuvres de Voltaire*, ed. M. Palissot. Paris: Stoupe & Servière.

  1877–85. *Œuvres complètes de Voltaire*, ed. Louis Moland. Paris: Garnier.

  1963–93. *Correspondance.* Bibliothèque de la Pléiade, ed. Theodore Besterman. Paris: Gallimard.

  1990. *The complete works of Voltaire.* Vol. LXIIIA, ed. W. H. Barber and Ulla Kölving. Oxford: Voltaire Foundation.

  1994. *Political writings*, ed. David Williams. Cambridge: Cambridge University Press.

  2002. *Mahomet. The complete works of Voltaire.* Vol. XXB, ed. Nicholas Cronk. Oxford: Voltaire Foundation.

Wagner, Wilhelm Richard. 1892. *Richard Wagner's prose works.* Trans. William Ashton Ellis. London: Kegan Paul, Trench, Trübner.

  1977. *Wagner on music and drama: a selection from Richard Wagner's prose works.* Trans. H. Ashton Ellis, ed. Albert Goldman and Evert Sprinchorn. London: Gollancz.

Wallace, Robert W. 2004. 'Damon of Oa: a music theorist ostracized?' In *Music and the Muses: the culture of 'mousikē' in the classical Athenian city*, ed. Penelope Murray and Peter Wilson, 249–67. Oxford: Oxford University Press.

Warner, Michael. 2002. *Publics and counterpublics.* New York: Zone Books.

Warstat, Matthias. 2005. 'Community building within a festival frame: working-class celebrations in Germany, 1918–1933'. *Theatre Research International* 30: 262–73.

Weissengruber, Erik Paul. 1997. 'The Corpus Christi procession in medieval York: a symbolic struggle in public space'. *Theatre Survey* 38(1): 117–38.

Weissman, Ronald F. E. 1982. *Ritual brotherhood in renaissance Florence*. New York and London: Academic Press.

Welschinger, Henri. 1880. *Le théâtre de la révolution, 1789–1799, avec documents inédits*. Paris: Charavay.

Wickham, Glynne. 2000. *English professional theatre, 1530–1660*. Cambridge: Cambridge University Press.

Wiles, David. 1981. *The early plays of Robin Hood*. Cambridge: D. S. Brewer.

  1988. 'Greek theatre and the legitimation of slavery'. In *Slavery and other forms of unfree labour*, ed. Léonie Archer, 53–67. London: Routledge.

  1991. *The masks of Menander: sign and meaning in Greek and Roman performance*. Cambridge: Cambridge University Press.

  1997. *Tragedy in Athens: performance space and theatrical meaning*. Cambridge: Cambridge University Press.

  2003. *A short history of western performance space*. Cambridge: Cambridge University Press.

  2007. *Mask and performance in Greek tragedy: from ancient festival to modern experimentation*. Cambridge: Cambridge University Press.

  2008. 'The poetics of the mask in Old Comedy'. In *Performance, iconography, reception: studies in honour of Oliver Taplin*, ed. Martin Revermann and Peter Wilson, 374–92. Oxford: Oxford University Press.

  2010. 'Seeing is believing'. In *Representing the past: essays in performance historiography*, ed. Charlotte Canning and Thomas Postlewait, 215–39. Iowa City: University of Iowa Press.

Williams, Raymond. 1975. *The country and the city*. St Albans: Paladin.

  1981. *Culture*. London: Fontana.

Wilson, Arthur McCandless. 1972. *Diderot*. New York: Oxford University Press.

Wilson, Peter. 2000. *The Athenian institution of the khoregia: the chorus, the city, and the stage*. Cambridge: Cambridge University Press.

Wilson, Richard. 2002. '"Is this a holiday?": Shakespeare's Roman carnival'. In *Julius Caesar*, ed. Richard Wilson, 55–76. Basingstoke: Palgrave.

Winkler, John J., and Froma I. Zeitlin. 1990. *Nothing to do with Dionysos?: Athenian drama in its social context*. Princeton: Princeton University Press.

Winston, Joe. 2006. 'Beauty, goodness and education: the arts beyond utility'. *Journal of Moral Education* 35: 285–300.

  2007. 'Introduction to special issue: drama for citizenship and human rights'. *Research in Drama Education* 12(3).

  2008. '"An option for art but not an option for life": beauty as an educational imperative'. *Journal of Aesthetic Education* 42(3): 71–87.

Xaxa, Virginius. 2008. *State, society, and tribes: issues in post-colonial India*. New Delhi: Dorling Kindersley.

Yarrow, Ralph. 2001. *Indian theatre: theatre of origin, theatre of freedom*. Richmond, Surrey: Curzon.

Zimmermann, Bernhard. 1993. 'Comedy's criticism of music'. In *Intertextualität in der griechisch-römischen Komödie*, ed. Niall W. Slater and Bernhard Zimmermann, 39–50. Stuttgart: Metzlerschen & Poeschel.

Zorzi, Elvira Garbero, and Mario Sperenzi. 2001. *Teatro e spettacolo nella Firenze dei Medici: modelli dei luoghi teatrali*. Firenze: L. S. Olschki.

Zorzi, Ludovico. 1977. *Il teatro e la città: saggi sulla scena italiana*. Turin: Einaudi.

Index

CPSIA information can be obtained at www.ICGtesting.com
Printed in the USA
LVOW10*1526091113

360676LV00021B/174/P

9 780521 193276

DATE DUE	RETURNED